Historic South Edinburgh

VOLUME ONE

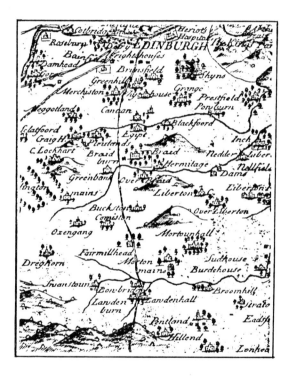

From John Adair's Map of Midlothian, 1735

Merchiston Tower

Historic
South Edinburgh

BY CHARLES J. SMITH

With a Preface by
C. S. MINTO
Formerly City Librarian
Edinburgh

VOLUME ONE

CHARLES SKILTON LTD
Edinburgh & London

VOLUME I

CONTENTS

LIST OF ILLUSTRATIONS

PREFACE

".... indeed it will be rather surprising if the student of local history does not at once attract to his aid the knowledge and professional skill both of the local librarian and of the local newspaper correspondent".

These words were written by the Scottish historian George Pratt Insh and were contributed to the *Quarterly Bulletin* of the Educational Institute of Scotland in an admirable series of short essays. Later these essays were incorporated in his *The Study of Local History and Other Essays* issued under the aegis of the Institute and it was on the publication of that small and interesting volume in 1932 that I first read them. I was then a budding librarian only recently over the hurdle of professional examinations. The recognition thus given to the part that even at that time local authority libraries up and down the country were able to play in assisting and encouraging research in local history gave both reassurance and a spur to an already held determination to take every opportunity to reinforce the collection of local material wherever my professional future might lead.

Dr Insh by the nature of his studies was concerned more particlularly with the smaller units of population, but his words are quite as relevant today as they were more than forty years ago and it is little wonder that they sprang so readily to mind when an invitation was received to write a preface to *Historic South Edinburgh*. Much of the author's research was done in Edinburgh Central Library's local history collections which have traditionally been, and remain, extensive both in the printed and written word and in auxiliary pictorial material; but one of the joys of the book lies in the resort that has been had to both local and national archival sources in the search for accuracy over an extremely wide and difficult field of coverage. Just how difficult that field must have proved becomes evident as one's reading progresses and the depth of both time and area unfolds. A first-class job has been done.

A secondary joy for me lies in nostalgia aroused by the account, in its due place, of the development of an area of the south side of the city which became very familiar throughout the years of childhood and youth. This came about as a result of my father returning to Scotland on his appointment in 1906 as Librarian to the Society of Writers to the Signet. We took up residence at the western, unfinished end of the new street of Comiston Drive. At the back of the house, but for the road, now closed, that led to the City Poorhouse, there was only fields and open country right to the slopes of the Pentlands. One of the common summer sounds that impressed itself on my growing consciousness was the unmelodious calling of corncrakes — a sound largely eliminated by changes in harvesting methods even before Greenbank came into being.

First schooling was at South Morningside school and later the Royal High, which latter involved travel by the N.B.R. Suburban line to Waverley or by cable car to the same destination. Life was unhurried and we neighbourhood youngsters made the most of the ample opportunities afforded by the area of rough, vacant building land at the top of "the Drive" to indulge in the popular games of the day — kick-the-can, alieveoy (relievo), rounders and the like. We had bikes, some of us, which we used for our own version of what would now be called cyclocross rather than for transport. What happened to the bikes met with very considerable parental disapproval as a result of which countryside excursions were made on foot for the most part. Our happiest hunting ground was the valley of the Braid Burn, roughly from where the abortive open air theatre was later built, to Dreghorn and we were soon familiar with such landmarks between there and "the Pents" as the Comiston Springs cistern-house where we never failed to look through the bars of the door at the sculptured birds and animals, the Caiystane, Hunter's Tryst and Swanston. Arrived at the hills, our principal occupation was searching for adders, lizards and "precious stones" along and around the Caerketton screes between bouts of seeing who could scramble up them fastest. However, as often as not, we got no further than the Burn itself with its abundance of waterside flora and fauna to be studied, admired and recorded. Happy, tiring days in a welcoming countryside, large tracts of which have now succumbed to urban spread. . .

In winter we frequented the Braid Pond for skating although it was common enough for skates to be donned along the frozen track for some hundreds of yards before reaching the Pond itself. We reckoned the ice at its best with an inch or so of water over the surface, a state of affairs which only pertained so long as you kept moving. If you stopped, the water depth increased with varying degrees of rapidity — as did the ire of the rangers whose legitimate aim it was to clear the ice before someone fell through. This happened frequently but there was no great danger involved as the average depth was around two feet. If abandonment could not be avoided there was always "Winchester's" at the south-east end for "skoosh" or biscuits in the unlikely event of our being in funds. There were also sledging opportunities galore and no end of whin bushes to be run into with painful consequences as sledge and rider parted company. During World War I more serious pursuits interfered with our ploys when allotments were provided at the top of Craiglea Drive and we were most of us enrolled to help our parents clear the ground in order to grow such long-established potato varieties as Golden Wonder, Great Scot and Kerr's Pink along with other vegetables. Two other memories of these years remain vivid: being taken into the back garden to see Halley's Comet in 1910 and to the front of the house to see a more mundane disturbing object by day — a Zeppelin — in 1916.

Shortly after the end of the war we moved house, still well within the confines of south Edinburgh, going to live in Nile Grove — one of several quiet residential streets with Biblical names — a little to the north of Morningside Station on the opposite side of Morningside Road. For an explanation of this curious nomenclative exercise I would refer you to Mr Smith's text (Chapter 11) where he deals with other examples.

So far as the Comiston excursions were concerned they tended to dwindle though happily still persisted for a year or two in the face of new-found diversions. Pride of place among these was taken by the Springvalley Cinema in Springvalley Gardens, though of the fare there offered on Saturday mornings I have but vague recollections. Among those that remain clearest are "The Four Horsemen of the Apocalypse", the French film "J'Accuse", W. S. Hart westerns, serials starring Pearl White and Hurricane Hutch whose motorcycle-powered flights over impossibly wide ravines held us spellbound till the next episode showed him landing safely on the other side with his fuming pursuers helplessly foiled yet again, and the Mack Sennett comedies. The demands of school work grew steadily more and more restricting of leisure time. Golf on the Braid Hills (public) and Merchants of Edinburgh (private) courses made other, more welcome, demands while the nearer proximity of the Blackford Hill and Blackford Glen offered new and irresistible temptations.

These informal and random memories of time past may have little relevance to formal history but those who, like myself, grew up to witness the vast expansion of the city southwards before and after the 1914-18 war are getting noticeably fewer. I trust, therefore, that these fragmentary records of a south Edinburgh childhood will not be considered too out of place as introductory matter to a work which I believe will be immediately recognised as definitive in its subject field.

C. S. MINTO

INTRODUCTION

Books on the history of Edinburgh abound, ranging from the classical source works of Arnot, Anderson, Maitland, Grant and Wilson to the many contemporary studies and pictorial expositions recording and contrasting past and present. The great watershed in the history of Edinburgh's development was the opening of the North Bridge in 1772. This realisation of Lord Provost George Drummond's long-held dream led to the exodus of Old Town citizens of means from the congested closes and high lands of the High Street northwards across the drained Nor' Loch to a new style of elegant residence in Craig's classical New Town.

But other eras and movements merit a place in the chronicles of the city. Another more leisurely exodus was to occur, this time southwards, early in the nineteenth century. Sir Walter Scott was amongst the many who had believed that the New Town would be built "to the south of the Town's College". Many of Edinburgh's citizens, notably prosperous merchants, professional people, artists and writers, while comfortably settled in their new dwellings in the New Town were nevertheless attracted by the pleasant rural seclusion of the city's sunward aspect to the south. Indeed, prior to the construction of the South Bridge in 1788, part of George Square had already been built and the opening of this new southern highway spanning the Cowgate stimulated a significant movement of people to the districts of Newington, the Grange and Morningside.

Historically speaking, the wide area on which Edinburgh's other "New Town" arose, the city's ancient Burgh Muir, was not entirely virgin soil. The lands to the south could lay claim to some antiquity, but their origins, elusively documented in the city's archives, were not so well known as those of the Old Town. Their history lay and still lies scattered in many sources not readily accessible to students of local history.

Glimpses of South Edinburgh's origins and development, of its earliest houses, notable residents and institutions, have also been recorded briefly, and in popular, frequently inaccurate, fashion, in a wide variety of booklets and articles. To bring such information together in one study has been the object of this work. A definitive history of any area is, of course, impossible: when an account of a district has been confined to print, new sources of information may quite unexpectedly come to light, or some venerable building (such as Gillespie's Hospital) may disappear almost overnight.

Prior to 1856 a history of South Edinburgh would have concluded at the city's centuries-old southern boundary, the Pow or Jordan Burn. The latter has thus been chosen as the natural dividing point between volumes one and two. While the chronicles of the lands along the northern bank of the Jordan Burn reach back into ancient times, their systematic development dates from 1586, when the city's Burgh Muir, extending from the South or Borough Loch to the Jordan Burn, was feued out by the magistrates in various lots, which were to become the residential districts of today. The lands south of the Jordan lay outwith the City's boundaries and were thus not included in the late sixteenth-century feuing scheme. Nevertheless they can also trace their origins into antiquity. Their development followed a different pattern from the neighbouring lands to the north, culminating eventually in the mushroom growth, in the late nineteenth century, of classical "villadom".

When Edinburgh people talk of the city's "South Side" they usually mean the relatively small area comprising South Clerk Street, St Leonards, Causewayside, Sciennes, Newington and the Grange. This part of Edinburgh has been described in *The South Side Story,* a valuable contribution to local history edited by John G. Gray. The present work extends the South Side, as defined above, to the east, south and west. Here South Edinburgh is taken to be that considerable part of the city which developed on the ancient Burgh Muir and beyond.

My inspiration to attempt a systematic historical study of South Edinburgh has had many sources, notably the privilege I have enjoyed of inaugurating a lecture course on the subject under the auspices of the Edinburgh Workers Educational Association. William Mair's fascinating *Historic Morningside* was also a powerful stimulus to research this district and its adjacent localities in greater depth. Any writer working on a history of Edinburgh will profit greatly by the invaluable resources of the Edinburgh Room of the city's Central Library and the professional skill and experience of its staff. For assistance in producing this study of South Edinburgh, in which much new ground had to be explored and obscure sources traced, I am indebted to Miss Sheena McDougall, A.L.A., Librarian-in-Charge of the Edinburgh Room and, from the work's earliest stages, to the painstaking guidance of her predecessor Mrs Norma Armstrong, M.A., F.L.A., now head of Reference and Information Services, who very kindly read the manuscript and prepared the bibliography and index. Mr Charles Finlayson, Keeper of Manuscripts in Edinburgh University Library has also offered valuable assistance.

I record my deep gratitude to my father for his constant interest and support, and to my brother, William R. Smith, B.Sc., M.B.K.S., L.R.P.S., for systematically photographing the whole area of study (even if, for economic reasons, only a fraction of his work could be published) and for much other practical assistance. He drafted the chapter on the Jordan Burn, of which he has made a special study. For the professional processing of many of the photographs used I am indebted to Mr Bill Weir of the Photographic Department of the Edinburgh University Library. I express my sincere appreciation also to Mrs Brian Smith, Mrs Margaret Hunter and, especially, Mrs Irene Combe who have successively typed the manuscript during its long period of gestation. My neighbour Mr Brian Smith also provided valuable assistance.

The tracing of much hitherto unrecorded information has meant discovering and drawing upon many primary sources. I have had many interviews with residents, often elderly, who have engaged in much correspondence. The people who have kindly and willingly assisted me in providing information and photographs are too numerous to mention by name, but I thank them all most sincerely. To one Morningside business man, Mr Gilmour Main who provided valuable information, photographs, and much encouragement, I express my especial gratitude, and likewise to Miss A. Beveridge of Greenhill.

I am also greatly indebted to the very many people, including administrators of various institutions, who kindly gave me or permitted me to copy old photographs and illustrations, many of which were unique.

Mr C. S. Minto, former City Librarian, has been kind enough to contribute a fascinating Preface, and has also cast an eye over the proofs, though any errors of course remain my responsibility.

Mrs Jean Desebrock, B.Litt (Oxon.) patiently edited the manuscript and transformed what were originally lecture notes into a more literary style. I am much obliged to her.

Finally, at a time when the economics of publishing a book on a localised subject constitutes a considerable financial risk, I am especially grateful to Mr Charles Skilton for his interest, guidance and encouragement from the time of his first acceptance of my manuscript, and for enabling it to see the light of day; similarly the helpfulness of the Carnegie Trust for the Universities of Scotland is appreciatively recorded.

Key plan of the Burgh Muir drawn by Dr William Moir Bryce

By courtesy of the Old Edinburgh Club (Vol.XI)

CHAPTER 1

The Burgh Muir · Sciennes · The Meadows

THE BURGH MUIR

The opening chapter of any chronicle of the origins and development of South Edinburgh must begin with the Burgh Muir, since it was upon this unpromising and rather forbidding area of the great forest of Drumselch that Edinburgh's "Southern New Town" was eventually to arise. In the course of over seven centuries, if the hills were not made low and the valleys filled and exalted, certainly the rough places were made plain.

While it is believed that the common muir of Edinburgh, originally the "Burrow Mure", was gifted to the city by David I in the first half of the twelfth century (the date 1143 has been suggested by some historians), unfortunately the actual charters and records have been lost. Many were removed when the ruthless Earl of Hertford sacked and set fire to the city in May 1544. David I's extensive gifts of land, especially for the foundation of abbeys and monasteries, earned him the title "A sair sanct for the Croon". In his foundation charter of Holyrood Abbey, granted in 1143, Edinburgh is first referred to as a Royal Burgh, and it is possible that this charter also included his gift to the city of the "Burrow Mure".

In David's time, immediately south of Edinburgh lay the dense forest of Drumselch and it was a major part of this which he gave to the city. The forest stretched from the north-east corner of Easter Craiglockhart Hill on the west to the lands of Cairntow and the Drum at Gilmerton on the east. It extended southwards from the South or Burgh Loch (now the Meadows) to the lower slopes of the Blackford and Braid Hills. Within this wide area was the Burgh Muir — bounded, in terms of present-day street names, by Leven Street, Bruntsfield Place and Morningside Road to the west, and by the east side of Dalkeith Road to the east. The south bank of the South Loch formed the northern boundary, the southern being the Pow (or later Jordan) Burn, flowing from Myreside, below Craighouse Hill, through Morningside, under the lowest point of Morningside Road near Braid Church, and onwards between the back gardens of Jordan Lane and Nile Grove, past Blackford and Newington, to join the Braid Burn at Peffermill. Here was a large marsh, the "Common Myre", beside the concourse of the two streams, and this area was gifted also as part of the Burgh Muir. The total area concerned was about five square miles. Exempted from the city's jurisdiction over the Muir were the Crown Lands of Grange, the Provostry Lands of Whitehouse, the Sergeantry Lands of Bruntsfield, and Merchiston. All such estates had

1

originally been granted directly by royal charter to their owners who held them independently by this right.

The forest of Drumselch was the home of countless "hartis, hindis, toddis [foxes] and siclike maner of beasts". Hence, for centuries it was a popular hunting ground for the Scottish Kings and their courtiers, riding out to its leafy depths from the Castle. It is here, legend has it, that David I, "a mighty hunter before the Lord," who often pursued wild deer, had an encounter which led him to found Holyrood Abbey. On a feast day, the King, against his confessor's advice, went hunting in the forest of Drumselch, "amids sic noyis and dyn of rachis [hounds] and bugillis [bugles] that all the beastis war raisit fra their dennys [dens]". The sport, presumably, was good, but when his companions were leaving the woods to return to the Castle, David was cut off. A ferocious deer, "the farest hart that evir was sene, with awful and braid tindis [antlers]", unseated the King from his horse. In danger, he grasped the deer's antlers—and, to his amazement, found himself holding a cross. At the sight of it the animal swiftly fled. In gratitude, David founded the abbey dedicated to the Holy Rood. The legend is commemorated by the small antlered head of a deer above the entrance to Canongate Kirk.

The Burgh Muir witnessed many battles and frequent musters of the Scottish army until, "the swords being turned [literally] to pruning hooks", it became a most pleasant, peaceful rural area. For long it was a valuable *cordon sanitaire* against invaders from the south. In 1335 Edward III of England crossed the border in support of the claim of Edward Baliol to the Scottish throne. In August of that year, a large body of foreign mercenaries under the command of Guy, Comte de Namur, also approached Edinburgh from the south, intending to join King Edward at Perth. Entering by the ancient "easter hiegait" (Dalkeith Road), they crossed the Pow Burn, but at the Burgh Muir were confronted by the Scottish forces under the Earls of Moray and March. Driven onwards into the city, the mercenary army was eventually defeated and its leaders given safe conduct back to England. In 1384 the Muir saw the first large assembly of a Scottish army, reputedly of thirty thousand men mounted on small horses, under the command of the Earls of Fife and Douglas. The object or outcome of the gathering is not clear. A century later, James III also mustered a large army which set out from the Burgh Muir for Lauder, there to suffer from the dissension of its leaders. Of all the great martial arrays on the Muir, none has been described with such dramatic detail and romantic poetry as that of August 1513, when James IV commanded "all able bodied men between the ages of sixteen and sixty to muster on Edinburgh's Burrow Muir", prior to marching to disaster at Flodden. Scott's colourful account of the scene in *Marmion* — quoted on the plaque beneath the Bore Stone beside Morningside Parish Church — describing an army of a hundred thousand men rallying round the Royal Standard hoisted at this stone, is more poetically vivid than historically true. Ten years after Flodden, and again in 1542, there were two further assemblies of forty and thirty thousand men, and on each occasion strife amongst the Scottish nobles made their campaigns abortive.

During these early centuries, part of this remote and isolated area was serving another more sombre purpose. Apart from providing vagrants and outlaws with a retreat from the city authorities, where they could camp out amidst the great oak trees or live in roughly built huts, the Burgh Muir served as the quarantine area for a constant stream of plague victims conveyed thither to prevent the spread of infection in the congested wynds and closes of the old town, there to seek recovery but most often to die.

A mid-seventeenth century traveller approaching Edinburgh from the south by the old Biggar road (through what today is Morningside), upon reaching the brow of Churchhill, in the small area known as Boroughmuirhead, would have enjoyed a magnificent panorama of the distant and then small city, clinging to the spine of the Royal Mile. The traveller would have noted the Burgh Muir was not without habitation. Near Burghmuirhead stood Merchiston Tower, to the east the Grange of St Giles could be glimpsed through its trees, and, looking towards the city, he would have seen Wrychtishousis, Greenhill House and Bruntsfield House standing like sentinels to guard his approach. To the south, three other castle-like mansion-houses stood in open country, the land rising steadily towards the Braids and the Pentlands. These were the castles of Braid and Comiston and, most prominently, the Craighouse, now known as Old Craig, on Craighouse Hill. Linking the "wester hiegait" (now Morningside Road) to the parallel Dalkeith Road, skirting the Burgh Muir to the east, was Cant's Loan, a narrow lane now on the line of present-day Newbattle Terrace, Grange Loan and West and East Mayfield. A traveller losing his way after dark on the isolated Burgh Muir might have reorientated himself with the help of the lights which burned on the tower of St John's Church, Corstorphine, and St Anthony's Chapel, prominently sited below Arthur's Seat.

In 1508 an outcry arose in Edinburgh over the tenure under which land on the Burgh Muir was held and the lack of supervision by magistrates of the various purposes for which it was being used. Ultimately the matter was brought to the attention of James IV who knew the area well. In the previous year it was probably he who had established there, in the grounds of what today is the Astley Ainslie Hospital, the little chapel of St Roque, around which James's ill-fated army was to muster before marching to Flodden. The King's response to a petition from Edinburgh's citizens was to grant to Provost, Bailies and Councillors power to lease "their lands of the Common Muir of Edinburgh, called the Burrowmure . . . to any persons, as to them shall seem most expedient, for feu duties to be paid thereupon yearly to our said Burgh". Those given a lease were subject to various conditions: they had, for instance, "to repair

3

THE·OLD·TIMBER–FRONTED·HOVSE·

Timber frontage constructed from trees felled to clear the Burgh Muir, drawn by Jessie M. King

By courtesy of Mrs Merle E. Taylor

4

every week with their victuals and other goods to the market of our said Burgh". They were also obliged to set up brew houses and to provide ale for the city authorities if requested.

Following James's charter of 1508, the magistrates encouraged the citizens to begin clearing the Burgh Muir of its great trees. Those willing to remove the felled timber to their houses in the old town were permitted to use it to extend their frontages by seven feet. Hence, before long, the High Street was reduced to fourteen feet in breadth, the minimum permitted in the wynds and closes of the town centre. As one commentator on the scene wrote: "The buildings which before had stone fronts were now converted into wood and the Burgh into a wooden city." Wooden fore-stairs became a special feature of many houses, particularly in the West Bow and the Lawnmarket. The purpose to which the timber from the Burgh Muir had been put soon created problems of obstruction and congestion, and in 1674 the Town Council forbade any further fore-stairs. In 1727, because many citizens still persisted, an Act was passed confirming the Town Council's edict and carrying heavy penalties. During the great clearance of the Burgh Muir, many timber-wrights were employed. It has been suggested that many of them lived along the northern edge of the Muir beside the site of the present-day Barclay Church and that this was the origin of the name of the little village there known as Wrychtishousis.

Today the pleasant, jealously guarded expanse of Bruntsfield Links is a reminder of the undulating slopes of the Burgh Muir, while the man-made hollows in the uneven ground opposite Alvanley Terrace recall one of the area's early uses as a quarry for the stone much used in the buildings of the Bruntsfield district.

While James IV's charter of 1508 resulted in much of the Burgh Muir being cleared and brought under control, no real development took place for almost another eighty years — over four centuries after David I had bestowed this potentially valuable land on the city. It was the tragic fate which overcame Edinburgh in 1585 which finally compelled the civic authorities to exploit their ancient gift. In that year the city was decimated by yet another of the regular epidemics of plague which harrowed and terrified the population for centuries. During this visitation, the authorities did everything possible to prevent undue spread of the infection and to provide for victims, and this proved costly to the municipal treasury, almost to the point of bankruptcy. At last the magistrates considered financial exploitation of the Burgh Muir. Hence, on July 20th, 1586, the Town Council agreed to feu out the Wester Burgh Muir, and in this area the districts of Greenhill, Morningside, East Morningside and Canaan were eventually if slowly to arise. Likewise, on August 9th, 1586, the magistrates "convenit in the Eister Mure of this burgh for rouping and setting of the waist part thereof . . ." It was in this eastern area that, more rapidly than in the west, Newington and Mayfield

5

were to arise. 1586, then, is the first milestone in the history of South Edinburgh. And it is with the developments which steadily followed until Edinburgh's "Southern New Town" had arisen, and with the lives of people who came to reside there, that this book is concerned.

SCIENNES

Over the centuries during which South Edinburgh slowly developed on the Burgh Muir, certain of its separate estates retained their own special links with particular features of the Muir. Wrychtishousis, as already mentioned, perhaps took its name from the settlement of timber-wrights employed in clearing the Burgh Muir of its great trees. The district and one-time village of Burghmuirhead were so called because they were situated at the highest point of the Muir. Sciennes originates from one of the less salubrious features of the Burgh Muir: it was for long the resort of "vagabonds, vagrants and outlaws" who found shelter beneath its great trees, and, because of its remoteness, an escape from the city authorities. It was a concern for the spiritual welfare and reform of such men that prompted Sir John Craufurd, a prebendary of Edinburgh's parish church of St Giles to attempt some kind of missionary contact with them. However much they had cut themselves off from the church and society, those who sought refuge in the rough lands south of the city apparently retained some devotion to St John the Baptist who, as "a voice crying in the wilderness", had himself sought refuge in the desert.

During the years 1511-12, Sir John Craufurd, then a Canon of St Giles, resolved to build in the wilderness of the Burgh Muir a little chapel dedicated to St John the Baptist, "the particular saint at whose altar the wandering rogue never failed to pay his devotion". He acquired four and a half acres of land near the west side of what is now Causewayside, and Sciennes House Place (long known as Braid Place). The area within which Sir John Craufurd erected his chapel can still be identified as the L-shaped piece of ground on the west of the Causewayside. From the south-east corner of Sciennes House Place it extended northwards to the little lane once called Sciennes Place. In 1511 this area was the site of the hamlet of Muresburgh, now represented by the triangle formed by Sciennes House Place, the Sciennes and Lord Russell Place. The chapel itself stood on the site of Sciennes Hill House (now 5 Sciennes House Place). A lamp was kept continually burning on the little tower of the chapel, as on that of the other Church of St John the Baptist at Corstorphine, as a guide to travellers after dark. By February 1513, the year of Scotland's disastrous defeat at Flodden, the chapel of St John the Baptist at Sciennes was completed. A Chaplain was appointed and the conditions of his tenure, laid down by Sir John Craufurd, included the provision of land and also strict requirements as regards his duties. He had to be "of laudable report and honest conversation", was bound to

6

continual residence "and the celebration of Mass daily at the High Altar of the said church", and was to be a man "who does not play cards, and is not a common gamester". To assist the chaplain, Craufurd appointed a hermit "of advanced age, good life and sound constitution, who shall always live at the said church and always wear a white robe, having on his breast the picture of the head of St John the Baptist and he shall be called his hermit . . . which hermit shall clean and purify the church from dirt and supply the chaplain with water, fire and salt. He shall have for his support an acre of land and a house."

Sir John Craufurd completed the foundation of the chapel of St John the Baptist by presenting to it a printed copy of a Breviary, a "Breviarium ad usum Sarum", as used at Salisbury Cathedral. At that time printed Breviaries were beginning to appear, superseding those written by hand. This original relic of Sir John Craufurd's early sixteenth-century chapel at Sciennes became part of the notable collection acquired by Master Clement Little, who presented it to the Town Council of Edinburgh in 1580, which in turn presented it to Edinburgh University ("the Tounis College"), founded in 1583. This collection formed the nucleus around which the University Library was built. Craufurd's Breviary is still preserved in the library's Manuscripts and Rare Books Department and has been exhibited in many countries. On the top of its title page is written: "Liber Bibliothecae Edinburgenae, ex Dono R.D. Clementis Little". There is a large woodcut of the Royal Arms of England and of St George and the dragon and, below this, in Sir John Craufurd's own handwriting, the words: "Liber domini Johannis Craufurd". The page also shows Master Clement Little's stamp with the inscription: "I am gevin to Edinburgh and Kirk of God be Maister Clement Little, Thair to Remain, 1580." Little's armorial stamp with a shield and the letters "MCL" are also shown.

Initially Sir John Craufurd acted as chaplain to his foundation, but the little chapel was to serve its original purpose for only four years. Events in the wider history of Scotland were to affect the history of Sciennes. Following Scotland's disastrous defeat at the Battle of Flodden in 1513, when the vast number of dead included men of all social levels, many titled ladies were widowed. In 1516 a number of these ladies decided to form a religious community and devote the remainder of their lives to prayer and penance. Amongst them were several from notable aristocratic families of Scotland. The Papal Bull granted by Pope Leo X on January 29th, 1517, and still preserved in Register House in Edinburgh, gives the names of the ladies who had sought and been granted permission to establish a convent at Sciennes. There would appear to have been three foundresses. The first named is Lady Jane Hepburn, daughter of the first Earl of Bothwell and widow of the third Earl of Seton, one of James IV's closest friends. *The Chronicle of the House of Seton* relates that Lady Hepburn "guidit hir sonnis leving gutrill he was cummit to age, and

7

Remains of the Convent of St Catherine of Sienna, drawn by William Douglas c. 1841

thairafter she passit and remanit in the place of Senis on the Burrow Mure, besyd Edinburgh, the rest of her lyvetyme. Quilk place sche helpit to fund and big as maist principale. She did mony gude actis.'' Lady Hepburn also waited until her daughter and her other son's children were married, giving them generous dowries, before entering the newly established convent at Sciennes, where she "liffit to gud age and deit in the yeir of God 1558 years in the said place of Senis". The other two foundresses of the convent were Elizabeth Auchinleck, widow of Sir William Douglas, son of the fifth Earl of Angus ("Bell the Cat") who was slain at Flodden, and "the Lady of the Bass", wife of Sir Robert Lawder whose extensive lands included the Bass Rock and the Grange.

On January 5th, 1516, in the Town Chamber House of the old Tolbooth, Sir John Craufurd met the Provincial of the Blackfriars (Dominican) monastery, then situated between the Cowgate and Drummond Street, and certain of the sisters of Sciennes and there translated and annulled his foundation of the Chapel of St John the Baptist, drawing up a disposition to Josina Henrison as the representative and first prioress of the new convent. This nun was possibly a Dominican sister of Scottish extraction brought to Edinburgh from another of the Order's convents in Europe. In the Papal Bull, the establishment of the convent in Sciennes is described as of great importance and benefit not only to the ladies who had founded it but also "to the whole people of the said Kingdom of Scotland". The foundation was also of historical significance in Scotland for a reason not appreciated at its establishment: it was the last convent to be built in Scotland prior to the Reformation. Just over three centuries later, in 1835, the nearby convent of St Margaret

8

in Whitehouse Loan was to enjoy the distinction of being the first convent to be opened in Scotland after the Reformation.

Craufurd, when bestowing his chapel and surrounding land upon the sisters of Sciennes, made several provisos. One was that upon "the failure of the ardour of the holy ladies to carry out their pious intentions", the chapel and its surrounding lands would revert to him. The final investment of the sisters took place on April 25th, 1517. The religious foundation was of the Dominican Order and dedicated to St Catherine of Sienna, the famous Italian saint of this Order. It was the French version of Sienna, Scienne, which became the name of the district. The site of the convent was the south-east end of Sciennes Road and its walls encompassed both sides of present-day St Catherine's Place. In the garden of 16 St Catherine's Place, a plaque proclaims that the surrounding stones are the last remains of the convent. One of the rules of the Dominican Order was that convent buildings "should be humble in design, with no pretentious ornaments", and that they should be enclosed by walls of sufficient height to ensure privacy and seclusion.

Not only was this the last convent built in Scotland prior to the Reformation, but it also had the shortest existence of any religious house. It was burned during the English invasion under Somerset in 1544 (as were the Grange of St Giles, Whitehouse and Bruntsfield House) and virtually destroyed in 1559, forty-two years after its foundation. During its short existence, however, Sir John Craufurd's proviso that the "failure of the ardour of the holy ladies to carry out their pious intentions" would result in its closure was certainly never invoked. Their ardour was so much a feature of their lives that, during the gathering storm before the Reformation in Scotland, the reputation of the nuns of Sciennes was unique. In Sir David Lyndsay's powerful and graphic play *Ane Satyre of the Thrie Estates,* a masterpiece of the Scottish theatre written when the Reformation was imminent (and revived during several Edinburgh International Festivals) he exempts the convent of Sciennes from his severe strictures on other such religious houses in Scotland. His character Chastitie, expelled from monasteries and convents elsewhere, finds a welcome at Sciennes:

> I traist scho bene upon the Burrow Mure,
> Besouth Edinburgh, and that richt mony menis,
> Profest amang the sisteris of the Schenis.
> Thare hes scho fund his mother Povertie,
> And Devotioun her awin sister carnall;
> Thare hath scho fund Faith, Hope and Charitie,
> Togidder with the virtues cardinall:
> Thare hes scho fund ane Convent yet unthrall
> To dame Sensuall, nor with Riches abusit,
> Sa quietlye those ladyis inclusit.

9

Metal plaque on the stones which are the last remains of the Convent of St Catherine of Sienna in the garden of 16 St Catherine's Place, off Sciennes Road

Photograph by Mr W. R. Smith

Along with the Breviary of Sir John Craufurd in Edinburgh University Library is a manuscript copy of the constitution of the Sisters of the Dominican Order which belonged to the convent at Sciennes. This indicates the austere rule which the nuns observed. Nevertheless, despite this and Sir David Lyndsay's acquittal of the sisters, the convent was to suffer the same fate as so many other religious houses when the Reformation occurred. The fateful day in Edinburgh was June 29th, 1559. According to one account, "the rascal multitude, leaving behind them the smoking ruins of the monasteries of the Black and the Grey Friars, rushed out in their thousands along the Cowgate, the Candlemaker Row and the other southern outlets of the city to the Sciennes, where, without opposition of any kind, they completed their vengeful work of destruction". Other accounts stated that the treatment of the sisters of Sciennes was not violent and that, having been warned of the approach of the mob, they escaped in time. A letter from Mary Queen of Scots appealing for mercy towards the nuns of Sciennes, since they were "aigit and decrepit", begged the Edinburgh authorities to show special consideration. In several subsequent letters the Queen sought to cancel the heavy fines which the nuns were required to pay to the Crown.

By 1567 the whole property of the convent of Sciennes had passed into secular hands and the aged sisters had been dispersed. The last prioress was Christian Bellenden who, with a few of the sisters, continued to live in the ruined buildings, then no longer a convent. Others returned to their homes.

In Sir Walter Scott's *The Abbot* (Chapter XI), a former nun, Catherine Seyton, tells Roland Graeme of the convent's fate:

"Our Blessed St Catherine of Sienna . . . This was her nunnery in which there were twelve nuns [the original charter provided for 30 nuns] and an abbess. My aunt was the abbess until the heretics turned all adrift."

"And where are your companions?" asked the youth.

"With the last year's snow," answered the maiden, "east and north and south and west, some to France, some to Flanders, some, I fear, into the world and its pleasures. We have got permission to remain, or rather our remaining has been connived at, for my aunt has great relations among the Kerrs and they have threatened a death feud if anyone touches us."

Scott also refers to this Convent in *Marmion*. In the autumn of 1513, during the muster of the Scottish army on the Burgh Muir, James IV is described as having made his way to "St Catherine of Sienne" — poetic licence, as the convent was not established until four years later.

Over the years after its closure the convent buildings became ruins and were gradually dismantled. For some time plague victims were housed in the remains, tended by the nuns who still lived there. The Edinburgh Town Council Records for July 1602 state that the buttresses and doors of the convent were used in the re-building of Greyfriars Church. The lands still belonging to the convent passed to a succession of owners, including, in 1645, William Dick of the Grange of St Giles. In 1735 the owner was Alexander Bayne, Professor of Scots Law at Edinburgh University, who sought permission to demolish the last remains of the convent. He was successfully opposed in this by Andrew Lauder Dick of the Grange of St Giles. Lord Cockburn, who during his boyhood had lived in an old mansion in Sciennes Road facing the Meadows, recalled having seen the ruins of the convent, and Grant, in *Old and New Edinburgh*, provides illustrations of them. But by 1879 the ruins had been swept away to make way for villas; all that now remain are the stones in the garden of 16 St Catherine's Place. George Seton, advocate and author of a history of the house of Seton, which had associations with the convent at Sciennes, lived at St Bennet's in Greenhill Gardens but a cairn of stones from the convent which he built in his garden there has long since disappeared. In Edinburgh University Library is an illustration of the seal of the convent, the original wax blocks of which are in Edinburgh's Register House and the British Museum. There is also a psalter, printed in Paris in 1554, which has an inscription on its fly-leaf: "This buik ptenis to Sister Marion Crafurde, in the place of Senis besyde Edinburgh."

On the north side of Sciennes House Place (formerly Braid Place), leading westwards from Causewayside to Sciennes and Sciennes Road, part of Sciennes Hill House (or Sciennes Hall as it was also known), built in 1741, still remains. The house was originally approached from an avenue running due south. Soon after its erection it became the residence of Robert Biggar. The ancestral home of the Biggars, one of the ancient families of Scotland, was Woolmet, a large three-storey towered mansion half a mile east of the Drum on the old Dalkeith Road, built in 1683. The Biggars left Woolmet at the end of the seventeenth century and the annals of this notable family became closely associated with Newington and Sciennes. Robert Biggar of Sciennes Hill House was one of the unfortunate shareholders in the disastrous Darien scheme. In about 1750 Biggar's two sons, John and Walter, built a linen factory in Sciennes which rapidly became a prosperous business. The British Linen Company presented them with a service of silver plate, so skilful were the brothers in their manufacturing process. John Biggar also resided in Sciennes Hill House and became something of a *littérateur,* assembling a valuable private library. His brother Walter lived in a villa on the site of what is now Bertram's engineering works. Through marriage, the brothers were related to various notable people of the time including the Duchess of Sutherland (who in her own right was the Countess of Cromarty), William Butter (Carpenter to the Royal Household in Scotland who featured in Kay's *Portraits*) and John Hullah (a notable composer). William Biggar, great-grandson of John Biggar of Sciennes Hill House, was himself a distinguished musician and composer, contributing to Scottish dance music "Mr Biggar's Strathspey" and "Mr John Biggar's Jig". He was offered the leadership of the Edinburgh Theatre Royal Orchestra. His wife was related to Dr Thomas Chalmers, the famous Disruption leader. Another member of the Biggar family was a descendant of the philosopher David Hume. The family's association with Sciennes Hill House ended in 1862.

The house, having already merited a place in the chronicles of South Edinburgh, was to earn inclusion in the wider history of Scotland, when, in the winter of 1786-7, it was the scene of the only recorded meeting between Robert Burns and Sir Walter Scott. At that time the house was the residence of Professor Adam Ferguson (commemorated by the building that bears his name in Edinburgh University's George Square complex). He regularly entertained his friends with "literary dinners" and at one of these both Burns and Scott were guests. The latter, then but a youth of sixteen, was probably attending with an adult friend. In a letter to his biographer Lockhart, written many years later, Scott wrote of the occasion: "As it was, I saw him one day at the late venerable Professor Ferguson's, where there were several gentlemen of literary reputation, among them the celebrated Dr Dugald Stewart. Of course we youngsters sat silent, looked and listened. The only thing I remember which was remarkable in Burns's manner was the effect produced upon him by a print of Burnbury's representing a soldier lying dead on the snow, his dog sitting in misery on the one side, on the other his widow with a child in her arms . . . Burns seemed much affected by the print, or rather the ideas which it suggested to his mind. He actually shed tears." Below the picture were some lines of poetry, and Burns asked who had written them. "It chanced", continued Scott, "that nobody but myself remembered that they occurred in a half-forgotten poem of Langhorne's called by the unpromising title of "The Justice of the Peace". I whispered my information to a friend present, who mentioned it to Burns. He then rewarded me with a look and a word, which, though of mere civility, I then received and still recollect with great pleasure." Another account has it that Burns, when he looked towards Scott in acknowledgment, remarked, "You'll be a man yet, sir." This historic meeting between Scotland's two most celebrated writers was the subject of a painting by Charles Martin Hardie, A.R.S.A. The other guests seen with Burns and Scott include Joseph Black, Adam Smith and John Home.

Sciennes Hill House was partially demolished and altered in 1868, becoming 5 Sciennes House Place, part of a tenement block which, viewed from the street, is obviously of much earlier date than the tenements on either side. It is the back of the original house, after restoration, which is seen from the street. The front is visible from the back green, entered from No. 7, and it still displays some architectural embellishment. The ceilings of the first-floor flats in No. 5 retain their decorated cornices and it is believed that, before sub-division, these rooms formed the large drawing-room in which Burns and Scott met. From the back green a tablet may be seen, placed there by the Association of Burns Clubs and the Sir Walter Scott Club, with the inscription: "This tablet commemorates the meeting of Robert Burns and Sir Walter Scott which took place here in the winter of 1786-87."

On the south side of Sciennes House Place, still visible through its railings, is an old Jewish burial ground, for long the only one of its kind in Scotland. Above it towers the sturdy local police headquarters, the city's coat of arms sculpted high on its north side. The little cemetery was originally entered from Causewayside, down a lane lined with picturesque gable-fronted houses and known as Jews' Close. The construction of a new block of tenements in about 1960 resulted in the close's disappearance, although the rear of the cemetery can still be reached through a pend running under the tenement, dated 1907. It was only with the opening of Braid Place that the cemetery became visible to the passer-by. It was owned by the Edinburgh Hebrew Congregation and established in 1816, and nearly four generations of Jewish families are buried there. It was closed in the 1870s. After this the Jewish community in Edinburgh acquired a small piece of ground on the north side of Newington Cemetery, but this was closed some years ago and a part of Piershill Cemetery was acquired. Newington is the district in which Edinburgh's Jewish community is strongest, its earliest members coming here from Germany and the Low Countries. They became successful in Edinburgh by trading in clothing, furs, and jewellery. Their first place of worship was in a lane behind Nicolson Street, and later in Richmond Court, long since demolished, which remained their meeting place for worship for over fifty years. After another period of twenty-five years, from 1868, in Bristo House, eventually demolished to make way for Edinburgh University's Music Department and the adjacent Men's Union in Park Place, there was a short sojourn at premises in Graham Street. Finally the foundation stone of the present fine synagogue in Salisbury Road, which seats two thousand, was laid by Viscount Bearsted on May 3rd, 1931.

Opposite the gates to the old Jewish Cemetery in Sciennes House Place the structure still remains of the district's tiny fire-station which housed two fire-engines. Emerging into Causewayside and proceeding southwards towards Grange Road, the southern boundary of Sciennes, a pend leads into Grange Court. This was for long a small community of quaint houses with outside stairs. By the 1960s the property had seriously deteriorated and this unique little area of Sciennes might well have been swept away. Happily, through the efforts of local town councillors and others, this fate was averted. The original houses have recently been skilfully restored and new ones built so that Grange Court's traditional old-world atmosphere has been re-created, providing a residential oasis of peace and character secluded from the busy thoroughfares close by.

Returning to the point where Sciennes turns sharply westwards to become Sciennes Road, in contrast to the more ancient religious associations of the district stands a modern engineering works. But this also has early associations. The extensive premises of Messrs Bertrams Ltd, the internationally renowned manufacturers of paper-making machinery, are known as St Katherine's Works. They have grown from a little building no larger than a blacksmith's shop, using primitive plant and tools, established in 1821. Not inappropriately, the works and foundry stand on the site of an early residence of Walter Chepman who, under the patronage of James IV, first introduced printing into Scotland.

The dominating landmark in Sciennes Road is the Royal Edinburgh Hospital for Sick Children, a landmark also in the progress of medicine in the city. The origins and development of the hospital from its foundation in Lauriston Lane in 1860 are described in a later chapter. Following its temporary establishment at Plewlands House in Morningside in 1890, it moved in 1895 to the present building in Sciennes Road, designed by George Washington Browne whose work is to be seen in many parts of the

14

city including south Edinburgh. The new hospital provided 118 beds and cost £47,000, of which £10,000 was donated by Lady Jane Dundas in memory of her sister Lady Caroline Charteris. They are commemorated by a hospital wing and by the Lady Jane Dundas and Lady Caroline Charteris wards. The opening ceremony on October 31st, 1895 was performed by Princess Beatrice of Battenberg, also commemorated by a ward. At its establishment it was estimated that seven hundred children would be admitted annually, with more than eight thousand being treated in the out-patients' dispensary. Since its foundation in 1860, a hundred and eighty thousand children had already benefited from the hospital's services. Many distinguished Edinburgh doctors and surgeons have been associated with the hospital from its earliest days, notably Dr Joseph Bell (appointed first "ordinary surgeon" in 1887), Sir Harold Stiles, Professor Sir John Fraser, Professor Norman Dott, Dr Gertrude Herzfelt and Professor Charles McNeil. Since the hospital's establishment at Sciennes in 1897, great changes have taken place in the nature and prevalence of children's illnesses, as also in treatment and hospital conditions.

Another famous Edinburgh institution in Sciennes was the Trades-Maiden Hospital, a post-Reformation educational institution established at a time when learning was sparse. In 1623 George Heriot's endowment for the establishment of a "hospital" (which meant a charitable institution, boarding, clothing and educating its pupils) set an example for other benefactors whose names are commemorated by numerous present-day Edinburgh schools, though the nature and function of these has greatly changed. Heriot's generosity was emulated by Mary Erskine, George Watson, James Gillespie, Jean Cauvin, John Watson, James Donaldson, William Fettes and Daniel Stewart. In all such hospitals provision was for the children of "decayed or deceased burgesses". The Trades-Maiden Hospital was to become the one exception. In 1674 Mary Erskine, widow of a druggist in Edinburgh's High Street, donated 100,000 merks to the town's recently formed Merchant Company, to be administered by it for "the maintenance of burgess' children of the female sex". The Merchant Maiden Hospital founded by the Merchants and Mary Erskine in 1677 was originally established just outside Bristo Port and then moved to a handsome classical building at the foot of Archibald Place. Finally, when the Royal Infirmary was built, the hospital transferred to the Hopetoun Rooms at the west end of Queen Street where it eventually became the Mary Erskine fee-paying school of today, latterly established at Ravelston.

After the foundation of the Merchant Maiden Hospital, the Incorporated Trades of Edinburgh, the great rivals of the Merchants, determined not to be outdone, gathered funds and obtained Town Council support for the opening of a hospital for "the needy children of the town's tradesmen, deceased or in difficult circumstances". Following its establishment, Mary Erskine was so impressed by the efforts of the

The Merchant Maiden Hospital in Lauriston Lane, drawn by Thomas H. Shepherd

Incorporated Trades that she donated so large a sum of money to it that she earned the title of co-foundress of "The Maiden Hospital founded by the Craftsmen of Edinburgh and Mary Erskine". The Trades-Maiden Hospital was first established in a building on the west side of the Horse Wynd, a narrow vennel running from the Potterrow to the Cowgate. Its site was that of the present-day Royal Scottish Museum and it faced the former Argyle Square on the north side of Chambers Street. The building was substantially altered in 1739. There was provision for fifty girls between the ages of seven and seventeen. A few years after the establishment of the Trades-Maiden Hospital at Horse Wynd, the governors apparently also purchased property on the nothern boundary of the Wrychtishousis estate and for some time the girls who were boarded there were known in the city as "the lasses of Wrychtishousis". By 1854 the building in Horse Wynd had greatly deteriorated and the girls suffered from the crowded conditions in the Old Town. The Governors (the Deacons of Edinburgh's various trades), after declining offers of purchase of the hospital and its property by various interested parties eventually agreed to sell to the government for £5,000. The site became part of a wider area acquired for the building of the Scottish National Museum, now the Royal Scottish Museum. Having insufficient capital to build new premises, the Governors of the Trades-Maiden Hospital purchased Rillbank House, situated to the east of what is now Sylvan Place, and commemorated by Rillbank Terrace. Its boundaries were the Meadows to the north and Sciennes Road (then Sciennes Loaning) to the south. Soon after the opening of Rillbank House, the Governors faced a mounting disquiet over the whole system of "institutions". In an attempt to modernise the hospital and its educational approach, they drew up detailed regulations for the running of the school and the conduct of its girls. But the original charitable purpose of the hospital was modified as admission came to be regarded as a source of prestige (as happened in the development of the Merchant Maiden Hospital to a much greater degree). Indeed, there was a proposal to change the name from the Trades-Maiden Hospital to Rillbank Institution for Young Ladies. In 1880 the Governors agreed to a radical change in education policy. Girls were still to be boarded, but they were to be sent out to other schools such as George Watson's Ladies' College and James Gillespie's High School for Girls, both of which had also begun as charitable institutions. A new era had begun. Nevertheless, the "lasses of Rillbank" were for long a lively feature of the Sciennes, contributing a colourful episode to its annals.

In 1891 the Governors received an offer from the Directors of the Royal Edinburgh Hospital for Sick Children for the purchase of Rillbank. This they declined, though another better offer followed, of £15,000, subsequently increased to £17,500 which was readily accepted. In 1892 they acquired Ashfield, a substantial villa formerly owned by Mr Henry Younger, the Edinburgh brewer, and situated on the west corner of Blackford Avenue and Grange Loan. Here the girls of the Trades-Maiden foundation resided, no longer in an atmosphere of institutionalism but as in a large family. They continued to be educated at George Watson's Ladies' College in George Square. By 1901, however, financial difficulties resulted in primary school girls being sent to James Gillespie's School, and eventually all girls went there. In 1971 Ashfield was sold and demolished

The Royal Hospital for Sick Children in Sciennes Road

to make way for the building of modern flats. Only the gate-lodge remains with the date 1874 inscribed on its north gable. Today the Trades-Maiden Hospital, with more than two hundred and seventy years of proud history, maintains its traditions in premises in Melville Street. Eligibility for admission is now not confined only to the daughters of tradesmen. Circumstances vary among the small number of girls who reside there. There are children who suffer from partial deafness or blindness, who come from all over Scotland. With the residential staff, the family atmosphere is retained. Education is obtained at various Edinburgh schools. Although circumstances have vastly changed since the earliest days in Horse Wynd, the motive of practical charity which inspired the establishment of the hospital is perpetuated by the present Governors.

Among the many treasures preserved in the little museum of the Trades-Maiden Hospital in Melville Street is one of great historical interest. This is the famous "Blue Blanket", given by James III to the Incorporated Trades in 1482, along with their charter. It was his and Queen Margaret's gesture of appreciation to the citizens of Edinburgh for their great loyalty. The Blue Blanket, a flag displaying a saltire with the crown and thistle, is one of the earliest on which the thistle appears as a Scottish symbol. The Queen is said to have personally embroidered it. Inscribed on the top and lower V-shaped sections of the flag are the words: "Fear God and Honor the King with a Long Life and a Prosperous Reigne . . . And we that is Tradds shall ever pray to be Faithfull for the Defence of His Sacred Majestes Persone till Death". The Blue Blanket was for long a great symbol for rallying the loyalty of Edinburgh's citizens to James III and later Kings. It is said to have been carried by Edinburgh's Incorporated Trades at Flodden and displayed by citizens to demonstrate their loyalty to Mary Queen of Scots.

Also in the museum are an English grammar compiled by an early teacher in the Trades-Maiden Hospital and a treatise which was read each month to the girls, instructing them how to behave. A detailed history of the Merchant Maiden and Trades-Maiden Hospitals by the Reverend Edwin S. Towill was published in the *Book of the Old Edinburgh Club*, Volumes 28 and 29. Many pictures of the succession of premises occupied by both foundations also remain, including one of the original Trades-Maiden building in Argyle Square.

In the latter half of the eighteenth century many Edinburgh citizens of means built themselves "huts" on the outskirts of the town. A "hut" has been defined by Chambers as "a small or mean house, a small temporary dwelling". An advertisement in the *Edinburgh Courant* of February 6th, 1775 refers to "Bruntsfield Hut", situated near "the head of Bruntsfield Links". The two-storeyed house, 13 Sylvan Place, reached from a little lane entered opposite the Out-Patient Department of the Sick Children's Hospital is of a much earlier date than its surrounding dwellings. Once known as Sylvan House, it came to be regarded by certain writers as "William's Hut". Laurie's Map of *c.* 1763 indicates three unnamed houses near the site of 13 Sylvan Place, as does another map of 1773. In the Ordnance Survey map of 1852, the house appears as a substantial villa with a large ornamental garden. The title deeds of the house indicate that it was known as William's Hut, erected by advocate Joseph Williamson in the grounds of Leven Lodge. Certain local historians, however, are reluctant to accept that 13 Sylvan Place is the original William's Hut without more documentation. Unfortunately the earliest title deeds have been lost.

THE MEADOWS

Strictly speaking, the history of Edinburgh's South or Burgh Loch and the Meadows which emerged from it is outside the scope of South Edinburgh, since the "Southern New Town" grew up on the Burgh Muir, which extended only from the south bank of the loch. Nevertheless, in relation to Sciennes and Bruntsfield the great sheet of water which separated these districts from the fringes of the old town merits some consideration. The boundaries of the ancient loch can still be identified. The east bank was at Hope Park Terrace and Buccleuch Street, the west where the Melville Drive becomes Brougham Street. The tree-lined walk from Hope Park Terrace to Brougham Street, passing behind the Royal Infirmary, was the north bank, while what became Melville Drive was the south. The approximate area of the South Loch was sixty-three acres. The east end at Hope Park was deepest while the southern stretch facing Sciennes became, in dry weather, no more than a marsh, where the copious reeds were the resort of wild fowl and other birds. Here there was also much tall grass known as "gyrs", and the many poor women who came to cut it for their cattle were called "gyrs women". At intervals from 1581 the civic authorities issued edicts against the women harrying the birds. The first such order proclaimed: "that na gyrs women nor utheris pas within the South Loch to cheir the gyrs thairof, hary the burd nestis, tak away the eggis of the saming befae Midsummer nixt, under the payne of skurgein". Thus this part of the South Loch might well claim to be one of Scotland's earliest bird sanctuaries. The west end was "the head of the loch" where, in 1700, there was the Fleck Yett or small sluice gate across the burn, the Loch-rin, which ran out at the north west and is shown in Kirkwood's map of 1817. Over the years the city authorities regulated the "clowse" or sluice to prevent the loch draining and becoming too shallow. The Lochrin street names of today thus originated with the town's South Loch.

Before Edinburgh's first piped water supply was brought from Comiston in 1621, the South Loch was the town's principal source of drinking water. In 1598 the Town Council decided to bring the water from the loch to four wells in the High Street, but there is no evidence that this

The South or Borough Loch, which became the Meadows, showing George Watson's Hospital

From Grant's "Old and New Edinburgh"

was ever done. Two years earlier, access to the loch's water was given to the Fellowship and Society of Brewers and several breweries were established beside the small group of houses at the east end of the Meadows in the district still known as Boroughloch. One of the principal breweries was Melvin's. The large premises of a former brewery still remain in the area, with "Boroughloch Brewery" inscribed above the old entrance. The brewers drew heavily upon the South Loch and, by the time the Society was dissolved in 1619, the loch had greatly shrunk. This was one of the main reasons why the Town Council considered the Comiston supply in 1621. During the centuries when the South Loch was the town's main water supply, amongst the many regulations laid down by the Town Council was that, during the successive epidemics of plague, those taking the victims out to be quarantined on the Burgh Muir were not to wash their infected clothing in the South Loch.

The date of origin of what, in the course of two centuries, was to become one of Edinburgh's most attractive public parks, the Meadows, was 1657. Then the Town Council decided to drain the South Loch. A small stretch of water, however, was to be retained at the east end for watering horses. Many ditches were dug. In 1658 John Straiton, a merchant burgess, was given "tack" of the loch for £1,000 Scots. He was also given all fishing rights, though the eels and perch from the muddy and polluted waters were evidently not of top quality or popular on Edinburgh's dinner tables! Straiton's considerable efforts to improve the now half-drained loch's surrounding amenities led to its being renamed Straiton's Park. But his various projects were not financially successful. He was succeeded by a series of other tackmen, a group of whom, in 1695, first laid out the walk around the South Loch, on the north and south banks, alongside which they were to plant ash, plane or fir trees. In 1722 a public-spirited man entered the chronicles of the district, one who was to be most closely associated with the Meadows and who gave his name to several streets. He was Thomas Hope of Rankeillour who took over the task of draining the loch and laying out an ornamental park. While the work proceeded, Edinburgh's citizens were denied access to the area for several years, so the Town Council requested Hope to construct a walk across the middle of the partially drained bed of the Loch. This was the origin of today's attractive and popular Middle Meadow Walk. In 1737 the Council obtained, as a feu from the Governors of Heriot's Hospital, part of Heriot Croft which Hope's new walk had skirted. Thus a broader tree-lined avenue could be constructed, beginning at the junction of Lauriston Place and Teviot Row (where two tall stone pillars were eventually erected) and extending to what became Melville Drive. The Middle Meadow walk was not extended uphill through Bruntsfield Links and to the top of Leamington Terrace until 1863.

Although Thomas Hope made a brave attempt to create a pleasant park from the receding South Loch, his efforts, especially in drainage, were unsuccessful and the Town Council took over responsibility for further development. Amongst the early landscape gardeners employed by Hope, probably in 1749, was William Burness, father of Scotland's celebrated national bard (who changed the spelling of his surname). The following year he left Edinburgh for a gardener's post on the Fairlie estate in Ayrshire. While in Edinburgh his other son Gilbert wrote that the father "wrought hard when he could get work, passing through a variety of difficulties".

Robert Burns knew the Sciennes and Newington districts well. Apart from the celebrated occasion of his meeting with young Walter Scott in Sciennes Hill House in 1787, he was a frequent guest at social occasions in many other houses.

Thomas Hope's efforts were appreciated, and in the district of Hope Park at the east end of the Meadows, Hope Park Crescent, Terrace and Square commemorate him. In Hope Park Square, immediately south of Boroughloch Square and facing the Meadows tennis courts, Hope, in about 1740, built as his own residence the house which is today No. 5, known locally as Hope House and now the property of Edinburgh University. Its high Dutch-style frontage dominates the other houses in the square, which retains its old-world character and atmosphere. Hope died here in 1771.

The houses on the north side of the square also have entrances in Meadow Lane. Where this lane enters the Meadows are the Hope Park

Halls, now a tennis pavilion. On the south wall of this building is the inscription, "Buccleuch Parish School 1839". Just west of this is a row of old stables now used as lock-ups. In this area the early days of the creation of the Meadows are easily recalled.

In 1804 Edinburgh Town Council began the reconstruction of the Meadows. A covered drain was laid which emerged in the King's Park. However, the disappearance of the old South Loch did not please everyone. James Haig of Lochrin Distillery in Wrychtishousis (situated at the corner of what are now Home Street and Gilmore Place) strongly opposed any interference with the Lochrin Burn, water from which he used, he said, "for cooling my worms" — meaning his spiral distillation tubing. Haig's complaint was upheld and the Lochrin Burn was left untouched, though eventually channelled underground to join the Water of Leith at Coltbridge. In 1842 the civic authorities, in a last effort to construct the Meadows, employed many Irish labourers in levelling operations, but were unwilling to spend much money on the project.

Among accounts written of the South Loch and Meadows, the most notable were by Hugh Miller, particularly interested in the area's geological features, and Robert Chambers, whose essay *The Meadow Walk Warriors* includes interesting anecdotes about "The Cage", the large summer-house at the south end of Middle Meadow Walk which became a rendezvous for old soldiers regaling each other with heroic deeds. "The Cage" was removed between 1821-8. In 1858-9 Melville Drive was laid out, named after the then Lord Provost Sir John Melville. At the same time the various walks and footpaths were improved at a cost of £1,500. By 1863 work on the Meadows had been completed, leaving them largely as they are today.

There are in the Meadows various memorials to important people and events. The two tall ornamental pillars, surmounted by lion and unicorn, at the eastern entrance to Melville Drive were presented to the city by Messrs Thomas Nelson & Son, the famous printers and publishers, in appreciation of their having been given temporary accommodation on the Meadows after their premises in Hope Park Crescent were destroyed by fire in 1876. They eventually moved to their Parkside works off Dalkeith Road which were demolished some years ago. The pillars at the west end of Melville Drive commemorate the Meadows' finest hour — when they were the scene of the International Exhibition of 1886. The pillars were erected by the Master Builders & Operative Masons of Edinburgh & Leith and consist of eighteen courses of stone. In each course is cut the name of the quarry from which the stone came: a durability test in later years. The pillars also display twenty-four shields bearing the Imperial Arms of Scotland, England and Ireland, the coats of arms of nineteen Scottish burghs and the crest of the Edinburgh Master Masons. This display of different kinds of Scottish stone was the idea of James Gowans, organiser of the Exhibition, who designed the twenty-six-foot-high pillars. In the imaginative, indeed unique, use of stone lay his particular genius. The octagonal sundial at the west end of the Meadows was also his creation. It was erected after the International Exhibition to commemorate its opening by Prince Albert Victor and was named after him. The sundial's original thirteen-foot-high brass column, cast by the Edinburgh & Leith Brassfounders and surmounted by an almost life-size sculpture of a brass-worker by J. S. Rhind, was removed after the Exhibition to the garden of Nicolson Square. Another Exhibition souvenir which is a unique feature of the Meadows is the whale jawbone arch at the Melville Drive entrance to Jawbone Walk. It was donated by the Zetland and Fair Isle Knitting stand.

Amongst the sports traditionally enjoyed on the Meadows' fine turf are cricket and athletics on the west section and soccer, tennis and bowls on the east. Another sport, which has much earlier associations with the Meadows, is archery. The ancient Royal Company of Archers, or the King's Bodyguard, were, till late in the eighteenth century, without premises of their own. In 1776 they feued a piece of ground just north of Boroughloch and there built the Archers' Hall in what is now Buccleuch Street. Their feu charter provided for the narrow, winding lane which still leads from the hall past Boroughloch to the Meadows. In order to raise money to pay for their hall, the archers for some years allowed it to be used on certain evenings as a dance-hall and tavern. The building, later restored, has a decorated facade with a large stone sculpted coat of arms above its entrance. It has housed a number of important and valuable paintings including the famous Raeburn portrait of Dr Nathaniel Spens in the Royal Company of Archers' uniform. The Company has practised shooting at Leith Links and Holyrood as well as in the Meadows. A silver arrow, presented to the Company in its early days by the Magistrates of Edinburgh, is still competed for annually. In recent years many organisations from districts surrounding the Meadows have collaborated to stage an annual Meadows Festival with a wide range of events for participation and entertainment.

CHAPTER 2

Newington · The Grange · Whitehouse

NEWINGTON

The Grange of St Giles, originally simple and austere in form, built on the Burgh Muir in the twelfth century, was the earliest habitation in the encircling dense Forest of Drumselch. It was also the first sign of "development" in the area. No doubt some early cultivation of its lands took place, though this monastic farmhouse or granary was to remain in isolation for several centuries. Even after Edinburgh's Provost and magistrates had, in August 1586, "convenit in the Eister mure of the burgh for rouping and setting of the waist part thereof," development of any significance did not take place for another two centuries.

Records reveal certain features of the 1586 feuing operation. The area subsequently to become Newington was very small, being less than a half-mile long and a quarter of a mile broad. Its boundaries in terms of today's streets were East and West Preston Street to the north, East and West Mayfield to the south (for long named Mayfield Loan and, earlier, Cant's Loan), the west side of Dalkeith Road to the east and Causewayside to the west. The area was divided into six lots running north-south, each eight and a half acres. The width of the four roads bounding the district was fixed at this time, Dalkeith Road at twenty-four ells and Liberton Road (Causewayside) at eighteen. In addition to these east and west roads there were to be "twa shorter passages ledand eist and west...the ane passage at the north beside the laird of Lugtoun's lands" and the other at the south "besyde the heid of the awld pairts of the said mure". Both cross roads were fixed at nine ells. The succession of the original and of subsequent early feuars is on record. Between 1586 and 1795 Newington remained pleasant open countryside and meadowland — indeed, one explanation of the name Newington is that it is derived from "new town meadow".

In the latter half of the eighteenth century an important event in the development of Edinburgh diverted the attention of people who might have considered moving south. The congestion and overcrowding of the old town, then still confined to the High Street and its honeycomb of high lands and closes, demanded expansion elsewhere. Sir Walter Scott was amongst those who thought that this would take place to the south and that "Edinburgh's New Town" would occupy "the extensive plain on the south side of the College". Some such development did take place: Brown Square and Argyle Square at the west end of Chambers Street, and

George Square on the verge of the Meadows (then the South or Burgh Loch), were built. But these were isolated projects. Despite the crowded conditions of the old town, people were reluctant to venture into the remote rural south to form the nucleus of a suburb. "Better a dwelling in a narrow wynd of the old town," one writer commented, "than a lodge in the wilderness." Then, through the long perseverance of one man, Lord Provost George Drummond, a development occurred which abruptly halted, temporarily at least, any further growth to the south. This was the opening of the North Bridge in 1772. A great milestone in Edinburgh's history, the North Bridge had been George Drummond's constant dream since his election as Lord Provost in 1725. He was one of the city's most influential Lord Provosts, and served for six periods of office. When at last his dream materialised, there began a great exodus of people of means from the High Street's historic closes, across the new bridge high above the old Nor' Loch and into the elegant terraces of Craig's New Town.

But development in the south of Edinburgh's other new town had merely been delayed. Before long it was, at first steadily, and then rapidly accelerated. The impetus came, as it did in the creation of the classical New Town, from the building of a new road and bridge, this time the South Bridge, completed in 1788. By the closing years of the eighteenth century, many people who had moved to Craig's New Town decided to build themselves country houses to the south. Others had begun to find that, while the elegance of the New Town's terraces was indeed attractive, these did not provide as much privacy as was desired. They therefore moved south to small villas, "snug boxes" with pleasant, spacious gardens in the rural seclusion of Newington, Grange and Morningside. A feu plan of Newington for 1795 shows that considerable sub-feuing had taken place and that houses had begun to arise. This plan also shows the "intended new road" which was to be Minto Street.

The most significant date in the development of Newington, however, is August 29th, 1805, when the whole of the estate was acquired by, and a charter was granted to, Dr Benjamin Bell, one of Edinburgh's most eminent surgeons. "The leading operator in Edinburgh and in Scotland," Lord Cockburn wrote of him, "a little, intelligent, agreeable, well-intentioned gentleman." Great-grandfather of Dr Joseph Bell, prototype of Conan Doyle's Sherlock Holmes, he was surgeon to the Edinburgh Royal Infirmary for twenty-nine years, becoming very wealthy through private practice. A serious accident, however, temporarily curtailed his professional work and during this time he took to farming at Liberton, where he was attended by another distinguished Edinburgh surgeon, Dr Alexander Wood. It was to "Lang Sandie Wood", as he was affectionately known to Edinburgh people, that Sir Walter Scott's parents took their young son when distressed by his lameness.

Dr Wood was a great philanthropist, with a deep concern for the city's poor. Even Byron had heard of his reputation and the poet immortalised him thus:

> Oh! for an hour of him who knew no feud;
> The octogenarian chief, the kind old Sandie Wood.

Wood was one of the doctors who attended Robert Fergusson during his last days in the Edinburgh Bedlam in 1774.

Wood was closely associated with Dr Benjamin Bell in the acquisition and development of the Newington estate, possibly through some financial relationship. In 1805 Bell built Newington House, "an austere-looking mansion" hidden by a high wall and thick plantations, entered from Blacket Avenue. His enjoyment of this residence and its surrounding eight and a half acres of pleasant lands was, however, short-lived: he died there in April 1806, probably before the mansion-house had been completed.

Bell was descended from landed proprietors at Blacket in the parish of Middlebie in Dumfriesshire, a fact commemorated by the names of modern streets. His son George, who succeeded to his father's property, soon sold Newington House and its lands to Sir George Stewart of Grantully, whose grandfather had married as his second wife Lady Jane Douglas, who featured prominently in the "Douglas Case", renowned in Scottish litigation of the eighteenth century.

During the seven years after Whitsun 1808, when Sir George had purchased Newington House, he was at liberty to dispose of the grounds for building purposes, provided that nothing was done to spoil local amenities, in which case the property would revert to George Bell. The proviso prohibited "the construction of breweries, the manufactory of soot or blood, tanneries, lime or brick kilns, or the construction of a steam engine," adding that "dunghills must not be established for commercial purposes." After Sir George's acquisition of Newington, the stone pillars and gates were built at the Minto Street and Dalkeith Road ends of Blacket Avenue and Mayfield Terrace. To ensure seclusion in this select area, the gates were closed at dusk. Anecdotes abound of residents and, more often, maid-servants returning home after dark to find themselves locked out. A porter's lodge was built at each gate and the remains of one may still be seen at the Minto Street entrance to Mayfield Terrace. The association of Newington with Sir George Stewart ended with his death in 1822. Five years earlier, the Newington section of Kirkwood's Map of Edinburgh (1817), revealed the considerable growth of the district. Most present-day streets had by then been laid out and named.

From 1822 onwards Newington House had a succession of owners. In 1826 records refer to Belleville, a large villa with its own land situated north of Newington House in Blacket Avenue, and this still stands. The name Belleville was often applied to Newington itself, possibly as a play on the name of its original developer, Dr Benjamin Bell. In 1852 Newington

Newington House

House was purchased by Duncan McLaren, a prominent Edinburgh draper. Having joined the Town Council in 1834, he became City Treasurer and played an important part in saving Edinburgh from bankruptcy. He was Lord Provost from 1851-4 and became a Member of Parliament. With another Lord Provost who resided in Newington, Sir John Melville, McLaren led the campaign for laying out the Meadows as a public park. His fellow campaigner's part in this enterprising project was commemorated by Melville Drive, while McLaren himself is remembered in Newington by Duncan Street and McLaren Road. His brother-in-law John Bright gave his name to Bright's Crescent. In 1863 Duncan McLaren acquired Mayfield, Rosebank and the village of Powburn at the eastern end of present-day West Saville Terrace. Known originally as Newlands, Mayfield was the property of Walter Porterfield, surgeon and burgess of Edinburgh, in 1735. He was succeeded by a number of owners before McLaren's acquisition. The latter soon began sub-feuing this land which

27

had long been used for farming. By the time of his death in Newington House in 1886, the terraced villas of Mayfield were largely completed.

A later resident in Newington House, during 1907-15, achieved distinction far beyond Scotland. This was Dr J. G. Bartholomew of the world-renowned firm of cartographers, established originally about 1826, which removed to Duncan Street in 1911. The facade of their premises here was constructed from the pillared frontage of Falcon Hall in Morningside, demolished in 1909, in which Dr Bartholomew had been the last resident before moving to Newington House. He founded the Royal Scottish Geographical Society in 1884 and remained its secretary until his death.

In 1915 Newington House was acquired by the Scottish National Institution for the War Blinded. After the end of the First World War it proved a most beneficial establishment, its workshops providing a valuable means of rehabilitation. After fifty years of service Newington House was demolished in 1966 and the land sold by the National Institution to Edinburgh University. The work for the war blinded is now carried on at Linburn, although premises used in Albany Street still perpetuate the name of Newington House.

After a pause in development between the early 1830s and about 1850, a report by Dr Henry Littlejohn, Edinburgh's first Medical Officer of Health, reveals that by 1865 Newington had become the most densely populated of Edinburgh's southern suburbs. Growth in the neighbouring Grange district and in Morningside and Bruntsfield had taken place more slowly. An important factor in Newington's growth was the introduction of public transport, horse-drawn buses in the 1850s and horse-drawn tramcars in 1871. By 1880 over one thousand horses were used in Edinburgh's transport system. Three years earlier, the valuation of Newington and Mayfield together was £1,358,000. With the establishment of the Edinburgh Suburban Railway and the opening of Newington Station in 1884, development of the district was greatly accelerated.

During its early development Newington had attracted primarily wealthy Edinburgh merchants, but by the close of the nineteenth century the pattern was changing and many professional people took up residence, including men distinguished in Edinburgh's literary and artistic circles. William Blackwood, founder of the publishing firm, lived at 2 Salisbury Road from 1805 until 1830, while he founded the famous magazine which bore his name. In Salisbury Place resided Dr Thomas McCrie, a Free Church minister in Potterrow who gave Blackwood his first best-seller, his *Life of John Knox*, published in 1811. William Nelson, the famous publisher, lived at what is now 10 Newington Road, which he named West Newington House to commemorate the original house of that name which had once stood in Causewayside. At Newington Lodge, now 38 Mayfield Terrace, resided David Octavius Hill, the first artist in Scotland to apply photography to portraiture. Hill's famous calotypes were an important stage in the evolution of photography. His painting of the first general assembly of the Free Church of Scotland at Tanfield in May 1843 is one of his classic works. In it Dr Thomas Chalmers, first Free Church Moderator, his collaborator Hugh Miller and Dr James Y. Simpson are prominently seen. Hill's establishment of a studio at Rock House on the Calton Hill with Robert Adamson began a long association of this house with photographic art.

Much valuable information about Newington, and in particular Causewayside, during the latter half of the nineteenth century is to be found in a very small book, *The Print of His Shoe,* published in 1906 by James Goodfellow who worked as a missionary in Newington for forty years. Goodfellow's illustrations are of unique interest, their subjects including the Grange Toll, Powburn and one of the Causewayside's important early houses, Broadstairs House. Standing between Salisbury Place and Duncan Street, and facing the Grange estate, this house may have taken its name from the broad flight of steps leading up to its entrance. Another name for the house was Wormwoodhall, though this seems to have applied to a separate part of it. Grant attributed the building of the house to the doctor of James IV or V and wrote that it remained in the possession of his family till the end of the eighteenth century, but there is no documentary evidence to support this account. By Goodfellow's time Broadstairs House had become a slum occupied by several families. Before the house was demolished in 1880, the last purchaser had to acquire not only the part known as Broadstairs House but also that designated Wormwoodhall before he could proceed with demolition.

In Newington, as in most of its neighbouring estates in South Edinburgh, many of the renowned old mansion-houses have long since disappeared, but certain other places of interest fortunately still remain. One of these is the Longmore Hospital in Salisbury Place, which owes its existence to John Alexander Longmore of Deanhaugh, whose grandfather Adam Longmore, of the Scottish Exchequer office, resided in Salisbury Road. After John Longmore's death in 1875, the residue of his estate was left to establish a hospital for incurables. His executors donated £10,000 to the Edinburgh Association for the Relief of Incurables on condition that the hospital to be built should be named the Longmore Hospital. In Salisbury Place the demolition of a row of houses with gardens in front and a boys' school known as Wilson's Academy provided an excellent site. The hospital was opened in 1875. While still bearing its original name, it has for many years now been a general hospital. Appropriately, the nurses' home stands opposite Adam Longmore's former residence in Salisbury Road.

While many distinguished persons have lived in Newington, there have been others who have earned a certain notoriety. None more so than Dr Robert Knox who, during the first half of the nineteenth century,

29

The stone pillars at the west entrance of Blacket Avenue, Newington, which once had gates closed every night at ten

Photograph by Mr W. R. Smith

resided at 4 (now 17) Newington Road (once named Arniston Place). He was a brilliant lecturer in anatomy at the Surgeon's Hall. After his wife's death, his sister came to live with him and, she being a competent hostess, the house ranked high in Edinburgh's social round. At his dinners and evening parties, in an atmosphere of gracious living and good music, Knox was a most cultured and charming host. But one evening during the week following February 12th, 1829, the hospitable calm of 4 Newington Road was rudely and noisily disturbed. Outside, a great crowd converged on the house and the background music in Knox's drawing-room gave way to the sound of shattering window panes from a fusillade of stones hurled by the crowd. Earlier that week, William Burke of the Burke and Hare "Resurrectionist" or body-snatching partnership had been hanged before a crowd of thirty thousand outside St Giles. His crimes were several murders committed in the Grassmarket and West Port area and the exhuming of corpses in various Edinburgh graveyards. His motive was supplied by Dr Robert Knox, to whom he presented the bodies, and who readily paid a good price in order to use them for dissection when instructing his medical students — who, according to his class registers, on occasion numbered five hundred in a day. Burke and Hare ensured that Knox was well and regularly supplied. The great crowd surrounding Knox's house, outraged by the crimes of Burke and Hare, considered

30

Knox to have been their prompter and accomplice. An effigy of the anatomist as a fellow-murderer was brandished outside his window, then hung from a tree nearby and a bonfire lit below it. Meanwhile Knox, disguised as a Highlander, complete with dirk and pistols, slipped out through a back door to safety. The city guard arrived and dispersed the incensed crowd.

A committee of inquiry exonerated Knox from complicity with Burke and Hare, but while Lord Cockburn was at pains to uphold his innocence, Sir Walter Scott was not so convinced, absenting himself from a dinner at which Knox was a principal guest and writing in protest to the secretary of the Royal Society of Edinburgh, of which Scott himself was President, against Knox's having been invited to read a paper entitled *On Some Dissections.* Scott resented "the boldness of one who had recently been trading so deeply in human flesh". However relieved Knox may have felt at having been proved not guilty, he nevertheless subsequently removed to Lauder, where he spent over twenty years, and died in 1862. He was the subject of many caricatures and cartoons including a set of prints entitled *Wretch's Illustrations of Shakespeare,* in one of which the Devil is seen with a pair of shears in his hands about to crop a plant, with the caption "A nox-i-ous weed". Knox has also been a popular subject for Scottish playwrights.

The anatomist was not the only Newington resident to bring notoriety to the district. Two sensational Scottish murder trials of the nineteenth century concerned the area. In one, Dr Edward William Pritchard was accused of poisoning his wife and mother-in-law and investigations led to a local chemists' prescription records. The other one involved a young schoolgirl from 5 Buccleuch Place, a pupil of Newington Academy in what was then Arniston Place. She became infatuated with one of her language teachers, a Frenchman named Eugene Marie Chantrelle, and they eventually married. Soon afterwards Chantrelle insured his young wife for £1,000 and a year later poisoned her. The victims of these Newington crimes are buried in Grange Cemetery.

Prestonfield House, strictly speaking outside the boundaries of Newington, is nevertheless on the fringes of the district and tends to be associated with it. The present house was built in 1687, a century before Newington was first developed. It was probably built on the site of a much earlier house of more primitive design. Originally named Priestfield, the estate first appears on record in a royal charter of 1153 when it was granted to the monks of Harehope in Northumberland, probably as a grange or farmlands, a possible explanation of the name. David II, returning to Scotland after eleven years of captivity in England, withdrew the lands from the monks on account of their support for his enemy, Edward III. In 1355 Priestfield was conveyed by Robert II to John, Earl of Carrick, Steward of Scotland. He in turn, as Robert III, granted the lands and those of the Grange of St Giles to Andrew Wardlaw, Archbishop of

(above) Grange Toll, Causewayside, c. 1854

Photographs by Tunny, by courtesy of Yerbury

(below) Grange Loan from Causewayside, looking west, c. 1854

Glasgow. In 1510 James IV bestowed Priestfield on Walter Chepman who, along with Andrew Myllar, introduced printing into Scotland. Chepman's "rent" was the delivery of a pair of gloves on each St Giles' Day, later translated into the sum of five shillings. There followed a succession of owners, one of whom, Sir Andrew Murray of Ardgask, was Principal Keeper of the King's Park of Holyroodhouse in 1567, before the estate was sold in 1677 to Sir James Dick, grandson of the ill-fated Sir William Dick of Braid, who changed its name to Prestonfield. From that date, the property has remained in the possession of Dick's descendants.

Sir James Dick, a prosperous merchant, was a staunch supporter of the Catholic claim to the throne, and in 1680 he was called to London by Charles II to attend his brother James, Duke of York. When James came north to reside at Holyroodhouse, not far from Dick's mansion at Prestonfield, a close friendship developed. The Duke of York, later James II, frequently visited Prestonfield House, his route thence, a footpath across the King's Park, coming to be known as the Duke's Walk. But Sir James Dick's friendship with his royal neighbour was to prove an embarrassment. When he became Provost of Edinburgh, he faced great opposition on political and religious grounds, and in 1681 the students of Edinburgh University burned down Prestonfield House, this action leading to a temporary closure of the University. James II sought to

Newington Station on the Edinburgh Suburban Railway

By courtesy of Yerbury

rebuild the mansion-house at public expense but Sir James Dick himself in the end had to bear the major cost. The new structure, which remains in its present form, was completed in 1687. The architect was the celebrated Sir William Bruce who had designed Holyrood Palace, and he employed the same craftsmen who had built the Palace. Sir James Dick died in 1728. His grandson William was Laird of Prestonfield in 1745 and is said to have entertained Bonnie Prince Charlie there.

Sir Alexander Dick, who succeeded to the estate in 1746, began a new era in the history of the mansion-house. He had many friends in medical, literary and social circles in Edinburgh. He was President of the Royal College of Physicians of Edinburgh for seven years and when his portrait was hung in the College it was a "mark of distinction never previously bestowed". One of his many enterprises at Prestonfield was the growing of rhubarb, which he considered to be of great medicinal value. He was probably the first to introduce it to Scotland. His land became famous for its crop, and inquiries reached him from far and wide requesting the secret of its cultivation. Perhaps this lay in the fact that his forebear Sir James Dick, the first Laird, when Provost of Edinburgh, had had Edinburgh's streets cleansed at his own expense and the copious horse

Grange House, rebuilt by W. H. Playfair in 1827

By courtesy of Edinburgh City Libraries

34

manure gathered spread on his land at Prestonfield. Sir Alexander Dick's rhubarb crop earned him a gold medal from the London Society for Promoting the Arts and Commerce. Perhaps they had been influenced by the request which Dr Samuel Johnson sent to Boswell, when in Edinburgh, in 1784, following a dinner at which the "learned Doctor" had been a guest at Prestonfield House. "Bring with you", Dr Johnson wrote to Boswell, "the rhubarb which Sir Alexander Dick so tenderly offers me." Boswell duly fulfilled his command, taking a package of rhubarb seeds to London. Johnson apparently consulted Dick professionally before his death. Some years ago, a Johnsonian commemorative dinner was arranged by an Edinburgh University society in Prestonfield House, at which the menu consisted of the "learned Doctor's" favourite dishes — and, for the sweet course there was, of course, rhubarb!

Dr Johnson was not the principal claimant upon Sir Alexander Dick's celebrated rhubarb crop. This distinction went to Professor James Gregory of Canaan Lodge in Morningside whose famous "mixture" included pulverised rhubarb as one of three constituents. Dick collaborated with Gregory in producing the requirements of the chemist Dr Thomas Steel who manufactured the mixture.

Prestonfield House underwent restoration in 1960, with the aid of a Ministry of Works grant. Now a hotel and restaurant, it retains the atmosphere of a venerable mansion-house with many traditional and interesting features.

THE GRANGE OF ST GILES

Of the several great manor houses which in early times stood out in the wasteland of the Burgh Muir, four, the Grange, Bruntsfield, Whitehouse and Merchiston, were outside the area of the Burgh Muir in 1586 feued out by Edinburgh Town Council.

Their origins went back far beyond that date. Most ancient was the Grange of St Giles. Because of other large properties acquired by its earliest owners, the marriages of their descendants and the associations of the house with influential families in the district, the Grange of St Giles may be regarded as the great source of development in South Edinburgh. Almost every street in the present-day Grange district has associations with the vast properties in various parts of Scotland owned by the Dicks and Lauders of the Grange. Likewise many Morningside place names are derived from those of families associated with Grange House.

There must be few places in Scotland which visibly bridge eight centuries of history, but this is true of Grange Loan, where two solitary stone pillars stand almost unnoticed in a modern residential district. A pedestrian enjoying a leisurely stroll on the north side of Grange Loan is

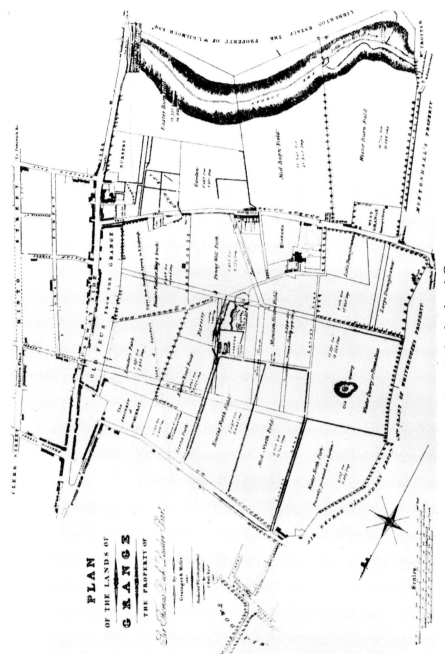

Plan of the lands of Grange

36

more likely than a passing motorist to observe, some hundred yards apart, the two early eighteenth-century rusticated pillars surmounted by griffins. These are the ancient Lauder griffins, the last noticeable remains of the great mansion-house which arose here on the Burgh Muir nearly eight centuries ago. This was "Sanct Geilies' Grange", or the Grange of St. Giles.

The origins of the house, as so much of Edinburgh's history, go back to David I, that "Sair Sanct for the Croon", whose widespread establishment of monasteries and churches was the result of a desire to provide centres of civilisation, culture and peace, and to bring areas of land under cultivation, the monks imparting their agricultural skill to their neighbours. Sanct Geilies' Grange was very much a case in point. David's only surviving son Henry shared some of his father's zeal and he founded, in 1150, the Cistercian monastery of Holme Cultrane, or Harehope, in the county of Cumberland, then Scottish territory. Soon after the foundation, David granted this religious community charge of Edinburgh's Parish Church of St Giles and "all lands pertaining" to it, including Sanct Geilies' Grange. There is some evidence, however, that in fact the Grange goes back further than 1150. David's brother and predecessor Alexander had built a new church of St Giles on the site of a much earlier foundation dating from 854, which had belonged to the Monks of Lindisfarne, the disciples of St Columba of Iona. It may well have been that these monks were given land out on the Burgh Muir by Alexander in about 1120, which was used as a granary or farmhouse serving the area of the Muir which they were bringing under cultivation. A grange was the name given to such a monastic farmhouse. The year 1120, then, is possibly the earliest date of Sanct Geilies' Grange, 1150 being the beginning of a second era when the farmhouse and its lands were conveyed to the monks of Holme Cultrane.

In 1323 David II, son of Robert the Bruce, expelled from Scotland all Englishmen possessing lands and benefices within the Kingdom. Amongst those forced to go were the monks of Holme Cultrane who had sworn allegiance to the English invaders some years before. The Grange lands were confiscated and given by the King to Sir Walter de Wardlaw, Archbishop of Glasgow, upon whose death they passed to his kinsman, the Laird of Riccarton. Remaining in the possession of the Wardlaw family for nearly two hundred years, the Grange was eventually returned to the Crown, and James IV subsequently bestowed it upon a leading Edinburgh burgess of an ancient family of churchmen and merchants, John Cant. As an early owner also of Comiston House, Cant provided the first link between Morningside and the Grange.

The Grange estate, in terms of present-day street names, extended from Sciennes Road in the north to Grange Loan in the south, and from St Catherine's Place in the east to Marchmont Crescent and Kilgraston Road in the west. While the original Sanct Geilies' Grange, farmstead of the monks of St Giles, must have been simple in style, with possibly a

Sword of Sir Robert de Lawdre, thirteenth-century ancestor of Sir George Dick-Lauder, 12th Baronet of Grange

The Bonnie Prince Charlie thistle, now in the possession of Sir George Dick-Lauder

The original twelfth-century keep or granary of the Grange of St Giles

By courtesy of Edinburgh City Libraries

The main entrance to Grange House in Grange Loan

turreted tower and keep, Walter Cant, owner in 1592, began a long process of modernisation which was continued by his successors.

In 1631 there was another link between Morningside and the Grange. After a hundred and thirty years of ownership by the Cant family, Grange House was purchased by Sir William Dick, Knight of Braid. The transfer of ownership was arranged in a somewhat modern setting during a round of golf between John Cant and Sir William on "the furzy hills of Braid"! After the game, both parties returned to Grange House to complete the legal formalities.

Sir William Dick was the greatest and wealthiest Scottish merchant of his day and became Lord Provost of Edinburgh. The acquisition by members of his family of the mansions of Craighouse and Plewlands provide yet further links between Morningside and Grange House.

When Bonnie Prince Charlie entered Edinburgh with his army from the north in the autumn of 1745, he approached the capital by way of Corstorphine, Slateford and Colinton Mains, then by the Braid Burn path to Braid Road and Morningside Road, turning eastward along Cant's Loan, now Newbattle Terrace, to avoid the gunfire from the Castle. As he passed along Grange Loan, on his way to the King's Park and Holyrood, no-one would have welcomed his arrival more enthusiastically as he skirted its wall than the owners of Grange House, William Dick, descendant of Sir William Dick of Braid, and his wife, Lady Anne Seton, both of staunch Jacobite families. During his residence at Holyrood, the Young Pretender visited Grange House. When one of Lady Seton's sisters presented him with a white rose, the Prince took the thistle from his bonnet and presented it to the ladies. The heirloom, sealed in a glass bell-jar, is proudly preserved by the present 12th Baronet, Sir George Dick-Lauder and his family. The white rose bush of the occasion, still flourishing when Grange House was demolished in 1936, was transplanted to a family estate in the north, but there, alas, failed to take root. Following his visit to the Grange, the Prince entertained the Dick family to breakfast at Holyrood and presented them at Court. A silver snuff-box formerly belonging to the Young Chevalier is also a treasured family heirloom.

In 1731 one of the Dick daughters, heiress of the Grange, married Sir Andrew Lauder, Baronet of Fountainhall. Their son Andrew in 1769 inherited Grange House and, soon afterwards, the Baronetcy of Fountainhall. He thereafter adopted the name of Lauder-Dick. This owner of the Grange chose, however, not to reside there and for some years the house and lands were rented to a series of distinguished tenants. Amongst these was Dr William Robertson who became Principal of Edinburgh University and Lord Provost of the city. He was a notable historian and close friend of Boswell and Dr Johnson. Many of his celebrated literary circle—David Hume, Robert Fergusson and Henry Mackenzie among others—were regular guests at the Grange.

39

With the death of Sir Andrew Lauder-Dick in 1820, his successor, Sir Thomas Dick-Lauder (who chose to reverse his hyphenated surname) began a new era in the annals of the already famous house. In 1827 it underwent great structural transformations. Builders, carpenters, masons and plumbers for a time took possession of the Grange. The architect was the distinguished W. H. Playfair whose work is so much a feature of Edinburgh. Within five years, the ancient monastic layout of Sanct Geilies' Grange, though partly preserved, gave way to the elegance of a handsome later-style mansion. The transformed Grange witnessed the development of a new style of life, centred on the wide cultural and literary interests of Sir Thomas Dick-Lauder, his deep involvement in Liberal Politics and his support for many causes of the time. Lord Cockburn, Dr John Brown and the Rev. John Thomson, the minister and celebrated artist of Duddingston, were among the Grange's most frequent visitors. While Sir Walter Scott was not often a resident at the house, he did make many visits. As a schoolboy at Edinburgh's High School he had been fascinated by the quaintness of the house and its gardens and by their air of antiquity. He is said to have climbed the pillars at the entrance to decide whether the Lauder griffins perched on top had protruding tongues of "veritable paint or veritable fire". In later years Sir Thomas Dick-Lauder and Sir Walter were close friends. In *Tait's Magazine* of November 1832, it was Sir Thomas who wrote the principal account of Sir Walter Scott's last days at Abbotsford and his funeral at Dryburgh Abbey.

Sir Thomas was closely involved in the passing of the Reform Bill and

Sir Thomas Dick-Lauder of Grange House and his lady
By courtesy of Sir George Dick-Lauder

many important political meetings to discuss the Bill were held at Grange House. He also presided over a rally of thirty thousand at St Ann's Yards, a field east of Holyrood Palace, and recorded his impressions of another mass rally held on Bruntsfield Links to celebrate the Reform Bill's eventual adoption in August 1832. Another article from his prolific pen describes the excitement and sadness experienced one night in January 1845 when, from the Grange tower, he watched the complete destruction by fire of the old Greyfriars Church. Amongst the numerous public causes he initiated and championed was the construction of the Queen's Drive in Holyrood Park. Sir Thomas Dick-Lauder's interests and knowledge were wide, his writings ranging from treatises on geology and natural history to political commentaries and works on Scottish history, particularly of Morayshire. His literary output was considerable. Amongst his best known works were *The Wolf of Badenoch* and *Legendary Tales*. Less well known but relevant to Morningside and most entertainingly written is his *Scottish Rivers*, the first chapter of which is devoted to none other than Morningside's own fascinating and ancient waterway, the Jordan Burn. Sir Thomas was also a sponsor of amateur drama and for a period "The Grange Salon Theatre" presented plays which he had written and which were performed by his family and friends.

This distinguished, talented and much loved owner of Grange House crowded much more than average achievement into a life a little shorter than man's allotted span. His contribution to the welfare and happiness of his family, his friends and his country was great and generous, inspired by Christian charity. He died on May 29th, 1848, at the age of sixty-four. Several hundred mourners from all levels of society in Edinburgh and far beyond saw him laid to rest in the family vault in Grange Cemetery, near the east wall and within the shadow of his beloved Grange House. They paid silent tribute to a great man and a cherished friend. The Grange tower in which he had written and initiated so much in the service of others was no ivory one. He belonged with distinction to the world of letters, and equally to the world of men and of action.

While the Dick-Lauder family retained ownership of the Grange for nearly a century after Sir Thomas's death, there were periods when it was largely unoccupied so that the fabric gradually deteriorated. When at first news spread of the ancient mansion's proposed demolition, individual and public protests appeared in the press. But, alas, in 1936 the demolition hammers began to fall. Nearly eight centuries after the monks had first built their Sanct Geilies' Grange on the bleak Burgh Muir and begun to bring its wasteland under cultivation, the elegant mansion which had arisen on the remains of their simple farm-steading was stripped of the treasures which expressed the life of the long succession of families who had dwelt there. By 1936 the cost of preservation and modernisation had become prohibitive. The Grange House saga was at an end.

While of the original estate only the griffins on their pillars remain

The dining-room of Grange House

The drawing-room of Grange House

By courtesy of the Edinburgh "Evening News"

readily visible to one passing along Grange Loan, two little harled rubble outhouses also still stand concealed at the end of a private lane off Lauder Road, once the north-east entrance to the mansion-house. Fortunately many relics of his ancestors are now in the possession of the 12th Baronet, Sir George Dick-Lauder and his family, whose home abounds in portraits of his forebears. There are also numerous original papers pertaining to Sir William Dick, Knight of Braid. The oldest of Sir George Dick-Lauder's treasured possessions is the large sword of Sir Robert de Lawdre, one of William Wallace's closest supporters in his successful struggle to liberate Scotland, who fought at Wallace's side at the victorious battle of Stirling Bridge in 1297. Sir Robert de Lawdre is mentioned in Blind Harry's poem on Wallace. The earliest Sir Robert de Lawdre on record was an Anglo-Saxon baron who assisted Malcolm Canmore to regain his throne from Macbeth. For this he was rewarded by the gift of lands in Berwickshire and Leader Dale, the name of which was changed to Lauderdale in his honour. One of his descendants accompanied Richard the Lionheart on his Crusade. Sir Robert de Lawdre in Wallace's time gained possession of the Bass Rock and Tantallon Castle, which he defended against England's Edward I. Members of the Lawdre, later spelled Lauder, family were also bishops of Dunkeld and Glasgow, and Lauder griffins appear amongst the carvings in Glasgow Cathedral. Next in antiquity among the present Baronet's ancestral relics is a finely carved oak chest, once the possession of Sir William Dick of Braid, Lord Provost of Edinburgh.

A sundial from Grange House, after finding a place in the garden of a former Edinburgh Town Councillor, now forms the centre-piece of the front garden of St Bennet's, the residence of Cardinal Gray, to whom the Councillor was related. Other relics of Grange House, including another sundial designed by W. H. Playfair and "the Monks' Seat", are in Edinburgh's Huntly House Museum. The most permanent daily re-minders of Grange House and its successive owners over many centuries are, however, the street names of the district in which the house once stood. Many such names have associations that are immediately obvious: Grange Road itself, Mansionhouse Road, Seton Place, Dick Place and Lauder Road. Others such as Tantallon Place, Cumin Place, Findhorn Place, Fountainhall Road and Relugas Road are derived from the estates which belonged to the Dick and Lauder families, whose ancestry goes back almost a thousand years.

The Church of St Catherine's in Grange, at the east corner of Chalmers Crescent and Grange Road, was built three centuries after the once nearby Convent of St Catherine of Sienna in Sciennes had been closed, and it perpetuates the name. It was the first church built in the Grange district and when opened on December 6th, 1866 it was known as the Chalmers Memorial Free Church of Scotland, so named to commemorate Dr Thomas Chalmers, the great Disruption leader and first

43

Moderator of the Free Church who had been buried only a few yards away in Grange Cemetery in 1847. After the Union of 1900, the church became the Grange United Free Church. In 1929, after the reunion of the United Free Church and the Established Church of Scotland, it changed its name yet again, becoming the Parish Church of St Catherine's in Grange. The church had its earliest origins in the meetings of Free Church adherents which took place in the dining-room of 13 (now 37) Mansionhouse Road. The possibility of establishing a Free Church in the Grange district had first been discussed by members of the Roxburgh Free Church who, with this end in view, had met in a hall in Causewayside, entered from Findhorn Place, which belonged to a school called Clare Academy. Amongst the distinguished ministers of St Catherine's in Grange were Dr Horatius Bonnar, the notable hymn-writer, and, in more recent times, the late Rev. Thomas Maxwell who wrote a valuable centenary history of the church with a scholarly account of the history of the district.

THE WHITEHOUSE

A short distance north-west of Grange House stood another ancient mansion-house, the Whitehouse, which gave its name to the present-day Whitehouse Loan and Terrace. Largely rebuilt and extended, the Whitehouse was to become the first Roman Catholic convent to be established in Scotland after the Reformation. It was occupied by the nuns of the French teaching Order, the Ursulines of Jesus, who afterwards opened a boarding school for girls. The lands of Whitehouse were originally named Hogstoun or Ogstoun after the family of Hog, the mid-fifteenth-century proprietors. The estate was bounded by what are now Whitehouse Loan, Whitehouse Terrace, Kilgraston Road and Thirlestane Road.

About the year 1505 the earliest mansion-house was built and it was in this year that the name Quhytehouse was first recorded. Much of the estate passed to James Hepburn, Earl of Bothwell, after the Reformation and later to Thomas McCalzeane of Cliftonhall who became Lord Provost of Edinburgh. About this time it also appears that Whitehouse was under the superiority of the Collegiate Church of Crichton in Midlothian.

A dramatic chapter in the annals of the Whitehouse was written in 1585, the year of the Great Plague. Thomas McCalzeane had recently died and the house had passed to his daughter, Euphamie, Lady Cliftonhall. During the severe outbreak of plague then ravaging Edinburgh, the Town Council instructed that some of the convalescent victims be "enclosed with keepers" in the Whitehouse and other large houses in this part of the Burgh Muir, the traditional quarantine area. Lady Cliftonhall strongly objected to the Whitehouse being so used. Her appeal to the Privy Council against Edinburgh Town Council was upheld and "the pestiferous persons, their guidis and baggage" were removed from her land and the house was "pungeit and clened of the said pest". But fate was to take a strange turn.

Five years after the outbreak of plague, the same Lady Cliftonhall of the Whitehouse was condemned as a witch and, unlike in ordinary cases of witchcraft when the victim was strangled first at the stake, this unfortunate lady was burned "quick [alive] to the death" on the south bank of Castlehill. The charges against her included consorting with other well known witches, obtaining the enchantment of a picture to cause the death of her father-in-law, attending a conventicle of witches at North Berwick and "seiking of ane pictour for the tressonable destruction of the King". Amongst the jurymen whose verdict sent the Lady of the Whitehouse to her death was her near neighbour Robert Fairlie, the Laird of Braid.

In 1596 the plague again returned to Edinburgh. This time the Whitehouse tenant Hew Crawford lost "5 of his puir bairnies through the pest", and later when the house was being disinfected it caught fire and all Mr Crawford's possessions were lost. He was accused of maliciously setting his own house on fire and forced to rebuild it by the proprietors, the Herries family.

Although Whitehouse was associated with the dreaded plague, in early times, being the district to which so many unfortunate victims were removed from the city, to hope for recovery or to die in isolation, a later account of the area, written by a resident, describes it as being "in the most healthy situation in Edinburgh, entirely screened from the easterly winds which are our greatest trial here . . . so healthy and agreeably situated indeed that it is called 'the land of promise'. It is the spot to which all the invalids are sent for their health."

The district seems to have been conducive also to notable literary work. Here, in the Whitehouse, Principal Robertson of Edinburgh University wrote his important *History of Charles V* and John Home his play *Douglas* (which so inspired one member of the audience during an Edinburgh production that he proclaimed loudly for the benefit of the many English people present: "Whaur's yer Willie Shakespear noo!") Here, too, Dr Blair is said to have written his famous *Lectures*.

In the early nineteenth century, the Whitehouse was to earn a notable place in the ecclesiastical, and, indeed, in the circumstances of the times, the wider history of Scotland. While the Convent of the Sisters of St Catherine of Sienna in nearby Sciennes had been the last built in Scotland before the Reformation, in 1834 St Margaret's at the Whitehouse was to become the first to be established after that tempestuous event.

At the beginning of the nineteenth century, the Catholic community in Edinburgh was small, following centuries of hardship after the Reformation. Among the little band of priests in the city was a man of outstanding and varied talents, the Rev. James Gillis, born in Montreal of parents who emigrated to Canada from Banffshire but had returned to Scotland. Deeply convinced of the importance of sound religious instruction for the young of the Catholic community, Father Gillis had for long attempted to persuade his superiors of the need for establishing a teaching Religious Order whose members could concentrate on the religious instruction of youth while also working amongst the sick and poor and devoting their lives to prayer. His plan was at last supported and he was permitted to tour Europe appealing for financial support from many of the royal families.

While the opportunity was awaited of purchasing a suitable house for the establishment of a convent in Edinburgh, two young Scottish nuns expressed their readiness to the Rev. Mr Gillis to join the proposed religious community. They had recently entered the Order of the Ursulines of Jesus at Chavagnes in France. One was Miss Margaret Clapperton of Fochabers in Morayshire, whose beauty was the subject of several ballads well known in the north in those days, the other Miss Agnes Traill, daughter of a Church of Scotland Minister, who, while studying in Italy with the object of developing her considerable talent for painting, had become a Roman Catholic in Rome in 1828.

In 1819 the Whitehouse lands passed to the ownership of Mrs Ann Oliphant, or Grant, widow of Francis Grant of Kilgraston in Perthshire (now commemorated by Kilgraston Road). She it was who in 1834 sold part of the estate, including the manor-house, to the Roman Catholic authorities for £3,000. After her death, her trustees feued other parts of the estate. In 1869 some of the land became the site of Esdaile College (in Kilgraston Road) for daughters of ministers of the Church of Scotland and of professors in Scottish Universities. In 1890, another portion of the land went to the Edinburgh Southern Cemetery Company for the laying out of Grange Cemetery.

The purchase of the Whitehouse and its immediate surroundings for the establishment of the convent was made possible by a great benefactor of the Catholic Church in Scotland, Mr. John Menzies of Pitfodels in Aberdeenshire who had become a close friend of the Rev. James Gillis (who was Bishop of Edinburgh and district from 1838). He also gifted Blairs College near Aberdeen to the Scottish Catholic bishops as a junior seminary for students to the priesthood. Mr Menzies came to live at Greenhill Cottage which stood near present-day Bruntsfield Hospital.

The convent, dedicated to St Margaret of Scotland, was ready for occupation on December 26th, 1834 and the two Scottish sisters who had returned from France were the founders of the new community. The work of the nuns soon began: they recited the Divine Office at the traditionally established hours of the day, educated girls of the "upper class" in the convent school and poor children in the Canongate district, and visited the sick, prisoners and the poor, especially those at the old Craiglockhart Poorhouse.

St Margaret's Convent in Whitehouse Loan, from an oil painting by S. Humble, c. 1840

Before long many Edinburgh citizens at first opposed to the opening of this the first post-Reformation convent in Scotland (many Catholics had indeed considered it premature) began expressing praise for its work. None showed greater kindness than their nearest neighbour Sir George Warrender of Bruntsfield House who, though a Protestant, gave the nuns access to his own grounds.

The chiming of the long-silenced bell of the old Convent of St Catherine of Sienna in the Sciennes had for long been a feature of the Burgh Muir, and the bell of St Margaret's centuries later picked up its echoes. The convent's beautiful chapel, designed by Gillespie Graham and today containing many interesting treasures and relics, was opened in 1835, but the great bell, a gift from Dublin, was not installed until 1858. Even then the ringing of church bells was permitted only by churches of the Church of Scotland. The sound of the bell, named Margaret, must have become familiar to many residents, not only in the immediate Whitehouse district but, on still evenings, also far beyond.

Proposed extensions to the Convent and plans for a girls' boarding school, drawn up by Edward Pugin in 1861, were put aside for several years because of lack of funds. The turreted villa in Strathearn Road, The Tower, was purchased in 1909.

Over the years, because of the community's French associations and as a result of Bishop Gillis' visits to Europe to seek financial help for St Margaret's, the Convent was visited by members of several royal families. These included the French Bourbon family, a former French Queen and, in 1871, the Emperor and Empress of Brazil.

Associations of the Whitehouse with literature and the arts continued when it became a religious community. After Bishop Gillis' death in 1864, the sisters, regretting their lack of a portrait of their founder, commissioned Sam Bough, R.S.A., a one-time resident of Jordan Lane, one of Scotland's greatest painters and an admirer of Bishop Gillis, whose sermons in St Mary's Cathedral in Broughton Street he had so often attended, to paint the portrait from memory. In the crypt under the Convent chapel rest the remains of Mr Hope Scott of Abbotsford, his wife (the grand-daughter of Sir Walter Scott) and their two children, Walter and Margaret.

CHAPTER 3

Bruntsfield House · Bruntsfield Hospital · Warrender Baths · The Links

BRUNTSFIELD HOUSE

While Grange House is now, alas, no more, its three neighbouring mansion-houses of the ancient days of the Burgh Muir, along with another of lesser antiquity, remain and share a common purpose: all are thriving educational establishments. Bruntsfield House is now the focal point of the modern, well-appointed James Gillespie's High School. The Whitehouse, just over a hundred yards southwards in Whitehouse Loan, is the Convent of the Ursulines of Jesus, providing a private school for girls. A mile westwards, on the other side of the Bruntsfield district, the venerable Tower of Merchiston, admirably restored, is the centre-piece of Edinburgh's important and bustling Napier College of Commerce and Technology.

Just how long a manor-house has stood on the site of Bruntsfield House is not known. Its name and that of the surrounding district is derived from Richard Broune who, records of 1381 relate, was the King's Sergeant of the Burgh Muir in the reign of Robert II. Broune's duties included collecting rents for Crown lands and summoning the lieges to the King's tribunals of justice. Such King's Sergeants also resided at Liberton, the Braids, Merchiston and other districts of Edinburgh. Instead of receiving payment for their services they were given tenancy of certain lands.

Whether or not an earlier mansion-house stood in Richard Broune's day where Bruntsfield House now stands is not known. In 1381 a royal charter conveyed the lands of "Broune's Field" from the tenancy of Broune to "our beloved and faithful Alan de Lawdre", a descendant of the great Scottish patriot and supporter of William Wallace whom we met in the Grange House annals, and ancestor of the Lauders of the Bass and Fountainhall, later owners of the Grange. Alan's father William de Lawdre had, in fact, been the first to receive the lands of Bruntsfield from the King, but on his death they were conveyed to Alan. Bruntsfield and its estate were held by the de Lawdres and subsequent owners directly from the Crown. Only in 1508 did Edinburgh acquire from James IV the right of feu. Alan de Lawdre's annual payment to the Crown for the possession of Bruntsfield was "a silver penny payable at the Burrow Mure on the feast of St John the Baptist . . . if asked".

49

The Bruntsfield estate remained in the de Lawdre family until 1603, save for a short period when it was confiscated on account of the family's involvement in the conspiracy of the Earl of Douglas, possession being regained by 1490 from Henry Cant, whose family had also been owners of Grange House. Sir Alexander Lauder of Bruntsfield was Lord Provost of Edinburgh from 1500 to 1504. His son Alexander succeeded him at Bruntsfield until his death at Flodden in 1513. In 1519 Edinburgh's Town Council expressed dissatisfaction with their vassals on the Burgh Muir for not making sufficient efforts to provide the means of brewing beer. William Lauder of Bruntsfield was one thus criticised.

The Bruntsfield estate extended to fifty acres. Records describe the destruction of the sixteenth-century house by the Earl of Hertford, who destroyed so many Edinburgh houses, during his ravages of Scotland in 1544. Many citizens, irrespective of age or sex, were brutally murdered by "Protector Somerset" as he was known. In these turbulent days Sir Alexander Lauder of Bruntsfield was slain at the battle of Pinkie Cleugh. A new Bruntsfield House was probably built by his successor. This house, in Z-formation and with towers, was sold by yet another Sir Alexander Lauder to John Fairlie, owner of Morningside's Braid estate and later of the Grange. Fairlie made substantial alterations to Bruntsfield House and his initials, combined in monogram with those of his wife Elizabeth Westoun, may be seen carved above the first-floor windows on the south side of the house, with the date 1605.

At the end of the seventeenth century another name enters the Bruntsfield annals, one so closely associated with the house that many people wrongly believe it to be this family's ancestral home. The name is Warrender. For some time the mansion-house was known as Warrender House, though in fact, the distinguished Warrender family became owners only in 1695 when they purchased the house from one of John Fairlie's descendants. Sir George Warrender, who became Edinburgh's Lord Provost in 1713, was the third laird of Bruntsfield to have enjoyed this honour. Unlike his neighbours at Grange House, he was no Jacobite, having been created a baronet by George I, the first of the Hanoverians.

The Warrenders owned Bruntsfield for over two centuries, during which time they acquired five smaller adjacent estates. These, along with Bruntsfield's acres, eventually became the extended Bruntsfield district of today. The smaller estates included one known as Baglap or Rigsland, a district of the western Burgh Muir and part of Bruntsfield Links, which in the mid-eighteenth century contained many quarries. One of these (a little west of Alvanley Terrace and the end of Warrender Park Terrace) was known as the City Quarry. It now provides a popular winter sledge run. Also acquired by the Warrenders was Brown's Acres, so named from its tenant, Robert Brown, Deacon of Edinburgh's Tailors.

In 1752, an anonymous pamphlet protested that the various land negotiations taking place would interfere with the grazing lands on the

Bruntsfield House, showing monograms of the initials of John Fairley (who restored the house in 1605) and his wife Elizabeth Westoun

Photograph by Mr W. R. Smith

Bruntsfield House before restoration as James Gillespie's High School

Links for the flocks of sheep which provided Edinburgh's citizens with ewe whey, apparently considered an important health tonic. Furthermore, those who enjoyed walking on Bruntsfield Links in safety from the golfers would lose their pathways. Part of Brown's Acres, one acre in extent, became known as Viewpark after the large mansion-house which once stood there. This was later sold for £10,000 to the builders of an extension to James Gillespie's Higher Grade School, and the studio for long occupied by the notable photographer Mr Swan Watson was also built on this land. In due course part of the adjacent Whitehouse estate was also exchanged for part of the Bruntsfield House lands, to the mutual benefit of both owners.

Sir George Warrender, laird of Bruntsfield House in 1869, was a Member of Parliament and a man of considerable business tact and foresight. He saw immediately the feuing possibilities of his estate. His original plan of feuing certain acres for the construction of terraced villas (three such first formed Alvanley Terrace in 1869) was altered to permit a great building project which gave rise to the streets which now surround Bruntsfield House. By about 1880, the high tenements of Marchmont had arisen. Each new street name commemorated some member of Sir George's family. Thirlestane and Lauderdale honoured his mother, daughter of the Earl of Lauderdale whose family seat was Thirlestane Castle. Sir George's wife Helen was the daughter of the 5th Earl of Marchmont, hence the name of the whole surrounding district. John Spottiswoode was another Warrender relation, while Arden was the family name of the Earl of Haddington who married one of the Warrender daughters. Alvanley, already mentioned, was yet another family name. Thus from a family tree a whole district derived its street names.

Power of observation was yet another of Sir George Warrender's attributes. It was he who first discovered the secret room in Bruntsfield House. The exterior of the house showed one window which the caretaker had not accounted for. First, in fear, he denied any knowledge of this mysterious region. Eventually, however, when pressed, he revealed a hitherto unknown room, entered from behind a tapestry. Inside all was intact and undisturbed since last it had been occupied: ashes were still in the fireplace, and . . . bloodstains on the floor! A skeleton, it is said, was also found below the window. The mystery was never explained.

Sir George, that distinguished member of the Warrender family who had done so much to improve Bruntsfield House and, by feuing out his estate, for the construction of the surrounding streets whose names now immortalise his family and the house itself, died in 1901. His lands then passed to trustees. Under the trusteeship, Bruntsfield House for long periods lay unoccupied. Fears began to be expressed for its future, not only by local residents but also by Bruntsfield and Marchmont expatriates in various parts of the world who wrote to the press. There were numerous rumours and counter-rumours of imminent demolition. In 1933 consternation reached its height when notices were posted in the district to the effect that the estate was to be feued for house-building. Demolition now seemed inevitable. Letters again flowed into the press. The president of the Old Edinburgh Club stressed that the house had pre-eminent architectural claims for preservation. An exile in Australia begged Edinburgh's citizens to stand firm against destruction, and appealed to the thousands of students who over the years had lodged in Marchmont to raise their voices.

A number of positive proposals were made for the future of Bruntsfield House, and W. Forbes Gray, the great authority on the history of South Edinburgh, urged the Lord Provost's Committee to intervene to ensure preservation. This committee discussed the matter over a series of lengthy meetings while their decision was eagerly awaited. At last, through the generosity of Sir Victor Warrender who offered to make over his life-rent interest in the property to the city, the Corporation were able, on January 9th, 1935, to obtain possession, the cost involved being £22,000.

In the transfer of Bruntsfield House to Edinburgh Corporation a number of provisos were made. The building of tenements was to be restricted, being permitted, for example, only on the south side of Spottiswoode Road, while the frontage of Warrender Park Road was to be preserved. The house and immediate surroundings were to be used for public purposes only, with a strict preservation of local amenities. But, despite all these safeguards, the future remained uncertain.

Further proposals appeared in the press, including suggestions that the house be used as an educational establishment, a hospital, or a social centre for the district, with bowling greens and tennis courts, and, in the house itself, lounges and a public library. This last proposal, adopted at a public meeting of local residents in the Central Hall in March 1935, visualised the estate as a community "pleasure ground". The establishment of a Danish-style Folk Museum was also suggested.

In July 1935 the Lord Provost's Committee agreed to make Bruntsfield House available to the City Public Assistance Committee for the transfer of young children from the Western General Hospital. This plan provoked protests in Bruntsfield, as did a further Corporation proposal that the house become a branch of Craigleith Workhouse.

At last, in 1937, the Corporation Education Committee decided to build a high school for girls which would incorporate Bruntsfield House. The plan seemed generally acceptable, but was laid aside as it was apparent that the country was on the brink of the Second World War. Like so many great mansion-houses, occupied and unoccupied, Bruntsfield, after the outbreak of war in 1939, was pressed into service, becoming an Air Raid Precautions and First Aid Rescue Centre.

In 1945, the war at last over, the city adapted the house to provide flats for homeless families, and in November of that year the Preparatory

Department of James Gillespie's High School for Girls moved to its new quarters in Bruntsfield House. By 1953 fifty people were still being accommodated here, and in the same year the house suffered a fire, which fortunately was confined to the attics.

In 1963, permission was granted by Edinburgh Corporation for Bruntsfield House to become the centre-piece of the new James Gillespie's High School for Girls, which for so long had been a prominent landmark high above Bruntsfield Links at the western end of Warrender Park Terrace. The new James Gillespie's, finally completed in 1966 at a total cost of £530,000 was designed by Rowand Anderson, Kininmonth & Paul, the architects who built the dome of Edinburgh University's Old College, the Museum of Antiquities in Queen Street and Adam House. Modern buildings are now clustered round Bruntsfield House, but the house itself has been carefully preserved in its essentials, although certain seventeenth- and nineteenth-century parts had to be demolished so that a new entrance and internal staircase could be built to facilitate use of the house as the school's administrative centre, with its staff rooms, club room and music room (which links most closely the original house and the modern buildings).

In the school's grounds the old stables and coach houses remain, while on the original main gate-house, opposite Bruntsfield Hospital in Whitehouse Loan, the arms of the Warrenders could, until its recent demolition, be seen. Near the gateway beside the old stables and coach-houses is a little grass-covered knoll, from which, it is said, James IV reviewed the Scottish army assembled on the surrounding Burgh Muir prior to Flodden. A tombstone commemorating a plague victim of bygone days, discovered in Spottiswoode Street built into the garden wall to the east of Bruntsfield House, is now preserved beneath one of the school classrooms.

Of Bruntsfield House, then, and of several other original features of this district to which the first tenant Broune gave his name, much happily remains. Perhaps the most impressive symbolic link with the earliest days of this hundred-and-seventy-years-old school, which after so many migrations at last found a dignified and attractive home at Brunts-field House, is the simple and moving ceremony, still observed in the Founder's Day Commemoration Service each February, during which the guest speaker is presented with a snuff box in memory of the generous and celebrated Edinburgh snuff merchant, James Gillespie. Such was the school's reputation that, while it was still a high school for girls, many parents enrolled their daughters soon after birth. In August 1972, however, as a result of sweeping changes in legislation, James Gillespie's ceased to be a fee-paying school for girls: it was renamed simply James Gillespie's High School, becoming co-educational and comprehensive. In 1975 James Gillespie's Primary School for Boys in Marchmont Crescent was closed and the premises given over for Further Education.

BRUNTSFIELD HOSPITAL

No account of Bruntsfield would be complete without reference to Bruntsfield Hospital. This unique centre of healing, properly entitled the Bruntsfield Hospital for Women and Children, was founded in 1885 by Dr Sophia Jex-Blake, one of the great pioneers among women doctors who made important contributions to the advancement of medicine. It was only in 1869 that Edinburgh University first admitted female medical students, and it was then the first British university to do so. There were certain reservations: separate classes had to be held for male and female students, the latter being very few in number. This meant that professors had to duplicate their lectures, with little extra payment, and many declined to do so. Miss Sophia Jex-Blake, soon after her entry to the then recently-established Queen's College in London in 1858, began campaigning for opportunities of higher education for women. After graduating at Queen's College as a teacher, she came to Edinburgh in 1869. Although able to pursue certain medical studies at Edinburgh University, she was forced, with her close friend Miss Pechey, to go to Berne in order to graduate as a Doctor of Medicine. She then obtained the Licentiateship of the King's and Queen's Colleges in Ireland which enabled her to practise in Great Britain. In 1889 the Universities (Scotland) Act at last granted women equal opportunities in the study of medicine, though full implementation of this Act did not come about in Edinburgh until 1894.

Nearly seventy years before Dr Jex-Blake's graduation, however, a certain Dr James Stuart Barry had taken an Edinburgh medical degree and subsequently become Inspector-General of Army Hospitals. On Dr Barry's death it was discovered that "he" had in fact been Dr Miranda Stuart Barry, a woman doctor who had originally, in disguise, been the first female medical student to penetrate the exclusively male citadel of Edinburgh's Medical School.

Dr Jex-Blake was convinced that there were many women who would prefer to be examined and treated by a doctor of their own sex, and she wished to provide more opportunities for woman doctors to train and work in a hospital. A ward of five beds for women patients was opened at her dispensary in Grove Street in 1885, and in 1898 the patients were transferred to Bruntsfield Lodge (formerly Greenhill Cottage opposite the main gateway of Bruntsfield House) which was Dr Jex-Blake's family home. On this site Bruntsfield Hospital was built in 1911. At first there were twenty beds; later two wards with fourteen beds in each were opened, with balconies facing the hospital's sunny and sheltered garden. Eventually further alterations provided for seventy-seven beds, seventeen of them for children.

Today the names of the hospital wards commemorate the founder and her early colleagues: there is the Beilby Ward (Medical), the Venters Ward (Surgical) and the Jex-Blake Ward (Medical and Surgical). Under

Greenhill Cottage, later Bruntsfield Lodge — which became the first Bruntsfield Hospital — the home of Dr Sophia Jex-Blake

By courtesy of Bruntsfield Hospital

the National Health Service, Bruntsfield Hospital has retained its character and maintained its proud traditions. At the time of writing, however, the retention of the hospital — and of its only other British counterpart, the Elizabeth Garrett Anderson Hospital in London, is a subject of debate and correspondence in the Press.

WARRENDER BATHS

While the name Warrender is perpetuated by many local street names, it has also been carried far beyond the boundaries of Bruntsfield by many distinguished members of the Warrender Swimming Club whose fame has spread across the world. Apart from its members of championship standard, innumerable other swimming enthusiasts have for more than eighty years enjoyed the excellent facilities of Warrender Baths in Thirlestane Road.

Edinburgh's records relate that in 1843 a public meeting was held in the Music Hall in George Street at which the then Lord Provost presided, and it was agreed "to further the opening of suitable baths for the working classes, the promotion of cleanly habits among the trades and working classes being essential for the removal of disease and the general improvement of that large and important class of people". This policy, gradually put into effect by Edinburgh Corporation, led to the opening of various public baths in the city, but Warrender Baths have quite a different origin. They were officially opened in 1887, by Sir George Warrender, M.P. of Bruntsfield House, the site having been donated by him. Some time prior to 1887 certain members of Glasgow's Bellahouston Private Baths Club had discussed with two Edinburgh friends the possibility of a private swimming bath being opened in Edinburgh. With the support of an Edinburgh business company and the active encouragement of Sir George Warrender, the baths bearing his name were duly opened at a cost of £11,000.

Originally the baths and the Warrender Club, which was founded soon after their opening, were part of a wider scheme for providing leisure facilities in the district. The premises housing the baths also had a billiard room and a reading room pleasantly furnished and decorated with pot plants. Apparently plants also hung from the roof above the swimming bath and one of the feats of more experienced and daring members was to clutch at a piece of greenery and convey it downwards *en route* from the high-dive. At first the baths enjoyed increasing support but by 1906 interest and financial resources had begun to fail and they were closed. Many Warrender Club members were on the point of joining the Portobello Club when in 1908 Edinburgh Corporation bought the Warrender Baths from their private owner for £3,000, less than a third of their initial cost, thus adding to the city's group of public swimming baths. Interest and support gradually picked up and the Warrender Club which had almost dispersed was re-formed and soon began to add to its former achievements. In 1913 another small club, the Dunedin, had been formed but this was short-lived. An interesting and colourful account of Warrender's early days has been provided by Alasdair Alpin MacGregor in one of his books recalling his early years as a student, living as did so many students in "digs" in Marchmont.

Amongst the distinguished swimmers who have been members of the Warrender Club was Miss Ellen King, who at one period enjoyed the unique honour of holding simultaneously the British Championship in three styles. Miss King was in the British Olympic Games team in 1924 and 1928. Another distinguished woman member, Miss Jean McDowall, was also in the 1928 Olympic team. Nearly half the swimmers representing Scotland in the 1970 Commonwealth Games were members of Warrender. But this famous Club's finest hour has undoubtedly been its former member David Wilkie's supreme achievement in winning the Gold Medal in the 200 metres breaststroke in the 1976 Olympic Games in Montreal. David received his early training at the Warrender Baths where his coach first discerned and encouraged his Olympic potential. He was made a life member of the Club in 1972 and suitably honoured by the Club at a special reception in 1976.

BRUNTSFIELD LINKS

The pleasant expanse of well-tended turf which is now Bruntsfield Links, happy playground of toddlers, young football enthusiasts and devotees of short-hole golf, must contrast sharply in appearance with the rough, overgrown, and forbidding Burgh Muir of centuries ago, of which this is the last open portion.

When the Muir was feued out in lots by Edinburgh Corporation in 1586, the Bruntsfield Links area, some thirty-five acres, remained the possession of the city. Its rocky surface was probably the main reason why, in later years, it was not used for house-building. Soon after 1586 stone-quarrying in the area commenced, the soft, grey sandstone being much in demand in later centuries for the building of villas and tenements in the immediate vicinity and in the centre of Edinburgh.

Bruntsfield Links, however, is important to Edinburgh not so much as the last vestige of the ancient Burgh Muir or, along with Craigleith, as one of the city's main quarries, but much more notably as the city's earliest golf course. Amongst the distinguished devotees of early centuries who earned for golf its reputation as a royal as well as an ancient game were James IV, James VII (James II of the United Kingdom), Charles I and Charles II, all of whom played over Leith Links, and the Marquis of Montrose who also displayed his powers there in 1627. While Charles I

The Golf Hotel, the original Golf Tavern
By courtesy of Mr Michael Shaw of the Golf Tavern

was in full swing at Leith Links, news was brought to him, it is said, of the rebellion in Ireland.

In the days of these Royal participants Leith was independent of Edinburgh, so Bruntsfield Links may claim to have been the city's first golf course. There is some evidence that James IV, in the happier days of his reign before the clouds of war gathered which led him to Flodden, included golf at Bruntsfield amongst his many recreational pursuits. The accounts of the High Treasurer of Scotland for 1503, however, show a constant purchase of new golf balls which rather casts doubt on "Jamie the Fourth's" skill with the club!

"Golf" and later "gowf" were the early terms for the game of which St Andrews traditionally claims to have been the original home. But the existence of similar words in early German and Dutch writings suggests that perhaps the game was not unknown on the Continent before its introduction at St Andrews. A Scottish statute of 1424, while prohibiting football, makes no reference to golf, but a later edict of 1457 does so, perhaps reflecting the game's first signs of popularity. Such censures were designed to preserve and promote the noble art of archery, a skill which could be drawn upon in the not unlikely event of war with England. With the advent of gunpowder, however, archery soon became obsolete in war and golfers enjoyed a new-found freedom.

Hugo Arnot, the Edinburgh historian, wrote:

Golf as far as we know is a game peculiar to the Scots. It is commonly played on rugged, broken ground, covered in short grass and in the neighbourhood of the sea-shore. A field of this kind in Scotland is called "the Links". The game is generally played in parties of one or two on each side, each party having an exceedingly hard ball, somewhat larger than a hen's egg. This they strike with a slender and elastic club of about 4 feet long, crooked in the head and having lead in it to make it heavy. The ball struck with this club will fly to a distance of 200 yards. The art is to play the ball into smooth ground. for the next stroke. The contest is to hole the course in the fewest number of strokes.

Modern devotees of the game will know these latter aspirations well!

Early in James VI's reign, club-making became an important craft and a letter issued at Holyrood in 1603 appointed William Mayne, burgess of Edinburgh, as maker of bows, arrows, spears and golf clubs to the King. So popular had golf become and so much were golf balls in demand that, according to another letter of the same King, "no small quantity of gold and silver is being transported out of His Highness' Kingdom for the buying of golf balls". Accordingly, certain Edinburgh golf-ball makers were given sole rights to manufacture these and only balls which bore their special stamp were to be used. The price of a ball — made of leather stuffed with feathers — in about 1600 was fixed at "four schillings money of this realm".

In 1744 the Edinburgh city fathers instituted a trophy, a silver club valued at £15, to be played for annually on April 1st by members of the Edinburgh Company of Golfers. This Company was granted a charter by the city magistrates in 1800 and many distinguished Scots of that time were members.

About this period another writer described the latest golf clubs as having "a face which is perfectly smooth, having no inclination such as might have a tendency to make the ball rise from the ground". Number 8 irons were yet to come!

"Far" or "fore" were the warning and optimistic cries issued before the ball was struck — or intended to be! "Far and Sure" became the motto of many golfing societies. It was also the well-deserved motto of the celebrated John Patersone, an Edinburgh shoemaker, considered the best golfer of his day, and the words are still to be seen inscribed high up on "Golfer's Land" on the north side of Canongate.

The story of Patersone, part of the essential history of the Royal Mile, is still related to Edinburgh's annual concourse of tourists. James VII, the Duke of York, while in residence at Holyrood in 1680 fell under the spell of golf. During an argument—at the 19th green no doubt—about whether golf had originated in England or Scotland, it was decided to stage an international contest. Two English devotees were to play the Duke and any Scottish partner he might choose, a large sum of money being at stake. The Duke, hearing of Patersone's fame, invited him to complete the foursome. The shoemaker feared he might let down his royal partner and was at first reluctant, but he eventually agreed. The scene was Leith Links and the Scottish court lined the fairways. The Duke and Patersone were easy winners. The latter with his large winnings — the Duke foregoing his share—built himself a fine house in the Canongate which his grateful royal partner decorated with the stone tablet visible today. This bears the Patersone coat of arms: a hand grasping a golf club, (the motto "Far and Sure" and the words "I hate no person" (being an anagram of the name John Patersone).

Arnot relates how the English writer Topham, on a visit to Edinburgh, believed that the city's more ambitious golf addicts played up and down the heights of Arthur's Seat, the Blackfords, Braids and Pentland Hills. On another occasion Arnot writes that in 1799 bets were laid in the Burgess Golfing Society that no two players could drive a ball over the one-hundred-and-sixty-foot spire of St Giles Cathedral. Two members accepted the challenge, each driving six balls from a special "tee" in Parliament Square. Several shots, apparently, soared well over the steeple and bounced down in Advocates' Close.

Amongst the more famous early Bruntsfield Links societies were the Burghers or Burgess Golfing Society (founded in 1735 and now the Royal Burgess Golfing Society, claiming to be the oldest properly constituted golf club in Scotland, whose private course is now at Barnton), the

Alexander McKellar, "Cock o' the Green", on Bruntsfield Links, from Kay's "Portraits"

Bruntsfield (1761, now the Royal Bruntsfield, whose course is at Davidson Mains), the Thistle (1815), the Honourable Company of Edinburgh (1844 or earlier, which moved to Muirfield), the Allied Golfing Club (1856), St. Leonard's (1857) and the Warrender (1858). Each club had its captain, treated with ceremonial honour. The traditional regalia of most clubs was a scarlet coat with distinctive facings and gilt buttons often bearing insignia.

Most of the early Edinburgh golfing societies had their champion or "Cock o' the Green". Bruntsfield's most celebrated one was Alexander McKellar whose legendary performances and dedication to the game at the beginning of the nineteenth century earned him a chapter and animated illustration in Kay's *Original Portraits*.

McKellar's addiction knew no bounds: he normally spent the whole day on Bruntsfield Links and was frequently found playing the short holes after dark by the light of a hand lantern. "By the la' Harry!" or "By gracious, this won't go for nothing!" were his mild and devotional exclamations as he addressed the ball, following a successful stroke by a ritual dance of delight.

McKellar owned a tavern in Edinburgh's New Town, which his wife was left to supervise, for McKellar himself was more often seen on the Links than behind his bar. But, provoked as golf widows have sometimes been known to be by the counter-attractions of their husbands' "other love", Mrs McKellar one evening set out to visit friends in Fife, leaving Andrew, for once, in charge of his own tavern. The lively conviviality of the band of golfing cronies whom he had invited for an evening in his hostelry had reached its peak when, quite unexpectedly, Mrs McKellar returned to the scene. The Queensferry Passage had proved impossible. Golf and golfers received the full blast of her tongue and McKellar's lively companions of the Links dispersed quickly into the New Town night! It is probable that "mine host", before extending future invitations to his cronies, took good care first to note the weather forecast for the Queensferry Passage.

No golf course is complete without its 19th green and Bruntsfield was no exception. The Golf Tavern, still a popular and comfortable rendezvous for those "who have wearied at the gowf", situated in the little street still called Wrights' Houses under the soaring steeple of the Barclay Church, proclaims proudly on a stone wall plaque that its establishment was in 1456. Legend, indeed, has it that a tavern existed here as early as 1399, when the first of Bruntsfield's golf pioneers may have set off round the links. There is, however, no official evidence of such antiquity or, indeed, of the claim in *A History of the Edinburgh Burgess Golfing Society* that charters vouch for a tavern on the present site in 1456.

In the year 1716 we are on firmer ground. Then James Brownhill obtained a feu of the land on which the eastern part of the little community of Wrychtishousis had once existed, eventually, as many of the cottages fell into ruin, becoming waste ground. The following year Brownhill built a house which he converted into a tavern named Golfhall. Some years later a bowling green was laid out nearby. Brownhill was exempted by Edinburgh Town Council from the duty payable on imported wines so long as these were vended and consumed in Golfhall — a privilege, it is presumed, for the convenience of Bruntsfield's golfers. In 1718 Brownhill, supported by his golfing clientele, agreed to pay £300 annually to Edinburgh's Lord Provost in lieu of duty due on imported wines and this payment is considered to be the origin of the Lord Provost's present-day expenses allowance. In the Golf Tavern today are preserved and displayed cartoons and portraits of early golfing days and personalities associated with the Links, and a number of original golf clubs.

At the beginning of the eighteenth century, in the vicinity of Bruntsfield Links, on a site now impossible to trace but apparently "about a mile south of Edinburgh", stood another golfers' hostelry called Rare Maggy Johnston's. Here "Maggy kept a little farm and had a particular art of brewing a small sort of ale agreeable to the taste, very white, clear and intoxicating." This was obviously a popular rendezvous and its hospitable owner merited a poem by Allan Ramsay.

Elegy on Maggy Johnston who died Anno 1711

Auld Reeky! Mourn in sable hue,
Let fouth of tears dreep like May dew.
To braw Tippony bid adieu,
Which we with greed,
Bended as fast as she cou'd brew.
But ah! she's dead.

When in our poutch we fand some clinks,
And took a turn oe'r Bruntsfield-Links,
After at Maggy's at Hy-jinks,
We guzl'd scuds,
Till we could scarce wi' hall our drinks
Cast aff our duds . . .

When we were weary'd at the gowff,
Then Maggy Johnston's was our howff;
Now a' our gamesters may sit dowff,
Wi hearts like lead.
Death wi' his rung rax'd her a' yowff
And sae she died.

In 1791 the Town Council considered the construction of a main road from Tollcross to the old village of Burghmuirhead, traversing the site of· the Golf Tavern and a section of the adjacent golf links. Pressure from the Burgess Golfing Society, who stressed that this area was hallowed ground, made the civic authorities alter their plans. The new highway was routed westwards, becoming the Bruntsfield Place of today.

This was but one of many threats to the Links both as a golf sanctuary and a most pleasant open space. In 1798 Sir Walter Scott, quartermaster and secretary of the Royal Edinburgh Light Dragoons, requested that the Town Council permit the use of the Links for drill exercises. Again the golfing societies stood firm, and Sir Walter was refused. During the 1914-18 War, however, military exercises were permitted on the Links. In 1827 an Edinburgh Corporation Improvement Act had precluded any future building on this last vestige of the Burgh Muir.

Eventually, with the steady construction of tenements around the Links and the need to lay out pathways for the convenience of local residents walking into the city, with some guarantee of safety from flying golf balls, and with some local people still claiming the age-old right to

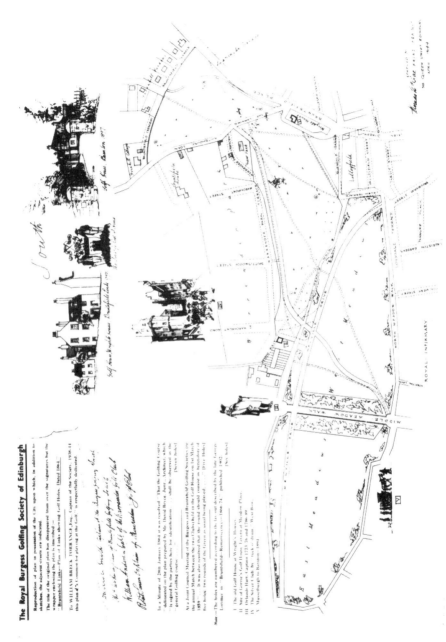

Plan issued by the Royal Burgess Golfing Society of Edinburgh

By courtesy of Mr Michael Shaw of the Golf Tavern

hang washing on specially provided iron poles, many Bruntsfield golfers considered that their style was being cramped. Thus when Edinburgh Corporation purchased the Braid Hills in 1889 and in later years laid out a first-class full-length golf course there, many of Bruntsfield Links' more ambitious players welcomed the freedom and new challenge of the Braids.

Bruntsfield Links, however, still has its large number of short-hole enthusiasts of all ages who worthily uphold the long and proud traditions of their famous course. Of a summer evening, competitions, as of yore, still attract many participants and spectators and generate an air of excitement which would have brought joy to the heart of Andrew McKellar, the "Cock o' the Green". On the southern portion of the Links the well-kept putting green provides a pleasant summer pastime for many.

The two-hundred-and-fifty-foot steeple of the Barclay Church towers high above the whole Bruntsfield district and is one of Edinburgh's great landmarks from afar. It was built as the Barclay Free Church in 1862-3, at a cost of £10,000, through a generous bequest from Miss Mary Barclay whose name the church commemorates. Other possible sites considered

The Barclay Church

65

for it were at Warriston, St Leonard's and the Grange. Designed by Frederick Thomas Pilkington, Barclay Church cannot fail to attract attention; it drew strong and controversial comments from critics of its day. Additional mouldings and sculpture proposed by the architect were not agreed by the first minister of the church and it was thus regarded by some as unfinished. The pointed style with the many small spires perhaps recalls something of the character of the ancient mansion-house of Wrychtishousis which once stood so nearby. In 1974 one of the church's lower pinnacles, forty feet in height, collapsed and was rebuilt in fibre-glass. Certain other parts of the steeple were replaced by the same material.

CHAPTER 4

Wrychtishousis

The ultimate establishment of the new James Gillespie's High School for Girls at Bruntsfield House recalls this school's association with another unique manor-house of the area, the ancient and impressive mansion of Wrychtishousis. Of this house Lord Cockburn wrote:

A very curious edifice stood on the very spot where the modern building is erected [Gillespie's Hospital in Gillespie Crescent, later the Royal Blind Asylum]. It was called Wryttes-Houses and belonged anciently to the family of Napier. It was a keep, presiding over an inferior group of buildings, most of it as old as the middle of the 14th Century, all carved with heraldic and other devices, and all delightfully picturesque. Nothing could be more striking when seen against the evening sky. . .Yet it was brutishly obliterated without one public murmur.

Another Edinburgh historian wrote:

A picturesque mansion of very great antiquity, quadrangular in form, striking in outline, with its peel tower, turrets, crow-stepped gables and gablets encrusted with legends, dates and coats of arms, for ages formed one of the most important features of the Burgh Muir.

Wrychtishousis is thought to have been built in the first half of the fourteenth century, perhaps on the site of an even earlier house on the edge of the Burgh Muir. It belonged to a branch of the Napier family, unrelated to those who owned Merchiston Castle. William Napier of Wrychtishousis was High Constable of Edinburgh Castle in 1390, succeeding the son of King Robert the Bruce.

Considered one of the oldest and by far the most interesting and picturesque of baronial dwellings on the fringes of Edinburgh, it was first known as Burgh Muir Castle or Barganie House. Its antiquity is indicated by the carved dated stones which were among the many emblems and mottoes which adorned the walls, doorways and lintels. One, dated 1339, must have been carved a few years after a great battle on the Burgh Muir, while another coincides with the Battle of Flodden. Other carvings included the heads of Julius Caesar and Octavius Secundus, while another commemorated the marriage in 1513 of a daughter of the Wrychtishousis Napiers to a son of their namesakes at Merchiston.

The origin of the name Wrychtishousis remains a mystery. The suggestion, already mentioned, that in the smaller houses surrounding the peel tower lived the wrights or joiners engaged in the great tree-felling

The original mansion of Wrychtishousis

project to clear the forest of the Burgh Muir has been doubted. After the demolition of Wrychtishousis in 1800, many of its sculptured stones were preserved. Four were built into the surrounding wall behind Bruntsfield Place, which was to become the wall of the playground around the original James Gillespie's School, and they are still to be seen there. Others were taken to Woodhouselee, a pleasant old country mansion on the southern slopes of the Pentlands, a few miles out of Edinburgh on the Biggar road, but alas now demolished. Two pediments were taken as far as St Margaret's Church in North Queensferry. Comiston House and Bloomsbury Laundry, at one time in Canaan Lane, are two other houses where stones from Wrychtishousis were preserved.

The little village which grew up around and took its name from the mansion-house of Wrychtishousis in Gillespie Crescent eventually, in the eighteenth century, spread eastwards across what is now Bruntsfield Place to the vicinity of the Golf Tavern and the Barclay Church. As the present-day street Wrights' Houses (running from the east corner of Barclay

Terrace down to Glengyle Terrace) recalls, it was this eastern part of the old village which survived longest. Several very old cottages near the Golf Tavern were demolished just a few years ago. Some original houses of the Wrychtishousis community to the west (near Gillespie Crescent and the beginning of Bruntsfield Place) were demolished in 1792 to make way for a wider highway from Tollcross to Morningside. On the west side of Leven Street (where it meets Gillespie Place) and at the top of Hailes Street (off Gilmore Place), a number of very old cottages and a little lane are the last reminders of the original village. The Wrights' Houses Toll Bar stood opposite today's Old Toll Bar public house.

James Gillespie, generous founder of the hospital bearing his name which was built on the former site of Wrychtishousis, was born in 1726. He was the younger of two bachelor brothers who ran a highly successful snuff business in Edinburgh's High Street. While James produced the snuff at his mill at Spylaw in Colinton, where he also resided, becoming known as "the Laird of Colinton", his brother managed the shop. Eventually to become extremely wealthy, they had been brought up to be modest and frugal in their tastes, and constantly industrious. These were especially the qualities of James Gillespie, but he was far from being miserly in his dealings with others. The domestic staff in his comfortable and substantial Colinton home were treated kindly, the "Laird" dining and mixing freely with them. He was a tolerant and considerate landlord to the many tenants on his estate. Hard work and personal frugality, coupled with a very successful piece of tobacco speculation during the American War of independence, were responsible for his steady accumulation of wealth.

One of Gillespie's few impressive possessions was his carriage and horses, in which he rode into Edinburgh from Colinton. The famous Edinburgh caricaturist Kay, in his *Original Portraits*, illustrates Gillespie's most prominent feature — his rather large and bulbous nose. This characteristic trade-mark of the snuff merchant prompted Lord Erskine facetiously to suggest, apropos Gillespie's grand carriage:

> Wha wad hae thocht it
> That noses had bocht it!

James Gillespie died in 1797 and was buried in Colinton Parish Churchyard beside his brother, who had pre-deceased him by two years. His generosity and concern for the poor found practical expression in his will. His trustees had the task of using over £12,000, plus the land in Colinton, "for the special intention and purpose of founding and endowing a Hospital or Charitable Institution, within the city of Edinburgh, for the aliment and maintenance of old men and women; and which Hospital should always be called, denominated and described by the name of James Gillespie's Hospital." A further £2,700 was bequeathed for building and endowing "a charitable or Free School,

Gillespie's Hospital

Kay's portrait of James Gillespie, the wealthy Edinburgh snuff merchant who founded Gillespie's Hospital, shown with his brother

within the City of Edinburgh or Suburbs thereof, for the education of 100 poor boys, to be taught reading, writing and arithmetic."

If, in proceeding with James Gillespie's last wishes, his trustees provoked public regret when they chose to demolish the venerable mansion of Wrychtishousis to provide a site for the hospital and school, certainly the public-spiritedness of the benefactor was never in question, and was deeply appreciated by the city.

Wrychtishousis was demolished in 1800 and James Gillespie's Hospital completed on its site in 1802. In accordance with Gillespie's wishes, the poor people entitled to admission were, firstly, his own former servants, if in need; secondly, persons of the name of Gillespie, fifty-five years of age and upwards, from any part of Scotland; thirdly, persons from Edinburgh and suburbs over fifty-five years of age; fourthly, failing sufficient Edinburgh applicants, those from Leith, Newhaven and other parts of Midlothian; lastly, failing sufficient applicants from any of these categories, persons over fifty-five years from any part of Scotland. Those to be admitted must not already be in receipt of a pension or help from another charity, and must be "only those who were decent, godly and well-behaved".

While the new hospital must have been welcomed by the first poor people to be admitted, the architects of the day were far from happy with its appearance. "A tasteless edifice in carpenter's gothic", was the criticism levelled by one.

The school, built separately from the hospital, was, after many modifications over the years as regards eligibility for admission and other matters, to become James Gillespie's High School for Girls. When it was opened in 1803, however, its first pupils were sixty-five poor boys. They were taught for six hours daily in summer and five in winter, "the Sabbath excepted", though Sunday evenings were, in fact, devoted to several hours of religious instruction in accordance with the founder's specific wishes. The first teacher was John Robertson. After some years, with an increased teaching staff, daily attendance averaged one hundred and fifty.

In 1870 the Endowed Institutions (Scotland) Act led to the Gillespie Hospital pensioners being granted a pension instead of accommodation and maintenance, and they were left to house themselves elsewhere. The vacated hospital became a fee-paying school for boys and girls. Generous bursaries were awarded by the Gillespie's Board of Governors enabling poorer children to attend either this enlarged and altered school or one of Edinburgh's early Merchant Company Schools. The demand for admission to the new James Gillespie's School was phenomenal: of 1,700 applications 700 had to be refused through shortage of accommodation. The school was of primary education level, serving as a feeder to Edinburgh's four Merchant Company higher-grade schools. In 1908, when the Edinburgh School Board took over the school and its buildings from the Gillespie's Board of Governors on lease (they were later

Old carved stones from the mansion of Wrychtishousis preserved in the boundary wall at Gillespie Crescent

purchased), higher-grade teaching began and the school was renamed James Gillespie's Primary and Higher Grade School.

During the First World War the school was used for military purposes and in 1922 it was sold by Edinburgh Corporation to the Royal Blind Asylum. The attractive and skilful basket-work and other items produced in the Blind Asylum workshops in Gillespie Crescent have long been in demand. In April 1971 the Royal Blind Asylum sold the premises and moved to Craigmillar where new workshops were built and administered by Edinburgh District Council. In 1975 the famous old Gillespie's Hospital building, so frequently featured by Shepherd and other artists, was, to the astonishment of many Edinburgh citizens, demolished almost overnight to make way for the building of small flats for old people. The Royal Blind Asylum adminstrative offices are still in Gillespie Crescent and the shop remains, now also selling work from other institutions for the blind and disabled.

In tracing the next stage in the development of James Gillespie's School and its transfer from the original Gillespie's Hospital building to its new location high above Bruntsfield Links, it is necessary to digress slightly and consider the foundation of another great school of the Bruntsfield district, Boroughmuir. At one point the history of the two schools is interwoven. Prior to 1900, non-fee-paying secondary schools in Edinburgh were unknown. Those seeking higher education had to attend one of the Merchant Company Schools, George Heriot's or the High School. But the demand for free advanced educational opportunities grew apace. Just before 1900, in an endeavour to meet this need, Edinburgh's School Board, dividing the city into two broad areas, north and south, provided three classrooms for higher grade education in the top floor of Bruntsfield Primary School and three in Broughton Primary School. As the demand continued to increase, plans were then made to build two non-fee-paying secondary schools and in 1904 Boroughmuir School at Bruntsfield Links (at the end of Warrender Park Terrace) and Broughton Secondary School were opened. Originally Boroughmuir was to have been named Victoria School, though eventually, considering its location, the name Boroughmuir was chosen. The new school on the links opened its doors in September 1904, the official opening ceremony taking place the following February.

Within ten years Boroughmuir proved quite inadequate, the demand for admission (as also at Broughton) exceeding all expectations. A new larger school for southern Edinburgh was therefore built at Viewforth, of a size and type which made it one of the finest in Scotland. Early in September 1913, the new Boroughmuir premises were opened and in January 1914, when the final transfer of pupils from the Bruntsfield Links building had been completed, the official opening ceremony was performed by T. McKinnon Wood, the Scottish Secretary of State. The ceremony was not devoid of one sign of the times: a suffragette in the assembled company threw a large paper bag of flour at Mr. Wood during his speech!

Another sign of the times (still in evidence today!) was economic: while the original Boroughmuir Secondary School and Broughton Secondary School had been built in 1904 at a combined cost of £51,000, excluding land costs, ten years later the Viewforth School alone cost £52,000.

For some years a Junior Student Centre at the new Boroughmuir "produced" twenty to thirty school teachers annually. While the school had been built to accommodate 1,150 pupils, the roll after several years greatly exceeded this number, especially just after the 1914-18 War when 1,700 pupils were in attendance. In recent years Boroughmuir Secondary School, short of accommodation, again took over the building at Bruntsfield Links as its Junior School, seventy years after it had been opened as Boroughmuir Secondary School. The school in Viewforth, as a result of recent educational legislation, is now known as Boroughmuir High School and has become comprehensive. From its foundation it was co-educational.

Former pupils of Boroughmuir have brought honour to their school in many spheres of life. They include a Moderator of the Church of Scotland, a Scottish Secretary of State, an H.M. Inspector of Constabulary for Scotland, a Director of the Scottish National Museum, an Edinburgh Director of Education and many more. In the field of sport, a former pupil was one of the first rugby players not from a fee-paying or public school to play for Scotland, while several boys whose soccer skill was developed with a rubber ball in the playground during lunch-break have become professionals. The Boroughmuir Basket Ball team has earned the distinction of competing in the European Championship, their leading player John Tunnah, a young Morningside resident, becoming, before his premature death, a Scottish internationalist and one of the greatest players in Europe. Of the innumerable former Boroughmuir pupils who served in the Second World War, no fewer than two hundred made the supreme sacrifice.

The removal of Boroughmuir School from its original building on Bruntsfield Links to Viewforth in 1914 proved timely for the development of James Gillespie's, which in due course was transferred from the old Gillespie's Hospital building in Gillespie Crescent to the vacated Boroughmuir premises. Soon after its establishment here, still as a mixed fee-paying school under the Edinburgh School Board, a post-intermediate department was added and a fusion effected between James Gillespie's and Warrender Park School. The latter building, at the top of Marchmont Crescent, served as Gillespie's junior division.

In 1929 further important changes took place. Pressure on accommodation and the ever increasing demand for a high school for girls led the Education Committee (the former School Board) to devote the

The old village of Wrychtishousis

Bruntsfield Links building exclusively to girls. It became James Gillespie's High School for Girls while the much smaller Warrender Park elementary school became James Gillespie's Boys' School, preparing pupils for entry to other Edinburgh secondary schools. About 1936 a new Infant Department for girls was opened adjacent to the main school on the Links, built on the site of a former well-known photographic studio close to the former Viewpark House.

CHAPTER 5

Greenhill

From Bruntsfield Links we retrace our steps by way of Bruntsfield Crescent (built in 1870), where in summer one may hear languages from almost every corner of the world as one mingles with the many young — and not so young — people enjoying the well-appointed and obviously popular facilities of the Scottish Youth Hostels Association's premises. Turning left into Greenhill Gardens, one is once more back in the past. The Greenhill district, through which Greenhill Gardens was for long the only highway, retains much of the pleasant secluded charm of bygone days despite the frequent passage of traffic.

Records of David II's reign in the fourteenth century refer to the conveyance of land by the owner of Braid estate in Morningside to "Heurie Multra of Greenhill", but more explicit references to this district date from 1586, in which year the western Burgh Muir was feued out by the city magistrates in six lots. Lot 5, eight acres in extent, went to Thomas Aitkenhead, a skinner or glover of Edinburgh eventually of merchant class who was for a period a bailie and Dean of Guild. Two small portions of neighbouring land were acquired when Aitkenhead's elder son fell heir to Greenhill, then described as "Laird's Hill". David Aitkenhead, who became the next owner of the Greenhill estate in 1619, was Lord Provost of Edinburgh for ten years. A staunch supporter of James VI and a controversial figure amongst Edinburgh's university students, he was also much involved in disputes over fishing boats from the European mainland invading Scottish waters.

The Greenhill estate was first feued for building in 1840, forty years before the mansion-house was demolished, and the villas in the northern half of Greenhill Gardens (from Bruntsfield Terrace to Chamberlain Road) were completed within ten years of this date. The southern portion of Greenhill Gardens (numbers 19 and 26 onwards) was built during a later phase and its eastern side was originally named Stuart's Green after its owner Stuart Forbes of Pitsligo.

The first ordnance survey map, of 1852, showing the environs of Edinburgh indicates some seventeen houses in the older northern end of Greenhill Gardens. Five of these on the west side (beginning from the Bruntsfield Terrace end) bore the names Greenhill Lodge, Viewfield Lodge, St Margaret's Cottage (the first to be completed, in 1849), Spring Bank and Hopefield Cottage. On the east side was Rose Villa. While these substantial villas were all built at about the same time, each was of a different design from its neighbours.

Greenhill House depicted in a
sculpted plaque at the corner of
Bruntsfield Gardens
and Bruntsfield Place,
the work of George Washington
Browne

An interesting account of the earliest days of Greenhill Gardens and of many of its distinguished residents and their achievements is preserved in the Edinburgh Room of Edinburgh's Central Public Library. This hand-written hardback notebook from the pen of John Smith, F.S.A. (SCOT.), author of many published historical works on Edinburgh who lived in nearby Viewforth Gardens, is entitled: *Greenhill Gardens, Bruntsfield Links, Edinburgh, with notes on some of its early residenters.* It is interleaved with photographs of the earliest houses and was written in 1929.

From this valuable record and other later sources we learn that in 1929 three of the earliest Greenhill Gardens houses already referred to retained their original names, Viewfield Lodge, St Margaret's Cottage and Hopefield Cottage. Today the houses themselves remain but they no longer bear their early names.

Greenhill passed from the Aitkenhead family in 1636 to John Livingstone, "an apothecary in Edinburgh" who ten years earlier had married Elizabeth Rig. The initials of Livingstone and his wife are still to be seen on a tombstone in a garden in Chamberlain Road. John Livingstone's enjoyment of the pleasant country lands of Greenhill was short-lived: in 1645 he was one of many victims of a particularly virulent visitation of the dreaded Black Death. So terrifying was this epidemic that "most of the citizens, even the soldiers in the Castle and prisoners in the Tolbooth fled the city in terror". Half the population of Leith is thought to have died.

77

John Livingstone was buried in the grounds of his estate and his tombstone is built into the west wall of a small enclosure in the front garden of Ashfield Nursing Home in Chamberlain Road. The enclosure takes the form of an unroofed mausoleum with a doorway once surmounted by a triangular pediment. Livingstone's gravestone bears the following inscription:

> This Saint whos Corps lyes buried heir
> Let all posteritie admoir
> For upright lif in Godly feir
>
> When judgments did this land surround
> He with God was walking found
> For which from midst of fers he's cround
>
> Heir to be interrd. Both he
> And friends by Providence agrie
> No age shal los his memorie
>
> His age 53.　　Died 1645

The tombstone is ornamented with a shield bearing three cinquefoils or gillyflowers flanked by the letters "I.L." and surmounted by a skull and crossbones and winged hour-glass. A scroll bears the words, "Mors patet: Hora latet."

This burial place was later to accommodate at least one other owner of Greenhill, although the Livingstone gravestone is the only one now in evidence. There were at one time other ornamental stones in the garden at Ashfield but, save for a sculpted head, these have all disappeared.

John Livingstone's widow Elizabeth died more than thirty years after her husband, in 1677. Nearly ten years earlier, the estate had passed to her elder son, also John Livingstone, who was a doctor of medicine. It seems to have been he who built the mansion-house of Greenhill on the site of the earlier and more simple dwelling. His plans must have been over-ambitious for he was led to borrow large sums of money he was unable to repay. He was forced to sell the house to his younger brother William, who stood security for him. John, having fled to Stirling, was eventually pursued by his creditors and forced to return to Edinburgh where he took refuge in Holyrood Sanctuary, "to his great charges and loss of his calling".

Greenhill House stood about a hundred yards north of the Livingstone mausoleum in Chamberlain Road. On the north corner of Bruntsfield Gardens, at its junction with Bruntsfield Place, the house is commemorated by a sculpted stone plaque, the work of Sir George Washington Browne, the architect who designed many of the late nineteenth-century buildings in Bruntsfield and Greenhill. Forbes Road

The private burial ground, in the garden of Ashfield in Chamberlain Road, of John Livingston, owner of Greenhill, who died of plague in 1645

Photograph by Mr W. R. Smith

was the drive which led to the four-storeyed "gable-ended and gabled manor-house". Many of its thirty-two windows were blocked up following the introduction of the Window Tax in 1696. This law, repealed in 1851, was severely criticised for its adverse effect on hygiene, restricting as it did light and ventilation. The Ordnance Survey map of 1852 indicates extensive grounds which included a dovecot and fish-pond.

By 1720 Greenhill House and its lands had passed from the Livingstone family and through a succession of owners to one Adam Fairholme, a burgess of the City of Edinburgh who had also fallen heir to the extensive Fairholme property in Liberton's Wynd in the High Street. According to the city archives Adam Fairholme was Treasurer of Edinburgh Town Council in 1752. The office of City Chamberlain, the important full-time salaried post which obtains today, was not finally introduced in Edinburgh until 1766. However, though the office which Adam Fairholme of Greenhill House held was that of City Treasurer and not City Chamberlain, nevertheless a century later Chamberlain Road was

The tombstone of John Livingston of Greenhill in his private burial ground

Photograph by Mr Brian Smith

named in his honour, commemorating him by the title then given to the city's purse-bearer.

Several Edinburgh historians have suggested that Adam Fairholme's son George was the Chamberlain after whom the street was named, but this appears to be incorrect. In 1643 a John Fairholme was City Treasurer, but he probably belonged to a different branch of the Fairholme family and was not connected with Greenhill. Certainly the George Fairholme who succeeded his father Adam as owner of Greenhill in 1771 might have been well qualified to succeed him also in managing the city's finances, for George and his brother William had for long resided in Holland where they became wealthy bankers. There George had also become a celebrated collector of art treasures, including an almost complete set of etchings by Rembrandt.

In 1790 George Fairholme made over his property at Greenhill to Thomas Wright but such was his attachment to the pleasant "village and lands of Greenhill" that he introduced the proviso:

> "Reserving never-the-less to me, the liberty and privilege of burying the dead of my own family and such of my relations to whom I, during my own lifetime, shall communicate such privilege, in the burial place built upon the said lands, and reserving likewise access to me and my heirs to repair the said burial place from time to time, as we shall think proper."

Fairholme's wish was apparently fulfilled: his death at his house in "George's Square" on February 1st. 1800 was noted in the *Scots Magazine* of March that year and several writers reported his interment in the Livingstone mausoleum in Chamberlain Road. However, there is now no memorial in the enclosure to confirm this, though he is commemorated more publicly in Kay's *Portraits*.

In 1806 the Greenhill estate and mansion-house was purchased by William Forbes, who in the same year succeeded his father as 7th Baronet of Pitsligo in Aberdeenshire. His father was the great Scottish banker of Sir William Forbes & Company's Bank in Parliament Square, then, at the beginning of the nineteenth century, the bustling business centre of Edinburgh. This bank, which in 1838 became the Union Bank of Scotland, was described by Sir William in his *Memoirs of a Banking House*, written in 1803.

Pitsligo estate, which the 7th Baronet Sir William Forbes regained in 1806, had been forfeited by the Jacobite Lord Forbes. Sir William's ownership of Greenhill and Pitsligo resulted in the naming of Forbes Road (off Bruntsfield Place) and Pitsligo Road (in the Churchhill district). Newbattle Terrace, as later noted, also derives its name from the Forbes family.

Sir William, when he took possession of Greenhill in 1806, was a widower of sixteen years. Once Sir Walter Scott's rival for the affections of the heiress and only child of Sir John Stuart of Fettercairn and Invermay in the north, Sir William was successful in marrying this fair lady and obtaining her considerable properties forbye. Sir Walter took defeat in good spirit and indeed later expressed appreciation for Sir William's considerable help during the illustrious Scottish author's financial crisis in 1826.

Sir John Stuart Forbes, who succeeded Sir William as 8th Baronet of Pitsligo, Fettercairn and Greenhill, was a generous benefactor in the

Greenhill district, especially to local churches. In 1873, some time after his death, his trustees sold Greenhill House and its land to the Right Reverend James R.A. Chinnery-Haldane, Scottish Episcopalian Bishop of Argyll and the Isles. He in turn disposed of it to Beattie's, a firm of builders, in 1882, donating the substantial proceeds to the Scottish Episcopal Church. The old mansion-house was demolished in 1884. Little time was lost in using the stone from three quarries opened within its grounds to initiate a great building programme of villas and tenements in the surrounding Greenhill and Bruntsfield districts. The dates high up on the walls of the tenements in Forbes Road, Bruntsfield Avenue and elsewhere signify how, within ten years of the disappearance of Greenhill House, a vast transformation had occurred in what for so long had been a quiet and remote village.

As one is about to enter Greenhill Gardens from the Bruntsfield terrace and Links end, one sees the first of many properties asscoiated with distinguished residents of the past. I select but a few for mention. On the right here, at the corner of Bruntsfield Terrace and Greenhill Gardens, stands the Tower House, originally No. 5 but now 8 Bruntsfield Terrace. Here lived and died George Cousin, surveyor, Edinburgh Town Council member for Newington in 1864 and an ardent social reformer.

Nearby, in 7 Greenhill Gardens, lived his brother David Cousin, an architect whose prodigious achievements are to be seen in many parts of Edinburgh. He was apprenticed to the celebrated Playfair who was then building Donaldson's Hospital and the National Gallery, and was himself later responsible for designing Chambers Street. As consultant architect to the Free Church he designed many of its Edinburgh churches, as well as the Free Church building on the Mound. He was defeated by Playfair in seeking the commission to build the Assembly Hall, but as University Architect he designed the music classroom in Park Place, behind the Medical School. Among his other achievements were the renovation of Old Greyfriars Church in 1854, after its severe damage by fire nine years earlier, the laying out of the east Princes Street Gardens and the designing of St Catherine's Convent in Lauriston Gardens, also the Corn Exchange in the Grassmarket (demolished some years ago to make way for an extension to the Heriot Watt University). In addition to supervising the feuing plans for the Mayfield district and planning the layout of Newington Cemetery (when completed in 1846 this was Edinburgh's second cemetery, after Warriston), David Cousin also found time to visit Paris to study the abattoirs at du Roule, Montmartre and Popincourt, which resulted in his preparing designs for Edinburgh's first extensive Egyptian-style abattoir at Fountainbridge. Despite so much spectacular public work, Cousin's main interest was the building of houses for the working classes. He died in the United States at the age of sixty-nine.

At 4 Greenhill Gardens there lived Professor Archibald Hamilton Charteris, founder of the Church of Scotland Deaconess Institution,

Training Home and Hospital, who is commemorated by the church next to the Deaconess Hospital in the Pleasance, which bears his name. Professor Charteris also started the Church of Scotland's magazine *Life and Work* in 1879.

On the same side of Greenhill Gardens, at No. 18, once known as Netherby, lived Horatio Ross of Rossie Castle near Montrose. He was a friend of Nelson, and famous as a crack shot.

Andrew Usher, donor of the great auditorium in Lothian Road which bears his name, lived in Greenhill Gardens in 1851 and died at 3 Greenhill Park. Though Mr Usher's gift of £100,000 for the construction of a great concert hall was announced in 1896, the Usher Hall was not completed until 1914. A gift of £10,000 to improve St Abb's Harbour was another expression of this great benefactor's generosity.

The Reverend Dr John Kirk, famed for his leadership of the Evangelical Union, built Hopefield Cottage at 17 Greenhill Gardens in 1851, and there resided until his death in 1886. An eloquent and moving preacher as well as a prolific writer on religious subjects, Dr Kirk was also a fervent promoter of the abstinence movement and his memoirs, edited by his wife, present a graphic account of the ill-effects on individuals and society of the excessive drinking prevalent in his day.

During his early labours in Hamilton in Lanarkshire, Dr Kirk was one of those expelled from the Congregational Union as a result of doctrinal controversies. Dr David Livingstone, the great Scottish missionary and explorer, supported him in his stand, and, when in Africa, was pleased to receive regularly from Dr Kirk his various religious publications. David Livingstone is known to have visited Hopefield Cottage and Mrs Livingstone, also a close friend of the Kirks, was, on her enforced return from Africa, made welcome at Hopefield. Amongst the many letters Dr Kirk received from Livingstone was one which gave him the difficult task of informing the explorer's eldest son Robert of Mrs - Livingstone's death.

Brighton Street Evangelical Church at Bristo was the first scene of Dr Kirk's long and arduous labours after he settled in Edinburgh in 1851. These were continued in the then remote district of Morningside. Kirk held regular open-air services on Bruntsfield Links, his large congregation occupying the natural amphitheatre of an incompletely filled-in quarry.

Kirk's son John, who became Minister of Gorgie Evangelical Union Church, succeeded his father at Hopefield and lived there until his death in 1923. Whatever the austerities of the Kirk household, one may assume that they enjoyed good food: the wife of the young Reverend John Kirk was an expert cook. In an effort to raise funds for her husband's church, Mrs Kirk sold hand-written copies of recipes for one penny. So much in demand were these that she was persuaded to publish them in book form, and *Tried Favourites* enjoyed immediate success. Having gone through more than twenty editions and sold nearly three-quarters of a million copies, it became a classic and was reprinted yet again a few years ago. Today the "Hopefield Cottage" name-plate has gone from the door of 17 Greenhill Gardens.

At 24 Greenhill Gardens (opposite Hopefield Cottage) resided one of Scotland's most celebrated sculptors, Aberdeen-born Sir John Steell, R.S.A., Sculptor-Royal for Scotland. The best-known of Steell's works is the Wellington Monument, a striking equestrian statue of the Iron Duke in front of Register House, completed in 1852. The unveiling ceremony of the hero of Waterloo's statue in Princes Street was a memorable occasion, attended by numerous war veterans. Among Steell's many other works, well known is his seated figure of Sir Walter Scott at the base of the great Scott Monument in Princes Street Gardens, completed in 1846 at a cost of £2,000. This work, showing Sir Walter's favourite Highland staghound Maida at his right foot, was the first marble statue commissioned in Scotland and it earned Steell a special award. Elsewhere in Edinburgh one may see other creations of Steell's: *The Ten Virgins* at the Standard Insurance Offices in George Street (reproduced by request for Dublin), *Allan Ramsay* in the west Princes Street Gardens, *Dr Thomas Chalmers* at the junction of George Street and Castle Street, *Alexander Taming Bucephalus* in the City Chambers forecourt and *Albert, Prince Consort* in Charlotte Square. Soon after the completion of this last work, Steell was knighted. Amongst his lesser-known creations is a bust of George Meikle Kemp, a fellow resident of Morningside, holding his pencil sketch of the Scott Monument, of which he was the architect.

At the southern end of Greenhill Gardens three silver birch trees stand at the edge of a grass plot. There is a belief in the district that the area was not built upon because it had been an ancient burial ground for plague victims and that the trees mark the graves of three nuns of the Convent of St Catherine of Sienna who had tended the sick here until they themselves fell victims. In fact the trees were planted very much later indeed by three university students of the district who named them after themselves. One of the students was said to be Hippolyte Blanc, later a distinguished architect who designed Christ's Scottish Episcopal Church at Holy Corner and St Matthew's Parish Church (now Cluny Parish Church) in Braid Road. The eastern side of Greenhill Gardens, alongside the plantation, was once named Stuart's Green. Originally it continued across what is now Strathearn Place, then a *cul-de-sac* entered from Whitehouse Loan. Eventually Edinburgh Corporation purchased a villa which was demolished to make way for a single tramline running through Strathearn Place and then eastwards by Strathearn Road and Grange Road. Previously the horse-drawn tramcars had turned off Grange Road into Hope Terrace and Whitehouse Loan, then passing along Clinton Road and round into Churchhill.

St Bennet's at 42 Greenhill Gardens was built, in an earlier form, by the advocate George Seton in 1856 and named by him. He resided here for thirty-four years. Author of *The Law and Practice of Heraldry in Scotland*, he also wrote *The History of the Family of Seton over Eight Centuries*, inspired by the fact that he was a descendant of Mary Seton, one of Mary, Queen of Scots' "Four Maries". It was probably his deep interest and pride in his family history which prompted him also to preserve the remains of the Convent of St Catherine of Sienna in Sciennes since several ladies of the Seton family, whose husbands had died at Flodden, had been amongst the first members of this religious community. Mr Seton had an explanatory tablet erected in 1872 in the garden of 16 St Catherine's Place (off Grange Road) where many stones were preserved when the convent was demolished. He also erected a small cairn of stones from the convent in the garden of St Bennet's, but over the years these have disappeared. Mr Seton was for some time President of the Morningside Athenaeum Club, established in the vacated North Morningside Church at the corner of Chamberlain Road and Morningside Road. Earlier in his career as an advocate he was one of Robert Louis Stevenson's rivals for the Chair of Constitutional Law at Edinburgh University. Seton obtained fifty-one votes against Stevenson's nine, the successful candidate receiving eighty-two.

St Bennet's was purchased by the Roman Catholic Archdiocese of St Andrews and Edinburgh in October 1890 for the sum of £3,800 as the Archbishop's house, and Archbishop William Smith took up residence there in 1891. The chapel, the Byzantine-style copper dome of which is something of a landmark at the east end of Churchhill, was built in 1907, the architect being R. W. Schultz. Its cost was met by the then Marquis of Bute, and some of the timber used in its construction was brought from Falkland Palace in Fife, one of the residences of the Bute family. It has been suggested that the architect's design for the chapel was inspired by Santa Sophia in Constantinople. Certain of its features were stipulated by the Marquis of Bute. The first stained-glass windows were installed by Cardinal Gray, the present Archbishop of St Andrews and Edinburgh, in 1955. The sanctuary and St Clare windows were executed by Gabriel Loire of Chartres in 1960. St Bennet's was substantially altered during its occupancy by the late Archbishop Andrew Joseph MacDonald, O.S.B., in 1934. Many relics of Scottish historical and sacred interest were at one time treasured in the house but these have now been transferred to libraries and other houses. One such relic was a chair which belonged to Cardinal Beaton of St Andrews, Cardinal Gray's long-distant predecessor in office.

While Cardinal Beaton was Scotland's last resident cardinal before the Reformation, Cardinal Gordon Joseph Gray, the present occupant of St Bennet's, enjoys the distinction of being the first resident Scottish cardinal since that stormy period. When appointed Archbishop of St Andrews and Edinburgh in 1951 at the age of forty-one, he became the

Holy Corner

By courtesy of Edinburgh "Evening News"

youngest Roman Catholic archbishop in the world. Born in Leith and educated at the former Holy Cross Academy, his forebears were millers in the district of Buckie and Portsoy on the north-east coast. He was also the first Catholic priest to become a graduate of St Andrews University since the Reformation, and was awarded an honorary Doctorate of Divinity of his former university in 1967. Since his appointment to his large archdiocese, Cardinal Gray has been responsible for the establishment of nearly thirty new parishes and the building of as many new churches. Perhaps the most courageous and enterprising feature of his career has been his adoption for missionary work of Bauchi in Nigeria, on the fringe of the Sahara, an area larger than Scotland. Many volunteer priests and generous financial aid from the St Andrews and Edinburgh Archdiocese for social and medical services are preparing Bauchi to become an independent Christian province.

Leaving Greenhill Gardens by Chamberlain Road, we pass the old burial ground of John Livingstone in the grounds of Ashfield Nursing

Home. The fine old villas of the area in their different styles give a distinguished architectural character to the still secluded Greenhill Park. We emerge at Holy Corner, so named because here stand four churches of different denominations, Congregationalist, Church of Scotland, Scottish Episcopalian and Baptist. The Congregation of North Morningside Church was established as a result of discussions held in 1860 to consider the formation of a United Presbyterian Church in Morningside, at that time a pleasant rural district remote from the city and a favourite place of summer residence for Edinburgh's wealthier citizens. Only two churches then existed south of Bruntsfield Links, Morningside Parish Church at the western corner of Newbattle Terrace and Morningside Free Church, which became the Baptist Church.

By 1862 the small band of people who for two years had been meeting for worship in a classroom of Merchiston Castle School in Colinton Road had resolved to build a church. One of their number was Mr Henderson, headmaster of James Gillespie's School then in Gillespie Crescent. In October 1862 the architect R. Paterson was commissioned to prepare plans for a church at an estimated cost of £2,200. Until this was completed, the congregation next arranged to meet, by permission of the Deacon's Court, in the Free Church School half-way down Morningside Road in the centre of the village, just beyond the site of the present Public Library. Numbering thirty-seven, the United Presbyterian Church congregation was officially constituted in July 1863, and on November 5th of that year the first service was held in the newly built church at the north-west corner of Chamberlain Road, on the site now occupied by the Congregationalist Church. It is interesting to note that among the congregation of the following year were Dr John Brown, author of *Rab and His Friends,* and Dr James Y. Simpson, famed for his discovery of chloroform as an anaesthetic. Architectural defects in the new church presented problems: the high roof made for poor acoustics and the building proved draughty. The congregation dwindled, despite the installation of a new ceiling, until numbers were still so small that the Minister's stipend was decreased. In January 1868 Edinburgh was swept by a violent gale in which the roof of the church was blown off and the congregation was forced to return temporarily to the Free Church School in Morningside. The problems of the excessive use of alcohol, against which Dr Kirk of Hopefield Cottage had led a prolonged crusade in the 1870s, are reflected by the North Morningside Congregation of this period in the controversy concerning the use of fermented wine in the Communion Service.

By 1879 the congregation had steadily increased and a larger church seemed necessary. Consequently two villas were purchased at the south-west corner of Chamberlain Road, and demolished to provide a site. In February 1880 the foundation-stone of the present church was laid. One important Morningside personality who took part in the ceremony was Dr

Clouston, Superintendent of Morningside Asylum, which had then been in existence for sixty years. The new church was opened on October 16th, 1881, at a cost of £13,500. Built in the Norman style of twelfth-century Scotland, with a prominent bell-tower, the architect was David Robertson. There was seating for one thousand people.

One of the greatest pastors of North Morningside Church was Dr Alexander Mair. Between his induction in 1873 and his retirement in 1902 the congregation increased from 162 to 800, which reflects also the growth of Morningside at that time. Mr Mair was the last Moderator of the United Presbyterian Church and he saw its union with the Free Church. In 1929 the North Morningside United Free Church then joined with the Church of Scotland. Church membership had increased over the years, especially under the ministry of the distinguished scholar and preacher the Reverend James S. Stewart who came to North Morningside from Beechgrove in Aberdeen and was eventually appointed Professor of New Testament Literature, Language and Theology at Edinburgh's New College. When Dr Stewart resigned his charge to take up this post in 1946, the congregation numbered over 1,750. The church has many fine stained-glass windows commemorating the First World War, distinguished ministers of the church and the thirty-seven members who founded its congregation in 1861.

When North Morningside Church moved to its new premises in 1881, the former building, which had cost £2,880 to build in 1863, was sold to the Morningside Athenaeum Company for £2,000. Here, with commendable enterprise, they opened the Morningside Athenaeum, providing a library, lecture theatre and concert hall. Some original programmes for winter evenings in this cultural centre are preserved in the Public Library's Edinburgh Room and reveal interesting enterprises of an apparently high standard. There were regular poetry readings and song recitals, and lectures sometimes on the most profound themes. The subject of the opening one for the 1882 session, given on November 2nd by George Seton of St Bennet's, who was Chairman of the Athenaeum's Board of Directors, was "Lecture on Contrasts of Life." The Athenaeum's unequalled contribution to cultural life in Morningside came to an end when the premises, unchanged from the days when they were occupied by North Morningside Church, were purchased by the Congregational Church in 1890.

The small group of Congregationalists in Morningside had rented accommodation in the Athenaeum from 1887 until their purchase of the whole premises three years later. In 1928 the original building was demolished, to be replaced by the present fine Congregationalist Church designed by the architect James McLachlan, F.R.I.B.A. The foundation stone had been laid on June 16th, 1928 by one of the congregation's pioneers, Mr Charles Price, M.P. for Edinburgh Central. The total cost of the hall (opened a year before the church was completed), church, manse

The original North Morningside Church on Holy Corner which later became the Morningside Athenaeum Club

and church officer's house was £24,000. The dedication service was held on October 29th, 1929. In 1974 the North Morningside Church of Scotland and the Congregationalist Church entered into an agreement of "linkage" and they are now served by one minister, combined services being held in both churches.

Opposite the Congregationalist Church is Christ Church of the Scottish Episcopal denomination, described by Grant in *Old and New Edinburgh* as being "eastward of Merchiston Castle and within the park where for ages the old doo'cot stood". In fact the congregation's first place of worship was in Merchiston Castle School. Christ Church was built in 1876-7 at a cost of approximately £10,500. In early French Gothic style, with a hundred-and-forty-foot high steeple, the architect was Hippolyte Blanc, F.R.I.B.A., R.S.A. The chancel with its noble circumambient aisle was built at the expense of Miss Falconar of Falconhall, the cost being just over £3,000. The font was donated by Mr and Mrs Finnie of Swanston Farm and the communion vessels by the son of Professor James Syme of Millbank in Canaan Lane.

The Reverend Arnold Patrick Spencer-Smith, curate at Christ Church in 1910, deserves special mention. He volunteered as chaplain to Shackleton's South Pole expedition in 1914 and died of scurvy at the Ross Barrier in the Antarctic.

In 1893, with the steady expansion of Morningside southwards, facilities were arranged at Morningside Hall in Morningside Drive for Episcopalians residing south of the Jordan Burn, and in 1896 a little iron church, "the tin kirk", was built at the south corner of Braid Road and Comiston Terrace.

Before crossing Colinton Road to the Baptist Church, observe the date 1873 on the west wall of the fine villa now occupied by the Bank of Scotland. At the junction of Colinton Road and Morningside Road a fountain, long since gone, was erected in 1869. Cut from Aberdeen granite and surmounted by an ornamental lamp, it was the gift of Mrs Nicol of Huntly Lodge in Morningside.

Near the south-east corner of Colinton Road, Morningside's small band of Baptist pioneers established themselves in 1894 in the high-steepled little church built twenty years before as the Morningside Free Church. When the Free Church moved to its larger building further up Morningside Road (now the Churchhill Theatre) their old premises were auctioned. It was said that Morningside's Roman Catholic community were interested in purchasing, but the Baptists' offer of £3,000 was not exceeded (although the church had originally cost some £7,000 to build). Seriously damaged by fire in December 1972, the church was virtually rebuilt, with many new features, and reopened on March 7th, 1976.

CHAPTER 6

Merchiston

From Holy Corner, Colinton Road leads westward through the ancient lands of Merchiston. On its north side is an old gateway with stone pillars each surmounted by a "lion couchant", recalling the district's earliest days. This is the Lion Gateway, once the entrance to Merchiston Tower. Constructed in the nineteenth century and erected on their present site in 1964, the pillars may have links with an earlier seventeenth-century gateway. A few yards westwards, through the portals of the Napier College of Commerce and Technology, the fifteenth-century tower itself may be seen, skilfully restored in 1964 to form the centre-piece of the college complex.

References to Merchiston (the name appearing variously as Merchamston, Merkesastone, Makerston and in other versions) first occur in the Exchequer Rolls of 1266. A Roll of King Robert the Bruce's reign cites William Bisset as in possession of the lands of Merchiston and Dalry. In the reign of David II, William St Clare of Roslin and Morton became owner. No subsequent successor is recorded until 1438, when Merchiston was acquired by Alexander Napier, merchant burgess of Edinburgh. The tower and its surrounding lands were to remain in the possession of the Napier family for much of the following five centuries and to be described as the "seat of a race second to none in Scotland for rank and talent". Alexander Napier, first Laird of Merchiston, was a successful merchant, wealthy enough to lend money to the Crown, in return for which he was granted the lands of Merchiston, and influential enough to entertain the French ambassador at Holyrood and escort Princess Margaret to France to marry the Dauphin Louis. He was Provost of Edinburgh from 1436-7.

After his death in 1454 his son Alexander in turn advanced the reputation of the "race second to none in Scotland" and was granted the additional lands of Over Merchiston. He became Comptroller of the Royal Household, Vice-Admiral of Scotland, and Scottish Ambassador to England and many European countries, negotiating the marriage of James III to Princess Margaret of Denmark in 1468. Among his other several offices was that of "Poulterer to the King", through his ownership of the poultry lands at the Dean. It was probably he, the second Laird of Merchiston, who, while he had quarters at Holyrood, built Merchiston Tower as a country house from which to farm his lands, although its precise date is not on record. In 1512 Alexander Napier was confirmed in Merchiston by James IV at a rent of "one silver penny yearly". A year later his eldest son and heir was killed at Flodden.

In common with the Grange, Whitehouse and Bruntsfield, Merchiston was Crown land and thus has a more ancient history than neighbouring areas of the Burgh Muir first feued out in 1586. The boundaries of the Merchiston estate were never clearly defined and were frequently altered. However, in terms of modern streets, Morningside Road may be taken to have formed the eastern boundary, while the irregular northern boundary included Dalry and Gorgie Muir. To the south-west, the ancient village of Tipperlinn and adjacent district of Myreside were included. A part of the land was known as Lady Acres. There are also early references to Merchiston Loch, though the exact

John Napier of Merchiston, inventor of logarithms

location of this is now difficult to determine. It is possible that it is the same as the ancient Jordanville Loch which extended over much of Myreside.

While Merchiston Tower was built as a country house, its strategic position on the old "wester heigait" from the south resulted in its being frequently under siege, especially during the struggle between Mary, Queen of Scots and her son James VI's supporters in 1572. A twenty-six-pound cannon-ball found embedded in the tower during its restoration is thought to have been a relic of this period. The Regent Mar installed garrisons in the Kirk of Corstorphine, Redhall and Craigmillar Castle to prevent food supplies reaching Edinburgh from the south, but Merchiston Tower was not so easily occupied. In May 1572 Sir Archibald Napier was ordered to surrender the tower but refused to do so. Three weeks later, "300 men with cannons came from Leith to the Burrow Mure". The tower's walls were breached and the customary attempt made to smoke out the occupants. But Merchiston held out.

Sir Archibald Napier died in 1608 and was succeeded by his son John, "fiar of Merchiston" and eighth of his line. He was the most illustrious of his great family, and also earned a place for himself among the world's foremost scientists. Born in Merchiston Tower in 1550, John Napier was sent to St Salvator's College at St Andrews University at the age of thirteen. He remained there for two years but left in 1565 without taking his degree. For six years he travelled widely in Europe. Returning to Scotland in 1572, he married and settled down to the life of a Lowland laird on the family estate of Gartness in Stirlingshire. A devout church-man and Commissioner to the Church of Scotland General Assembly, his first published works were on the political aspects of religion. In 1593, the appearance of his *Plain Discovery of the Whole Revelation of St John* earned him a high reputation throughout Europe as an influential theologian. At a time when invasion was a constant fear of European nations, Napier also applied his inventive mind to the design of powerful new defensive weapons, publishing a paper, *Secrette Inventionis,* which anticipated by centuries the tank, armoured car and submarine. Other suggestions included lenses to concentrate the sun's heat on the enemy. His plans were personally submitted to James VI, for whom he felt a special loyalty.

While his theological and military writings earned John Napier a high reputation, it was his publication in 1614 of a small book consisting of fifty-seven pages of text and ninety pages of tables which was to bring him lasting renown. This was his *Mirifici Logarithmorum Canonis Descriptio,* the result of years of studying astronomy and mathematics in his small room in Merchiston Tower, which astonished the world's scholars. Indeed, Napier's system of logarithms helped to point the way towards modern mathematical sciences. It was Britain's first significant contribution to the advancement of science, placing Napier, alongside Copernicus, Galileo

Title-page of the first edition of Napier's famous work on logarithms

and Kepler, with those "whose genius consolidated the labours of their predecessors and laid down the lines of future advance". Napier was also the first to conceive the idea of the decimal point.

During his residence at Merchiston Tower from 1608 until his death there on April 4th, 1617, John Napier became renowned in the district as the "Wizard of Merchiston", many local people believing that he dabbled in Black Magic. His method of dealing with pigeons from a neighbouring house which invaded his property and decimated his crops perhaps confirmed this belief: he fed them with peas and grain that had been steeped in alcohol, thus apparently reducing their great capacity for destruction. It was during the time of the pigeon invasion, tradition has it, that the area south of the tower became known as Dowcroft and the little lane (now Albert Terrace) leading from Morningside Road to Tipperlinn as Doo Loan.

John Napier's father, Sir Archibald, had been master of the Scottish Mint for thirty years, during which time he discovered gold in the Pentland Hills, "not in vaynes but rather in rocks neere the tops and heights of the mountaynes". This gold, with that from Leadhills, was minted in the Scottish coinage till the Union of Parliaments in 1707.

John Napier's son and heir Archibald was raised to the Peerage as the first Lord Napier and created a Baronet of Nova Scotia by Charles I in 1627. He married Lady Margaret Graham, sister of the Marquis of Montrose, and, although he had signed the Covenant, later pledged his loyalty to Montrose. This led to his imprisonment in Edinburgh Castle in 1641. Three years later he was confined to Holyrood with his son and son-in-law, each under a penalty of £1,000, and, when the two others escaped, Lord Napier was fined £10,000. He himself eventually got away to join Montrose, but after the Battle of Philiphaugh had again to make his escape, this time to Atholl. Lady Napier, after her brother's execution and ignominious burial as a criminal on the Burgh Muir, had his body exhumed and his heart extracted and placed in a casket of steel "which was to undergo many adventures".

The first Lord Napier's son Archibald was sued for payment of his father's debt of £10,000. As he was unable to pay, Merchiston Tower was confiscated and given in 1647 to John Cant of Morton and Comiston, son of Walter Cant of the Grange of St Giles. Thus, after nearly two centuries of unbroken succession, Merchiston passed from the Napier family. A further century was to ensue before they regained possession. In 1656 the Napiers of Merchiston were excepted from Cromwell's "Act of Grace and Pardon" and several of their creditors were given small parts of the estate. In 1729 the then owner of Merchiston went bankrupt, the lands being purchased by the Governors of George Watson's Hospital who, in 1752, sold to Francis, Lord Napier "the mansion-house of Merchiston & pertaining offices". Merchiston Tower had returned to its ancient owners. Soon afterwards, however, it was sold once more and various owners resided in the tower towards the end of the eighteenth century, including, in 1785, Dr Robert Blair, Professor of Practical Astronomy at Edinburgh University, appointed to the Chair "during all of his life time". He possessed neither observatory nor astronomical instruments, his post being "a complete sinecure for forty-three years". Extensive alterations were made to the tower between 1802 and 1817, as revealed by Kirkwood's

The restored Merchiston Tower, now part of Napier College
By courtesy of Napier College

map of the latter date. In 1818 Merchiston was again acquired by the Napiers, through the 8th Lord, William John, who had served at Trafalgar.

In 1833 the tower was let to Charles Chalmers, founder and first honorary member of Merchiston Castle School. Originally a publisher at Hope Park, Chalmers, brother of the famous Dr Thomas Chalmers, later conducted classes for boys intending to enter Edinburgh University. It was this small private school which was transferred to Merchiston. Shortly afterwards the tower was considerably altered, a castellated Gothic-style extension of two storeys and a basement being built on to the south front. Lord Cockburn in his *Memorials,* published a few years later, was to comment that, "Merchiston Castle has been greatly injured by a recent and discordant front". In 1914 the ancient mansion-house and its grounds were sold by Colonel the Honourable John Scott Napier to Merchiston Castle School Limited. The Napier dynasty, extending over more than five centuries, was at an end. In 1930, after nearly a century of educational achievement at Merchiston Castle, this notable boys' boarding-school moved to its present attractive rural setting at Colinton, retaining its name. Merchiston Tower and grounds were then purchased by the Edinburgh Merchant Company Education Board and finally, in 1935, the property passed to the Provost, Magistrates and Council of the City of Edinburgh.

After its acquisition by the city, there were many proposals for the tower's future use. None, however, proved practicable and, apart from its use by the National Fire Service during the Second World War, it remained for long unoccupied, though in 1949 preservation work was carried out on it. In 1956, it was suggested that the venerable tower should be the centrepiece of a new technical college named, most fittingly, after the famous scientist, John Napier of Merchiston. Two years later plans for the enterprise were approved and a substantial grant towards the cost of restoration was offered by the Ministry of Works on the recommendation of the Historic Buildings Council for Scotland. Restoration began in 1958 under the direction of the Edinburgh City Architect's Department and with the guidance of the Ministry of Works and Royal Commission on Ancient Monuments. The slow, intricate and skilful work was to take six years. In the course of restoration the architects and their advisers studied a wealth of interesting information which enabled them to piece together the original appearance and function of the fifteenth-century tower. A detailed account of the work carried out and the data recorded has been provided by Stuart Harris, Depute City Architect, in Volumes XXXI and XXXIII of the *Book of the Old Edinburgh Club.* He comments on the "ill-conceived and wretchedly executed alterations carried out principally in the seventeenth and nineteenth centuries", noting that, "with the exception of the seventeenth-century upper-works above parapet level, all work later than the original was distinguished by its shoddiness and scamped workmanship. The original masonry is, by contrast, well and substantially built." Highlights of the restoration were the discovery of the entrance drawbridge and the preservation of an original seventeenth-century plaster ceiling.

In 1962 a painted timber ceiling was discovered in Prestongrange House. Inscribed "1581" it is the earliest dated example of a type of ceiling fashionable in Scotland in the late sixteenth and early seventeenth centuries. Since it could not be preserved in Prestongrange House, it was brought to Merchiston Tower where it now forms the principal feature of the Napier College Board Room on the third floor.

The Napier Technical College was opened in 1964 at a cost to the city of two million pounds. The inaugural ceremony was performed by the late Sir Edward Appleton, Principal and Vice-Chancellor of Edinburgh University and, fittingly, a scientist of world renown. It was renamed the Napier College of Science and Technology in 1967. After its amalgamation with the College of Commerce at Sighthill in 1974 it became the Napier College of Commerce and Technology.

In designing the college, the most important problem confronting the architects was the visual relationship between the tower and a large new building over sixty times its size. That this was skilfully and imaginatively solved is immediately evident to all — including, one may confidently assume, the long generations of Napiers, one of whom had inscribed on a ceiling within the ancient tower, "A hundred and eight forebears handed these down to us unconquered". He would surely be proud of the manner in which his heritage has been preserved.

In the vicinity of Napier College, especially to the west, down Colinton Road there are a number of fine Victorian villas of more interest architecturally than historically. None of these, however, has attracted as much attention as one which once stood in Napier Road and which was described in a recent architectural publication as "astonishing". Known as Rockville, alias Pagoda House, Sugar Loaf or the Chinese House, it was built by Sir James Gowans as his own residence, 3 Napier Road, in 1858, but sadly demolished in 1966. Lammerburn, standing opposite at 10 Napier Road was also built by Gowans (in 1859) and is of similar design, recalling the eccentricity of Rockville.

James Gowans was born at Blackness in 1821. His father, a stone-mason, predicted the vast building programme about to begin with Edinburgh's expansion to the south and west and moved to Dean Street in Stockbridge. James was educated at Hamilton Place Academy which he left to enter the emergent architectural profession. He began training under David Bryce who was to become an expert in the Scottish Baronial style. The young apprentice was also to become one of Scotland's — indeed Europe's — most distinguished and controversial architects. His training completed, Gowans turned to railway engineering, and his early work included laying the entire track from Edinburgh to North Berwick. He later obtained the working of Redhall quarry from his now prosperous father. This quarry was first used in 1650 and the red sandstone Redhall Castle was one of the earliest creations from its stone. Gowans soon formed very definite views about contemporary architecture. While a French architect had forecast that cement, concrete and iron would eventually replace stone, this seemed hardly imminent in Edinburgh and Gowans was determined that stone should remain to the fore. His fascination with the tactile qualities, textures and colours of stone was defiantly expressed in Rockville, but he was always deeply interested also in building houses for working-class people. The 1861 census had revealed that 13,000 Edinburgh families lived in single rooms, 120 of these without windows, Gowans pressed for houses well lit by windows and surrounded by green spaces. "Light and air," was his slogan. A row of cottages in Rosebank built in 1855 opposite Gardiner's Crescent was one of his several working-class housing schemes in Edinburgh.

Medieval architecture fascinated Gowans, who made a study of pre-Reformation abbeys and churches, believing that the architect should

Rockville, Sir James Gowans' house in Napier Road, Merchiston

analyse the masterpieces of the past in order to make his own synthesis which served modern conditions and used the materials of his time. When building Rockville, he declared that he had "no desire to create novelty" but merely wished to demonstrate the effectiveness and economy of his simple but radical technique, the use of two-foot-square modules in the form of sandstone grids filled with small stones or rubble and arranged at fixed angles. In the construction of the square three-storeyed house with its massive stone chimneys and Gothic gables, he used different types of stone from many areas, including fragments from the Braid Hills and even stone from China. As a result, a wide range of colours was discernible in the house and its lodge which revealed salmon pink, crimson and olive interpersed with glittering quartz. It was the Rockville tower, five storeys or sixty-four feet high, which resulted in the name Pagoda House. Surrounded by an acre of sunken garden, the house had very large rooms, all designed in multiples of two feet to enable the use of standard doors and other fittings.

A detail of Rockville

If Rockville was the prototype, Lammerburn, built the following year, was a smaller and less elaborate replica. Gowans' other works in this style in Edinburgh were 23 and 25 Blacket Place, built in 1861, and, designed in his later years, 1 to 4 Lockharton Gardens and 64 to 82 Colinton Road. A farm-labourer's cottage at Gowans' estate, Gowanbank in West Lothian, also bore his unmistakable stamp, as did Lochee Station in Dundee. Gowans resided in Rockville for twenty-five years, during a lucrative period of his life when he was engaged in much building. By 1867 he had become the largest lessee of quarries in Scotland. In 1871 his past experience with railways earned him the contract for designing the track for the new Edinburgh Street Tramways Company at a cost of £300,000. In the mid 1870s he was one of several leading professional men of Edinburgh who, almost exactly a century ago, it is interesting to note, proposed a new theatre, winter garden and aquarium as part of a larger scheme for a public recreation area between Cornwall Street and Cambridge Street. As part of this plan, and after touring European capitals to study their theatres and opera houses, Gowans designed the New Edinburgh Theatre in Castle Terrace, opened in 1875 at a cost of £80,000. Though it was less elaborate and smaller than originally conceived, the theatre company nevertheless went bankrupt two years after its opening and the building was sold for £26,000 to the United Presbyterian Church and was later to become their Synod Hall. Eventually converted into a cinema, it was demolished some years ago to make way for the city's projected and controversial opera house and International Festival complex. The tall block of flats at 25 to 36 Castle Terrace was also built by Gowans.

In 1885 Gowans became Edinburgh's Lord Dean of Guild, supervising all new building in the city. His interest in working-class housing continued and his concern for "light and air" led him to campaign against pollution from the numerous mills on the Water of Leith. The highlight of his last years was his chairmanship of the executive committee of the International Exhibition of Industry, Science and Art held in the Meadows in 1886. Exhibits came from all over the world. The main exhibition hall was one thousand feet long by three hundred feet wide. Unlike similar exhibitions elsewhere, this one was lit after dark by 3,200 electric lamps fed from nine dynamos. Two-and-a-half million visitors attended. The cost of staging the mammoth event was £40,000 and the profit £20,000. Queen Victoria visited the exhibition in August 1886 and before departing bestowed a Knighthood on Gowans. A large public gathering was held in the Meadows to honour him and his family. For him it had been a great personal triumph, but his achievement had taken its toll in strain, both physical and financial, and his health began to fail. He moved with his family from Rockville to a house in nearby Blantyre Terrace and there died in June 1890. He was buried in Grange Cemetery.

After Gowans' departure, Rockville was used by Morningside College which had moved from the former Morningside Hydropathic building in Morningside Drive. Eventually acquired by Sir John Harrison, City Treasurer and son of Lord Provost Sir George Harrison, Rockville was to remain the Harrison home for fifty years. After their departure the house was sub-divided, but in the end once more was occupied as a complete private residence. In 1966 it was sold to a builder and its demolition soon afterwards, with the permission of the Edinburgh Town Planning Committee, has been described by one of Gowans' biographers as "an act of gross vandalism, revealing a complete ignorance of architectural history".

Proceeding down Colinton Road we come to George Watson's College, the modern design of which does not readily suggest the school's origins as one of the many great seventeenth-century educational foundations of old Edinburgh. This was an era when many generous benefactors made education more widely available to children of all social classes. George Watson was born in Edinburgh in 1654 and was sent by his parents to Holland to study book-keeping. In 1676 he became private secretary to Sir James Dick of Prestonfield House. The experience gained in managing Dick's estate and complex financial affairs was valuable and George Watson later became one of Scotland's first eminent accountants. Through his various successful business enterprises in Edinburgh and abroad he acquired considerable wealth and he was one of the early benefactors of the Merchant Maiden Hospital. When he died on April 3rd, 1723, Watson's will provided for generous bequests to the Merchant Company of Edinburgh, specific sums being set aside for the Merchant and Trades-Maiden Hospitals and Heriot's Hospital. Watson stipulated that his beneficiaries were to bear the name Watson or Davidson. A further sum of £144,000 Scots was left for the foundation of a new hospital in the city "for entertaining and educating the male children and grandchildren of decayed merchants in Edinburgh". The governors of the proposed new hospital at first favoured a site at Thomson's yards opposite Lady Yester's Church, east of the University Old College. This scheme was later abandoned and a new site considered south of George Heriot's hospital, between Lauriston Lane and the Meadows. Although this proposal was accepted, certain governors were uneasy, arguing that the new school would be too distant from the town.

The architect William Adam was engaged, whose estimate for the simple three-storeyed building was £4,168. Stone was to be quarried from the site. The new George Watson's Hospital was opened in 1741, eighteen years after its founder's death. High on the roof of the school sailed the ship which was the emblem of the Edinburgh Merchant Company, signifying successful trading.

Today another ship surmounts the main entrance to the new college in Colinton Road. By 1869 eighty-three boys were being boarded in the new hospital and twenty were attending as day pupils. Their rigorous day began with cold baths at 6.30 a.m. and morning prayers in chapel before breakfast. In 1870 the foundation became a day school for some eight hundred boys and two years later 1,160 boys were attending. By this time, however, the school had vacated its original building, sold to Edinburgh Royal Infirmary in 1869, and moved to the old Merchant Maiden Hospital premises built in Archibald Place in 1818. In 1926 this building was also sold to the Royal Infirmary, but George Watson's College continued to to use it until 1932, when it moved to a new building in Colinton Road on a site once part of the playing fields of Merchiston Castle School. The chapel of the original George Watson's Hospital, along with certain other parts, was incorporated in the Royal Infirmary.

The removal of the expanding college from Archibald Place to Colinton Road had first been contemplated in 1924 when the Royal Infirmary managers had expressed a desire to acquire the site. Opened in September 1932 at a cost of £200,000, the new college consisted of three main buildings designed by architect George L. Martin.

In 1974-5, George Watson's amalgamated with George Watson's Ladies' College in George Square to become a co-educational establishment retaining its original name. There are now 2,500 pupils, some of whom are boarded in nearby villas owned by the college. The long years of distinguished achievement in academic work, athletics and sport, especially rugby, are described in *George Watson's College: History and Record, 1724-1970,* edited by Hector L. Waugh.

CHAPTER 7

The Village of Burghmuirhead · Churchhill

On our right, just beyond the Baptist Church as we proceed towards Churchhill, is a little lane leading to an open space now used as a car park. At the end of the lane a collection of small buildings and their adjacent walls remain from earlier days. In the car park stands a large, solid and sombre-looking villa, of a style common in Morningside and other parts of the city. Now the well-appointed premises of the Masonic Lodge Abbotsford, this impressive if gaunt house was for over a century known as Grangebank and, surrounded by pleasant gardens, it presided over the old village of Burghmuirhead.

Located much further south than the district around the present-day post-office which still bears the name, Burghmuirhead was originally part of the lands of Greenhill, which constituted one of the several lots of the old Burgh Muir feued out by Edinburgh Town Council in 1586. The first feu-charter referring to Burghmuirhead as such is dated 1587-8 and is made out to Andrew Stevenson. This small estate remained in the possession of the Stevenson family till 1670; two members whose names remain on record were Andrew Stevenson, Minister of Dunbar, and his son Dr, later Sir, Archibald Stevenson.

John Scoon, a "meal-maker in Gorgie", obtained possession of Burghmuirhead in 1670 and built a number of houses there. In 1692 he feued out the southern portion of it to William Archibald, a writer in Edinburgh, who built additional houses. By the end of the seventeenth century Burghmuirhead had become a sizeable village, but still within the lands of Greenhill. John Scoon eventually sold his property to William Jamieson, a slater, and the transaction included "that high house covered with slate in Burghmuirhead, with cellar, and little close built within the great close adjoining the said high house on the south, bounded by the King's Highway on the east . . ." This Highway was, of course, the old "wester hiegait" skirting the Burgh Muir, eventually to become Morningside Road. Scoon's sale also included another dwelling-house "upon the north side of the said high house". While this latter house has long since been demolished, the "said high house" is that still to be seen and which had become known by 1852, and probably earlier, as Grangebank, although occasionally referred to as Burghmuirhead House. This house is thus nearly three centuries old.

In 1735 Adam Fairholm, owner of Greenhill estate (and the City Treasurer or Chamberlain already referred to), feued out two small cottages in Burghmuirhead village to John Mann, "gardener at

Foulbriggs", and a subsequent Greenhill owner conveyed another part of Burghmuirhead to John Mann's daughter. The latter married Thomas Steel, a surgeon of Burghmuirhead, and the Steel family, several of whom were doctors or chemists, resided in the village as owners of Grangebank House until 1819. Kirkwood's map of Edinburgh for 1817 shows the whole area of Burghmuirhead as "Dr Steel's property" and Grangebank House is indicated.

The first Ordnance Survey Map of Edinburgh, that of 1852, shows the district of Burghmuirhead as triangular in shape, the base extending from the south-east corner of Colinton Road to the northern end of Abbotsford Crescent, with the apex at the meeting point of Morningside Road and Albert Terrace at the brow of Churchhill. Grangebank House is shown as surrounded by a wide area of well-planned gardens, which included a bowling green. Grangebank Cottage, apparently a substantial dwelling-house in 1852 and probably the house described as "upon the north side of the said high house", stood a little to the north but was eventually demolished. A post office is marked in at the south-east corner of Colinton Road (on a site near the present-day Napier Restaurant), but it has now been replaced by that further north at the entrance to Montpelier Park.

In much earlier maps of Edinburgh and the Lothians, many of the then separate districts to the south of the city, which eventually expanded and amalgamated to form "Greater Morningside", are clearly shown. Timothy Pont's map, *Lothian and Linlithgow* (1660) indicates Wrychtishousis, Grange, Merchiston, Tipperlinn, Craighouse, Blackford and Braid as distinct locations. J. Adair's *Map of Midlothian* (1735)—so wide-ranging as to include East and West Lothian, the Borders and Clydesdale—shows the districts indicated by Pont and also Greenhill, Whitehouse, Canaan, Plewlands, Comiston and Greenbank. John Lawrie's map of Edinburgh and environs for 1763 adds Burghmuirhead. Among the most valuable and interesting sources from which one may trace the dates of Morningside's earliest houses and details of their successive owners are the old Edinburgh Directories. A complete series of these, the first dating back to 1773, is contained in the invaluable collection of historical records preserved in the Edinburgh Room of the city's Central Public Library. Perhaps, however, the first Edinburgh directory was *Constables' List of Inhabitants* (1682). Those listed resided mainly in the Old Town. They were grouped under each "quarter" for which a constable was responsible. The people who earned a place in this earliest directory were titled or prominent in some sphere of public life, or were merchants or tradesmen of some standing. Morningside was then well outside the confines of Edinburgh, and in fact was no more than a short row of cottages. The great mansion-houses of Grange, Bruntsfield, Whitehouse, Greenhill, Merchiston, Craighouse, Braid and Comiston encircled the village, each with its own rural estate or farmlands.

The first attempt to produce a more comprehensive directory resulted in *Williamson's Directory for the City of Edinburgh, Canongate, Leith and Suburbs,* first published for 1773-4. Again the city's residents listed were only those of some standing — judges, lawyers, "public and private gentlemen and other eminent traders". Compiled by a succession of publishers and providing a simple alphabetical list of all such inhabitants, with their street and occupation entered, this type of directory continued to be published annually until 1807, when the first *Post Office Directory* appeared. It was not until 1832 that the city's residents (and, again, mainly those of standing) were grouped street by street as in directories of today. The streets were further grouped into districts. Bruntsfield Links, Burghmuirhead, Morningside and Canaan constituted District 42, while Leith and Newhaven formed the last District 55.

In the 1833-4 Directory, the pull-out map of Edinburgh for the first time extended to the Jordan Burn, the city's traditional southern boundary. Previous directory maps had reached no further south than Wrychtishousis. In the Directory for the previous year, the total number of residents listed under "The Forty-Second District", divided into the sub-headings of Bruntsfield Links, Burghmuirhead, Morningside and Canaan, was seventy! These were primarily the occupants of the district's principal houses, or important tradesmen and shopkeepers. From these old directories and maps, the successive owners of Grangebank in the village of Burghmuirhead can be traced.

Grangebank passed from the Steel family in about 1850. Among subsequent owners we may note a John Bartholomew in 1859, founder of the now world-renowned firm of cartographers in Duncan Street, who died here in 1861.

In 1892 St Theresa's Orphanage for Girls was established in Grangebank, latterly becoming a Catholic school of the same name which is well-remembered by a number of Morningside residents who were pupils. This school closed just after the outbreak of the First World War. After a period during which it remained unoccupied, Grangebank was purchased by the Lodge Abbotsford in 1920. This Lodge, originated at a meeting held in Springvalley Hall, Springvalley Gardens in 1905, continued in that meeting place until 1914 when alterations forced them to meet in other parts of the city until the purchase of Grangebank. After considerable renovation, their three-hundred-year-old premises were ready for occupation in 1921, but further extensive repairs were required in 1955. Deciding in 1963 to remain at Grangebank rather than move to new premises, the members of Lodge Abbotsford have since effected further tastefully executed improvements, especially to their refectory. It is interesting to note the Lodge's Gaelic inscriptions on the venerable interior walls of Grangebank. "That high house", last remaining reminder of the old village of Burghmuirhead, is happily still preserved.

CHURCHHILL

At Churchhill we reach the summit of the ancient Burgh Muir. From this vantage point, anyone venturing further from Edinburgh in early times would have enjoyed a magnificent, uninterrupted panorama on every side. To the north, gazing back across Bruntsfield, the Castle would rise sharply against the sky, dominating the old town, with the Forth and Fife like a theatrical backdrop, while the crown steeple of St Giles would tower like a milestone above the spine of the Royal Mile descending steeply to Holyrood. To the west, Merchiston Tower would stand isolated amidst its surrounding orchards and farmlands, the open countryside beyond stretching as far as the eye could see. To the east, the turreted Grange of St Giles, the little chapel of St Roque and the Convent of St Catherine of Sienna would be the principal landmarks against the huge bulk of Arthur's Seat, and, on the horizon, Berwick Law, the Bass Rock and the Lammermuirs. To the south, down over the brow of Churchhill where today the villas, church steeples and tenements echo the roar of the ceaseless stream of traffic through the bustling suburb of Morningside, our traveller would have gazed on a very different scene: a farm cart and horse, perhaps, passing at leisurely pace between a row of cottages straddling a narrow country road descending steeply to the Jordan Burn; a hawthorn-lined lane leading to Braid, Comiston and Biggar, and, beyond, rising gently to the Pentland Hills. The mansion-house of Braid would lie hidden out of sight in the depths of the Hermitage; the ancient castle of Comiston might just be visible through its surrounding woodland; old Craighouse would be prominent on the eastern slope of Craiglockhart hill, while the white-washed walls of the old inn at Hunters' Tryst would be the last outpost under the shadow of Caerketton and Allermuir.

Following our long journey and digressions into the outlying approaches to Morningside, it may seem time we took at long last the road down into the heart of Morningside itself. But not quite yet. Churchhill and its immediate vicinity may justly lay claim to a chapter in our story, for here is much germane to the origins of our modern suburb.

The section of Morningside Road from the Baptist Church to Churchhill was originally known as Waverley Terrace, while the continuation to the corner of Abbotsford Park was named Marmion Terrace. Both names had their origins in the legends woven by Sir Walter Scott around this district with its famous Bore Stone, in which, it was for long believed, the Scottish Standard was raised prior to the muster of the Scots army about to depart for the ill-fated battle of Flodden in 1513. Colourful and romantically stirring as were such names as Waverley and Marmion, the authenticity of their associations is questionable. Both names were lost, being incorporated in Morningside Road, in 1886.

On the left, above the frontage of the shop at the north corner of Morningside Road and Abbotsford Park (originally the residence of the early medical superintendents of the Morningside Asylum), the name Marmion Terrace was once to be seen, but the passage of time and much paint has now almost obliterated it. This shop once belonged to a grocer named O'Hagan and was the subject of one of a classical series of old Edinburgh photographs by Balmain (now reproduced by Yerbury, the well-known Edinburgh photographers). Towards the end of the nineteenth century there was a small private school in Marmion Terrace known as "Mr Baillie's School". A copy still exists of a prize certificate awarded in July 1877 to Robert T. Patterson for Map Drawing; it is signed, "James Baillie, Headmaster". It is possible that the premises occupied by this school were those eventually acquired, and occupied until a few years ago, by Yerbury's.

Through the commendable enterprise of Edinburgh Corporation, Churchhill came to be widely known not only to the citizens of Edinburgh but also to innumerable visitors from all parts of the world attending the city's annual International Festival. For here, on September 25th, 1965 was opened the Churchhill Theatre, soon afterwards to become an officially approved Festival centre.

The establishment of this excellently appointed theatre ended one chapter and began another in the history of amateur drama in Edinburgh. When the Little Theatre in the Pleasance, scene of so many successful amateur productions, was sold by the Pleasance Trust to Edinburgh University in 1960, the city's many amateur companies — and their large number of patrons — were far from happy. Alternative facilities were not readily available. Strong and repeated representation was made to

The Churchhill Theatre, once the last premises of Morningside Free Church

Edinburgh Corporation for positive assistance. In 1960 Morningside High Church (which, until 1929 and the formation of the United Free Presbyterian Church, had been the last of a long succession of premises occupied by Morningside Free Church) became vacant as a result of its union with Morningside Parish Church at the corner of Newbattle Terrace. The spacious red sandstone building was purchased by Edinburgh Corporation for £6,000.

The cost of converting the former church into a first-class theatre was £67,000; the architect was George L. Walls. Apart from the excellent stage, seating and dressing-room facilities, there are two halls suitable for "theatre in the round", the mounting of art or photographic exhibitions, public meetings and social functions. The Churchhill Theatre opening ceremony in 1965 was performed by the distinguished Scottish actor, Tom Fleming, and the theatre curtain rose for the first time on an inaugural production by the Scottish Community Drama Association of Oscar Wilde's *The Importance of Being Earnest*. First used for an Edinburgh International Festival production in 1966, the Churchhill Theatre now enjoys an established place in the official Festival programme of drama and ballet. For the rest of the year, the theatre is constantly booked by a wide variety of amateur companies and other associations which enjoy facilities unique in Britain.

As we turn into Churchhill Place, which, beyond its short row of substantial tenement flats, becomes Churchhill, it may be recalled that this street was formerly a narrow lane named Napier Terrace, probably after the distinguished mathematician laird of nearby Merchiston Tower. The street (and also the district of Morningside) was later to be known as Churchhill because there came to reside here the famous Dr Thomas Chalmers, who built the first house on the hill overlooking Morningside in 1842 and named it, originally, Kirkhill (as indicated on the early maps) and, subsequently, Churchhill. This villa, now number 1 Churchhill, was re-named Westgate by a later owner, a name it still bears. A bronze tablet to the left of the front of the house briefly states: "In this house Thomas Chalmers died, 31st May 1847." Behind this simple statement lies one of the stormiest chapters in the history of the church, and indeed of Scotland herself, for Dr Chalmers, of course, was one of the leaders of the Disruption which in 1843 tore the Church of Scotland apart.

Born in Anstruther, Fife, in 1780, of which busy fishing village his father was Provost, Thomas Chalmers studied at St Andrew's University, where he later lectured in mathematics and chemistry before being appointed as Professor of Moral Philosophy. Divinity was, however, the subject in which he was most qualified. Entering the Church of Scotland ministry, he served in a number of country parishes before his appointment to Glasgow's important Tron Church in 1815. Here his sermons, frequently on the relationship between science and religion, gave an early indication of the eloquence and fire which were to lead to his

Dr Thomas Chalmers of Churchhill, leader of the Disruption

recognition in later years as the most outstanding preacher of his day. This great talent was to play a decisive part in his leadership of the Disruption. He came to Edinburgh University as Professor of Theology in 1828 and his impact on the Capital was soon felt. His first residence in Edinburgh was in Forres Street, from which he moved to 7 Inverleith Row. In 1841 he went to live temporarily at 2 Morningside Place, where he was so impressed by the rural-retreat atmosphere of Morningside that he decided to build a house for himself in Churchhill. A man who led a deeply spiritual life, he perhaps had some feelings of guilt when he contemplated taking up residence in what was then a rather exclusive preserve of the wealthy who were able to spend the summer away from the city in the quiet rural environment of Edinburgh's southern suburb. He wrote in his dairy: "Mean to build at Morningside; but let me not forget the end of the World and the coming of Christ."

Nothing, however, of the life of the idle rich entered the house which Dr Chalmers duly occupied at Churchhill. In the quietness of his study, the room to the right of the main door (looking in from the street), the remote peacefulness of **Morningside** was a stimulus to the man who, day

110

after day, laboured relentlessly at his desk on a succession of sermons, speeches and articles which were to spur on events soon to burst upon Scotland like a revolution.

For some years a keen point of debate in the Church of Scotland had been Patronage, the right of the State or certain influential persons (aristocrats or land-owners) to veto the appointment of a church minister chosen by a congregation. The age-old issue of Church versus State was involved. Most Church of Scotland leaders believed that, while recognising and professing loyalty to the Crown, the Church should be allowed independence in spiritual affairs and in the appointment of its ministers. This belief was outlined in a General Assembly resolution of 1834.

There were many test cases, notably at Auchterarder where Lord Kinnoull presented to a congregation a minister who was quite unacceptable to all but two members. The case was referred to a civil court and Lord Kinnoull's appointment was upheld. This decision was confirmed by the House of Lords. Other similar cases followed, and in each the local congregation's wishes were disregarded.

At a large meeting in London in 1838, attended by nine Church of England bishops. Dr Chalmers, in a speech of unprecedented eloquence, asserted the Church of Scotland's claim to freedom in the appointment of ministers, a matter in which he said, "The King cannot . . . the King dare not" interfere. His rousing, defiant words drew a great response.

The growing conflict between Church and State became a national issue. In Parliament, Robert Peel re-asserted the rights of the Crown. Many congregations in the Church of Scotland were, however, already flouting the law. The crisis was imminent. Some church leaders might have accepted a compromise, but not so Dr Chalmers: he and other prominent church leaders prepared to bring the issue to a head at the General Assembly of 1843.

The Assembly was to convene on May 17th in St Andrew's Church in George Street: forecasts and rumours of what might happen swept the country. The Assembly, it was generally agreed, would be stormy, yet on the evening of May 16th it was estimated that at most a mere twenty to thirty ministers, finding Parliament's ruling unacceptable, might secede from the established Church.

Dr Chalmers and his colleagues had not been idle. They had already booked Tanfield Hall at Canonmills, having confidently predicted what was going to happen. Seating was available for three thousand. The day of the Assembly dawned. The seats in St Andrew's Church began to fill up. Outside in the city the atmosphere was hushed and electrified. Many stayed off work and there gathered outside St Andrew's Church a vast crowd which included people from all over Scotland and many who had arrived specially from abroad. They had not long to wait.

The Assembly was hardly seated when the Moderator, Dr Welsh, rose, and, in the presence of the Lord High Commissioner, the Marquis of Bute, read the famous words: "We protest that, in the circumstances in which we are placed, it is and shall be lawful for us . . . to withdraw to a separate place of meeting . . . with an assured conviction that we are not responsible for any consequences that may follow from this . . ."

With this, the Moderator laid the protest on the table and, lifting his hat, bowed to the High Commissioner. He left his chair of office and proceeded to the door. Dr Chalmers, who had been close beside him throughout, immediately followed, accompanied by several other prominent ministers. Those in the gallery cheered the departure of the pioneers of the Disruption, then fell silent, waiting . . . How many others would follow? The stream of support began: first one minister left his seat, then another, and another; bench after bench became empty; a great mass crowded round the exit doors. Those who remained watched spellbound. Outside in George Street, as Dr Welsh, Dr Chalmers and their supporters appeared, the words were excitedly taken up by the crowd: "They come . . . They come!" Those who counted their number, expecting a mere twenty to thirty, were amazed: the procession seemed unending. No fewer than four hundred and seventy-four ministers quit the Assembly. Before the eyes of the onlooker, the established Church of Scotland had been torn asunder.

At Tanfield Hall the first Free Assembly was constituted and Dr Chalmers was unanimously elected Moderator. The historic scene at Tanfield was recorded by David Octavius Hill, R.S.A., in a large oil painting, on which he was engaged for twenty-three years. It was purchased by the Free Church for £1,500 and now adorns the Presbytery Hall of their Offices on the Mound.

A few weeks after the Tanfield Assembly, Dr Chalmers resigned his professorship of Divinity at the University. When the Free Church College was built on the Mound, it was he who laid the foundation stone of this great landmark, designed by W. H. Playfair. Dr Chalmers was also appointed first Principal, on June 4th, 1846, almost exactly one year before his death. After the reunion of the United Free Church and the Church of Scotland in 1929, the Free Church College on the Mound became New College, and it was incorporated in Edinburgh University's Faculty of Divinity.

Many writers have recorded sad scenes throughout Scotland as people watched long-serving and beloved pastors gather together their chattels and families and leave their manses to face the unknown. It was estimated that, in one day, those who quit their charges signed away more than £100,000 per annum in stipends. One third of the total membership of the Church of Scotland left to join the Free Church, and they were perhaps the most active and interested members. The Disruption had, indeed, seemed a mortal blow.

Such, then, was the impact on Scotland of the man whose sudden death at the first house in Churchhill is so briefly commemorated on an inconspicuous plaque. Throughout his long, determined campaign, fought mostly from his quiet study in rural Morningside, *The Scotsman* followed with intense interest his principles and policies, at times supporting him in leading articles, at others criticising him severely, but never diverting him from his convictions. The newspaper *The Witness,* edited by Hugh Miller, was an influential and more reliable supporter of Dr Chalmers and his followers. (Copies are preserved in the Edinburgh Room of the Central Public Library.)

Morningside experienced the effects of the Disruption no less than other parishes, as several churches in the district still bear witness. One of these is Morningside Parish Church, just over the brow of Churchhill (at the north-west corner of Newbattle Terrace). The establishment of this church had been pioneered by Dr Chalmers, who had also preached the inaugural sermon. At the Disruption, the Reverend Thomas Addis resigned his charge and, with many sympathetic parishioners, established the first Morningside Free Church. So many people left the Parish Church to follow Dr Addis that the decision, taken just before the Disruption, to build a parish manse had to be postponed.

These first Free Church members were, for a time, a congregation without a church: in the long pilgrimage which followed they were to occupy no fewer than five different places of worship before settling in the High Church opened at Churchhill in 1894.

For the first two Sundays after the Disruption, the Morningside Free Church adherents continued to meet in the Parish Church. On being threatened with expulsion, however, they sought permission to occupy the Old Schoolhouse opposite the western end of what is now Falcon Avenue. The committee of management of this little village school, then privately run, refused permission (not without a long and violent debate, it is recorded).

Dr Addis sought Dr Chalmers' advice and the latter immediately offered the use of his house in Churchhill. Thus, for three Sundays, a congregation of three hundred Free Church members in Morningside worshipped in Dr Chalmers' large villa, the considerable gathering occupying every room in the house. Dr Chalmers himself preached from the landing half-way up the staircase, while listeners sat on the upper and lower stairs and on forms in the lobbies and adjacent rooms.

In 1843 Morningside's Free Church gained their own premises — a large circular tent pitched at the south corner of Abbotsford Park. The four hundred who gathered there each Sunday, however, found the summer heat uncomfortable. The reaction was a mixture of annoyance and relief when the canvas church had one day suddenly to be vacated, "a mischievous boy" having cut the guy ropes so that a gust of wind collapsed the tent on the occupants' heads.

By common impulse many of the congregation marched down

113

Churchhill to the Old Schoolhouse, this time being granted admission. Here they continued to meet until the first Morningside Free Church building had been completed. This apparently stood a little back from the road near what is now 74 Morningside Road, and was opened in 1844. The little church is said to have been designed as a replica of Tanfield Hall at Canonmills where the first Free Church Assembly met. The site was provided by Mrs Steel of Grangebank House at Burghmuirhead. For some time road repairs near the new church prevented proper access by the front door and members of the congregation had to clamber over the back walls to gain entrance from Abbotsford Park. This inconvenience was drawn to the attention of Sir George Clark of Penicuik, Members of Parliament for Midlothian, and the main road entrance was soon cleared. Strangely, there is no evidence of the exact site of this church either on old maps of the period or in contemporary street directories. Nevertheless, the church opposite the entrance to Churchhill served the Free Church congregation for thirty years, during which period a Free Church School was established near the present-day Public Library, and a manse in Morningside Place.

The second Free Church building, designed by McGibbon and Ross, was opened to the north of Churchhill in 1874 at a cost of £7,000. After twenty years, the accommodation of this church proved inadequate for the steadily growing Free Church congregation. Several sites proposed for a new church proved unsuitable and Sir John Stuart Forbes of Greenhill House refused to grant a site within his lands. A proposal to build a large church adjacent to Dr Chalmers' house was also rejected. Finally, the church which is now the Churchhill Theatre was built, two villas which occupied the site having been purchased and demolished. This spacious red sandstone building of Italianate style was opened in 1894. The vacated high-steepled church near the corner of Colinton Road was purchased by Morningside's small group of Baptist pioneers for £3,000, less than half the original cost of building.

The journeyings of Morningside Free Church were at last at an end. Morningside High Church remained its meeting place until the establishment of the United Presbyterian Church in 1929. Subsequently the Church of Scotland congregation re-united with Morningside Parish Church in 1960 and, after one hundred and twenty years, the wheel had turned full circle. Dr Alexander Martin, who succeeded Dr Addis as minister of Morningside Free Church, became Principal of New College on the Mound and played an important part in the move towards re-union with the Church of Scotland, achieved in 1929.

Dr Chalmers' funeral procession to Grange Cemetery on June 4th, 1847 is said to have been the largest of any in nineteenth-century Scotland. Innumerable memorials to the great Disruption leader are still to be seen in Edinburgh and other parts of Scotland, ranging from statues to churches bearing his name. One of the latter which he might well have

114

treasured above all other reminders of his life's work is the Territorial Church (on the right-hand side as you descend the West Port, almost opposite Portsburgh Square). Dr Chalmers saw this church completed just before his death and he immersed himself in its outstandingly successful pioneering work amongst the illiterate and abandoned poor of the Grassmarket district. At the corner of West Port and Lady Lawson Street stood another church, the Chalmers Memorial Church, something of a landmark, but this lay closed for many years and was eventually demolished. The Chalmers Hospital in Lauriston Place is named not after Dr Chalmers but in memory of George Chalmers, an Edinburgh plumber, who died in 1836, bequeathing the largest part of his estate of £30,000 for the erection of a hospital "for the sick and hurt". It was built in 1861.

Leaving Dr Chalmers' house, which for a period in later years became a girls' school, and continuing eastwards along Churchhill, we may glimpse the white-walled East Morningside House beyond the green-domed private chapel at St Bennet's. This venerable mansion-house, the entrance drive of which leads from Clinton Road, was built by Gavin Bailie, an Edinburgh merchant, in about 1726. On his death in 1734, Bailie is described as "of Morningside" and this is the earliest reference to the name of the district yet found in the City Records. The name may have been derived from the fact that the original entrance to the mansion-house faced east to "the morning side of the sun". The lands of East Morningside stretched from what are now Churchhill Place, Churchhill and Strathearn Place in the north to Newbattle Terrace in the south, and from the corner of Newbattle Terrace to Churchhill in the west to Whitehouse Loan in the east. Comprising eighteen acres, this land had been feued by the city as part of the Burgh Muir in 1586. Andrew Stevenson, an Edinburgh merchant, obtained first possession with part of the Wester Muir. Stevenson's grandson later disposed of three acres to Sir John Stuart Forbes of Pitsligo, Laird of Greenhill, and the remaining portion to Thomas Beg, another Edinburgh merchant. In 1697 the estate passed to Sir William Menzies of Germaine, whose son in turn sold it, in 1725, to Gavin Bailie, who built the present mansion-house soon afterwards. The west wing of the house was added in about 1850. It was because Sir John Stuart Forbes of the adjacent lands of Greenhill obtained part of East Morningside, and because of the subsequent marriage of one of his descendants, Harriet Forbes, to the 21st Baron Clinton, that the present-day Clinton Road was so called in 1858. Morningside Parish Church still pays a nominal feu duty to the Clinton descendants. The name of Pitsligo Road also recalls that Forbes of Greenhill and Pitsligo once owned part of East Morningside.

Whilst the story of Churchhill is associated with the ecclesiastical history of Scotland, that of East Morningside introduces us to one of the great literary figures who lived in Morningside. Many interesting and distinguished people have resided in the spacious and majestic mansion,

East Morningside House
Photograph by Mr W. R. Smith

East Morningside House, but none has received more widespread publicity than Miss Susan Edmonstone Ferrier whose three novels *Marriage* (1818), *Inheritance* (1824) and *Destiny* (1831) had considerable impact and influence on the literary world of her day and on early nineteenth-century high society in Scotland and, indeed, beyond.

Most of her first book was written at East Mórningside House, in the oak-panelled study with its seventeenth-century pitch-pine fireplace. This room, still well preserved, is now the study of a distinguished medical specialist, a forerunner in research into certain types of heart disease.

Susan Ferrier, whose novels drew the warm praise of Sir Walter Scott and once gained for her the title of "Scotland's Jane Austen", was born in a flat in Lady Stair's Close, off the Lawnmarket, on September 7th, 1782. She was the youngest of the ten children of James Ferrier, Writer to the Signet and younger son of John Ferrier, Laird of Kirklands in Renfrewshire. Her mother was Helen Coutts, a famous beauty of her day, who, before her marriage, had lived in Holyrood Palace. Susan's early schooling was obtained at Mr Stalker's Academy for Boys and Girls in George Street. The Ferrier family subsequently moved from Lady Stair's

Close to 25 George Street, and while there James Ferrier acquired East Morningside House as the family's summer residence.

Through the influence of John, 5th Duke of Argyll, whose estates he managed, James Ferrier was appointed a Principal Clerk of Session at the Edinburgh Law Courts. There he became a close friend of a legal colleague, Walter Scott. One of the many treasures preserved in the East Morningside House is a chair bearing the inscription: "To my friend James Ferrier for happy days and hospitality at East Morningside House — *Walter Scott.*"

Susan Ferrier grew up in the midst of the brilliant Edinburgh literary circle at the close of the eighteenth century. In addition to Walter Scott, her father's close friends included Robert Burns (Ferrier, indeed, was among the first to welcome Burns to Edinburgh), Henry Mackenzie (author of *Man of Feeling*), Dr Blair and many others. From an early and impressionable age, therefore, the future novelist absorbed the stimulating atmosphere of the literary scene, which must have awakened her own potential. The raw materials for her novels she found elsewhere: not in Edinburgh, but in a Highland castle.

After her mother's death, Susan, then fifteen, made the first of many journeys with her father to Inveraray Castle, the Duke of Argyll's principal residence on Loch Fyne. These visits were to rouse in her the first stirrings of a lively imagination and be imprinted on a highly perceptive mind. While her father attended to his duties at the castle, Susan observed and experienced a whole new world of fashion and high life, encountering a fascinating variety of people who to her seemed larger than life and who, in time, found their way into her novels. There were "red-haired Highland Chiefs, sniffing, sneezing and condemning everything that was not Scottish, and there were London ladies who brought their parrots, lap-dogs, macaws and doctors." So one of Miss Ferrier's biographers described the scene. It was a potential novelist's paradise. Nevertheless, young Susan might well have kept her impressions secretly and silently to herself (no doubt many of those who, to their embarrassment, later appeared in her books would have been much relieved had she done so) rather than present them satirically (though never wholly unkindly) to the Scotland of her day, had it not been for her friendship with the Duke of Argyll's young niece, Charlotte Clavering.

Charlotte, seven years Susan's elder, was herself something of a *littérateur*. Full of high spirits, she too relished the eccentricities of her uncle's guests and suggested that she and Susan collaborate in writing a novel of the Inveraray scene. A start was made in 1810, but Charlotte Clavering in the end contributed very little to the work; it was Susan who completed the novel, which was finally entitled *Marriage*. Much correspondence was exchanged between the collaborators. The moral message of the book, Susan Ferrier wrote to her friend, should be "to warn all young ladies against run-away marriages . . . I expect," she

117

The novelist Miss Susan Ferrier, who lived in East Morningside House

added, "it will be the first book every wise matron will put into the hands of her daughter. I hear the enchanting sound of some sentimental Miss, the shrill pipe of some antiquated spinster, or the hoarse grumbling of some incensed dowager as they severally inquire for me at the circulating library, and are assured by the master that 'tis in such demand that though he has thirteen copies, they are insufficient to answer the calls upon them but that each of them may depend upon having the very first copies that come in!!!" In some trepidation she went on: "One thing let me entreat of you: if we engage in this undertaking let it be kept a profound secret from every human being. If I was suspected of being accessory to such foul deeds my brothers and sisters would murder me and my father bury me alive." Charlotte Clavering, with a touch of devilment, gave Susan every encouragement in these "foul deeds", writing that she was quite transported by one of the characters Susan was developing. Later, however, Susan declared that she had become so apprehensive over another of her characters that she feared she would have to drown herself if her authorship were ever discovered.

In addition to the Inveraray circle, three ladies who lived next door to the Ferriers at 26 George Street, the Misses Edmonstone of Duntreath, who almost nightly "engaged in pitched battles over whist with their father and his friends", had their place in the novel which was taking shape.

At first entitled *The Chiefs of Glenfern,* the novel was submitted in 1817 to the famous Edinburgh publisher, William Blackwood, the central, stimulating figure of a distinguished circle of Edinburgh writers including John Wilson (alias Christopher North), John Galt, Michael Scott, John Gibson Lockhart and James Hogg (the Ettrick Shepherd). Blackwood accepted the novel with little delay, writing to Miss Ferrier: "The whole construction and execution appear so admirable that it would almost be presumption in any one to offer corrections to such a writer." Not many writers receive such unqualified acceptance on the submission of a first novel!

Under the title *Marriage,* the book appeared in 1818. Miss Ferrier, in correspondence with Blackwood, negotiated and accepted a fee of £150. (This correspondence is preserved in the National Library of Scotland.) The novel, portraying with little disguise so many living people, laying bare their vulgarities, their selfishness and absurdities, was, not surprisingly, published anonymously. Susan's father, who had no time for female authors, was ill in bed at the time. On asking her to read to him, Susan obliged by taking up *Marriage.* She was eager to obtain his reaction before that of the general public. With the page carefully concealed behind a bedside curtain, she read on — to her father's apparent satisfaction. When he requested that she obtain another book by the same author, whose work he considered the best he had yet heard, Susan thought fit to point out that it had been written by a woman. Mr Ferrier refused to believe it: the book had been so good. His daughter then confessed her authorship.

In the literary world of Scotland and beyond, the appearance of Susan Ferrier's first novel was an event. Attempts were made to identify the author. London critics attributed the book to Scott, who, in later years, wrote: "I retire from the field, conscious that there remains behind not only a large harvest, but labourers capable of gathering it in . . . If the present author, himself a phantom, may be permitted to distinguish a brother, or perhaps a sister, shadow, he would mention, in particular, the author of the very lively work entitled *Marriage."* The mystery novelist was compared to Jane Austen and John Galt, and she was praised for diverting the Scottish novel into new channels.

Inheritance, Miss Ferrier's second anonymous novel, followed six years after *Marriage,* in 1824. While the first novel had been regarded as the work of an author of great promise, the second was generally considered to have fulfilled that promise, revealing a more skilful construction of plot and a much improved style. This novel Miss Ferrier sold to Blackwood for £1,000 (having rejected an earlier offer of £500). It seems that she had considered the sum of £150 received for *Marriage* as

William Blackwood's offer of £150 for Susan Ferrier's novel "Marriage"
By courtesy of the National Library of Scotland

an under-payment. Scott also praised this second novel warmly. Another critic considered it "the best of its class at the present day." Others now saw a definite attempt at a style modelled on Jane Austen, though lacking that delicacy of treatment.

120

Destiny, or the Chieftain's Daughter, the third and last novel, was published in 1831. Critics saw in it signs of a decline — of which the authoress herself was perhaps only too well aware. Influenced by the adverse criticism, she resolved to write no more fiction. *Destiny* was dedicated to Sir Walter Scott, now her close friend, who, it was said, had persuaded Blackwood to pay Miss Ferrier a record £1,700 for it. The book was widely read. Set again in the Highlands and full of quaint caricatures, it was later considered to have anticipated Dickens and Trollope. Miss Ferrier had positive views on the role of the writer in society. "The only good purpose of a book", she wrote, "is to inculcate morality and convey some lesson of instruction as well as delight." Whether or not her three novels put this into practice must be judged by her readers — and these she still has. The anonymity of her authorship was retained until 1851 when she allowed her name to appear on new editions.

Described as "dark, tall, handsome, a brilliant conversationalist and herself no blue-stocking", Susan Ferrier never married. She was a most kind-hearted person, and especially helpful to Sir Walter Scott in his last years. When amidst his friends at Abbotsford, his speech increasingly impaired, she would tactfully help him over difficult moments in conversation. She herself suffered from near-blindness in her last days and was forced to spend much time in a completely darkened room. She died at her town house, 38 Albany Street, in 1854, at the age of seventy, and now rests in the family grave in St Cuthbert's Churchyard in Lothian Road.

Much, though not all, of Miss Ferrier's writing was done at East Morningside House (*Inheritance* was written largely at Stirling Castle). After her mother's early death and the marriage of her brothers and sisters, she acted as housekeeper to her father till his death in 1829. Each spring she loved to make the long journey from Edinburgh's New Town to the pleasant rural setting of East Morningside House, with its orchards and freshly cultivated farmlands.

On one occasion she wrote: "We are once more settled here, for seven months to come I suppose, and glad I am to find myself out of the smoke and dust of town which always disagrees with me at this season."

In the winter of 1829 she wrote from East Morningside: "The storm seems to be awesome and appears to be endless. Last night was almost as bad as any we have had — nine trees blown down at Morningside — the stack of chimneys of this house was discovered to be hanging on a thread. Except the Walkers and James on a Sunday we never see a soul."

Old maps of Edinburgh which include Morningside illustrate how remote was the setting of East Morningside House when Miss Ferrier lived there. Kirkwood's map of 1817 (this was the year before her first novel was published) shows the wide expanse of farmland between Whitehouse Loan on the east and Morningside Road (the old "wester hiegait") on the west. To the north, there was also open countryside around the neighbouring mansion-house of Greenhill, though, in the south, several villas in the lands of Canaan and the Eden district were quite close by. The first Ordnance Survey Map of Edinburgh, published in 1852, still showed the East Morningside estate as quite extensive, and as yet with no other houses. Clinton Road and Strathearn Place did not yet exist. This map clearly indicates the fine avenue of beech trees leading from Grange Loan (from the gateway near the present-day high voltage electric power plant) straight to East Morningside House. In Clinton Road it is still noticeable that one section of the southern boundary wall of East Morningside House was more recently constructed than the adjoining parts. This section was originally open and through it the main drive and avenue led up to the mansion-house.

The house, with its immensely thick walls, is set in spacious, well laid out gardens with stately trees. The grounds retain their rural atmosphere within the main gates, where little has changed in two hundred years, and they contain two interesting relics of earlier days. The ivy-covered square dovecote near the south wall at Clinton Road, which has two hundred and thirty-two nesting places — a reminder of times when pigeon-pie was a popular dish — merited description in Volume XXV of the *Book of the Old Edinburgh Club*. Its timber and slate roof inclines to the north, unlike those of most other dovecotes which are south-sloping so that the pigeons can bask in the sun. The entrances for the birds are also unusual: there are twelve openings in four rows, with landing ledges in a wooden frame set in a window cut into the angle of the south and west walls.

It is related that there was much rivalry between the dovecote at East Morningside and that at nearby Merchiston Tower. James Wilson, the famous naturalist who lived in Woodville at the top of Canaan Lane, a contemporary, close neighbour and friend of Susan Ferrier, once asked her in a letter whether she poisoned visiting pigeons to preserve her vegetables. One is reminded of how, two centuries earlier, the distinguished mathematician John Napier overcame the problem of invading pigeons by feeding them with grain soaked in alcohol. East Morningside House did not exist, of course, in Napier's time.

In many large Scottish estates, the dovecote has survived the manor house, perhaps on account of the special importance attached to it and the traditional belief that, if the dovecote were pulled down or allowed to deteriorate, the lady of the house would die within a year. James I decreed it a felony to destroy a dovecote and James VI introduced a law forbidding the building of a dovecote beside any house which did not possess a certain amount of surrounding land and adequate victuals cultivated in fields.

Close to the dovecote's south wall and hard against the Clinton Road boundary wall is a very old willow tree which was successfully grown from a cutting brought from Napoleon's garden at Longwood on St Helena. Carefully supported by splints, the tree still flourishes and a glimpse of it may be caught from Clinton Road. A white rose bush said to have been in the garden when Bonnie Prince Charlie and his soldiers passed along Grange Loan in 1745 *en route* to Grange House and Holyrood Palace, and at which they stopped to pick blooms to adorn their bonnets, was reportedly transplanted many years ago to a garden in the North of Scotland, where it failed to survive.

The professions of law and medicine have been well represented among those who have owned or resided in East Morningside House. Susan Ferrier's nephew, James Frederick Ferrier, who often visited the house, was Professor of Civil Law at Edinburgh University. John Montgomery Bell, Writer to the Signet, who for a time lived here, composed much fine church music and took part in compiling the Scottish Church Hymnary. His father was professor of conveyancing at the University. Lord Fleming, Senator of the College of Justice, and a generous benefactor and active supporter of many causes, lived in East Morningside House for a long period. He and Lady Fleming are commemorated by a seat placed in Whitehouse Loan, which is inscribed "Rest and be Thankful. This seat is placed here in memory of Lord and Lady Fleming who lived in East Morningside House from 1924 till 1944." Following Lord Fleming's death, a succession of medical men have resided at the house.

For well over a century, East Morningside House enjoyed the rural remoteness of its secluded and spacious estate. In the nineteenth century, however, several other mansion-houses arose in quick succession in Clinton Road.

Directly opposite East Morningside House on the south side of Clinton Road, there stood until 1962 the stately Scottish Baronial-style mansion of Woodcroft. The original entrance gateway pillars bearing its name remain at the end of the fine avenue of beech trees which once lined the main driveway from Grange Loan to East Morningside House.

Woodcroft was designed and built in 1858 by Colonel Sir David Davidson after his retirement from long and distinguished service in the East India Company. Standing in five acres of land purchased from the East Morningside Estate, the house was of fine pink sandstone quarried from its own grounds, and considered equal in quality to that then obtainable from Craigleith.

In his autobiography, *Memorials of a Long Life,* published in 1890, Colonel Davidson writes that he selected "an amiable site on the ridge running east from Burghmuirhead, on which the Scottish army had camped before marching to Flodden, and commanding a view of the Blackford, the Braid and the Pentland hills stretching one behind the other like the scenery of a stage." Standing three hundred feet above sea level, Woodcroft must then certainly have enjoyed a magnificent southern panorama. Dr John Brown, author of the Scottish classic *Rab and His Friends,* was greatly impressed by Woodcroft. "The best house in

Edinburgh," he once called it, "and built of the rock on which it stands."

Born in Haddington in 1811, young David Davidson had there been a close friend of the local doctor's daughter, Jane Welsh, later to become the famous Jane Welsh Carlyle, wife of "the Sage of Chelsea". While awaiting the completion of Woodcroft, Davidson had lived temporarily at St Margaret's Cottage in nearby Greenhill and there was visited by Jane Welsh Carlyle, on which occasion they exchanged reminiscences of their youthful days in Haddington. He also visited the Carlyle residence in Chelsea's Cheyne Row, where he met Alfred Tennyson. The meeting is said to have resulted in a most animated discussion.

When Woodcroft was at last completed, the motto over its main doorway, "Meliora semper cogita", was suggested by Jane Welsh Carlyle. It was the same motto that had been inscribed on her childhood home in Haddington. Frequent recollection of their early days at Haddington was at first a regular feature of Colonel Davidson's correspondence with Mrs Carlyle. This for some time she appears to have enjoyed, readily indulging in the nostalgia. Later, however, she began to find his constant references to the "old days" increasingly upsetting and he was requested to write in such vein no more. The point, it seems, was taken.

Colonel Davidson became a prominent figure in the military life of Edinburgh, stimulating the development of the Edinburgh Volunteers and, in 1860, commanding the leading brigade of rifles at the Royal Review in Holyrood Park.

In his autobiography, Davidson refers to the building of Dr Thomas Chalmers' house at Churchhill. This was the first house to be built in the district to the west of Woodcroft.

Following Colonel Davidson's death in 1900 (he was in his eighty-ninth year), Woodcroft had a succession of owners. Towards the end of the Second World War, a part of the extensive grounds was requisitioned for the erection of a Post Office Telephones training centre. The old mansion-house was demolished in 1962 and three years later, on July 9th, 1965, there was opened by the Right Honourable Anthony Wedgwood Benn, then Postmaster-General, an important STD telephone trunk-call centre for south-east Scotland, operating in conjunction with sub-centres at Aberdeen and Dundee. Approximately half a million calls a week to all parts of the world pass through this most modern exchange, which retains the name Woodcroft.

Soon after the original Woodcroft was completed in 1858, two other houses of similar design were built to the east of it. Of pink sandstone from the East Morningside estate, they were again in the elaborate Scottish Baronial style.

That called Avalon, immediately adjacent to Woodcroft, bears the date 1860. Little is known of the original owner, Miss Fleming. The name of the house was probably chosen by a later owner.

A monogram carved in the stonework above the main door is now indecipherable, though the mottoes and philosophical injunctions inscribed on the walls may still be read. On the front is, "He yt thollis overcummis", on the west wall, "Feir God and honor ye King" and on the rear, "Ponta labore quies".

The wrought-iron coat of arms on the small gate to the left of the main entrance in Clinton Road is also of interest. The same heraldic design may be seen in many of the books published by W. Green & Son, the legal publishers of St Giles Street, in the stained-glass windows of Gracemount House off Lasswade Road (now an Edinburgh Corporation Youth Centre) and in the entrance hall of Avalon. These are the arms granted by the Lord Lyon in 1908 to Charles Edward Green of St Catherine's, Gracemount and Burnhead, who purchased Avalon in 1920. They show the scales of justice and an open book, and, surmounting these, a mailed fist holding aloft a sprig of holly. The accompanying German motto is, "Erst Wägenden wagen".

Born in 1886, Charles Edward Green was the eldest of the four sons of William Green, founder of the legal publishing house. On his father's death, he withdrew from his study of medicine at Edinburgh University to take over as sole partner of the firm. He continued to further the family's academic ambitions, however, by materially assisting his three brothers to graduate in medicine, law and architecture.

Charles himself never lost interest in medicine, the study of which he had obviously relinquished with regret, and the book he wrote on the possible causes of cancer attracted some attention in medical circles. Devoting himself assiduously to publishing, he produced four large encyclopaedias on medicine, accountancy, Scottish law and English law, the last of which was at the time the largest single work in the English language. From his own pen he published a standard work on East Lothian.

Charles Green's enjoyment of Avalon, with its magnificent garden and pleasant surroundings, was short-lived. He died at the age of fifty-four — within a year of purchasing the house. His widow (the younger daughter of John Dalrymple, an Edinburgh merchant) continued to live at Avalon until her death many years later. Possibly it was she who named the house Avalon, after the legendary paradise of King Arthur fame. Does the mailed fist and branch of holly in the coat-of-arms perhaps have some symbolic link with Excalibur, King Arthur's sword rising above the water?

After Mrs Green's death, Avalon became the residence of a distinguished medical specialist, as it remains at present. The mansion-house and grounds are well preserved and unspoilt, though the notable collection of orchids now in an unheated greenhouse, no longer flower. It is interesting to note that the garage door is said to have come from St Giles' Cathedral. A sundial which once stood in the garden now graces a public park in Brechin.

Immediately to the east of Avalon, and entered from Whitehouse

Loan, stands The Elms, the last of the trio of impressive mansion-houses on the south side of Clinton Road. It was built by Alexander Hamilton, W.S., formerly of Glasgow, in 1858. His monogram is carved above the main door with a motto reading "In arduis fortitudo: 1858".

In 1884 The Elms became the residence of Andrew Hugh Turnbull, who was prominent in the world of Scottish insurance and was a director of the Royal Bank of Scotland. His wife Margaret was the youngest daughter of Adam Black, a former Lord Provost of Edinburgh. Black was elected to Parliament in 1856 at the age of seventy, and served for ten years. He was for some time the publisher of *Encyclopaedia Britannica* and the *Edinburgh Review.*

Passing from private ownership in 1957, this eminently suitable mansion-house became a Church of Scotland Eventide Home the following year. With additional purpose-built accommodation, The Elms now provides thoughtfully planned facilities for old people.

Facing Clinton Road, but entered (through a spacious and attractive garden) from the Whitehouse Loan, is ClintonHouse, built in 1877 by Mrs Kerr Ross, widow of Lieutenant-General James Kerr Ross, who served under Wellington.

Mrs Kerr Ross was a devoted member of Morningside Parish Church and a generous benefactress of the Dorcas Society and other charities for the poor. She presented the Communion Table to the church in 1877, when she first came to Clinton House, and the Kerr Ross Bequest of £1000 has brought relief and comfort to many beneficiaries over the years. A stained-glass window in the north transept of Morningside Parish Church was placed there by Mrs Kerr Ross in memory of her husband in the year of his death, 1872.

Of considerable musical talent, Mrs Kerr Ross at the age of ninety-one composed a march to celebrate the Diamond Jubilee of Queen Victoria, which the Queen graciously accepted. When she was two years past her century, this venerable and still alert owner of Clinton House bought a grand piano and continued to practise daily. She died in 1909 at the age of one hundred and three.

William Mair, in *Historic Morningside,* refers to The Elms as having been the residence of two distinguished brothers, George Wilson, M.D., F.R.S.E., founder and first director of the Scottish Industrial Museum (which became the Royal Scottish Museum) in Chambers Street in 1861, and Sir Daniel Wilson, author of one of the great classics on the history of Edinburgh, *Memorials of Edinburgh in the Olden Times.* In fact, George and Daniel Wilson lived not in The Elms but in Elm Cottage in Blackford Road, opposite the gates of The Elms. Divided into east and west, it is now numbers 1 and 3. "Elm Cottage West" is still indicated on the wall of number 1.

Professor George Wilson, son of a wine merchant, graduated in medicine, but his special interest was in chemistry. He published several books on this and related subjects, all the results of original research. His labours were directed particularly towards the foundation of a Scottish Industrial Museum, which was achieved in 1855. Soon after this he was appointed Professor of Technology at Edinburgh University. By the time of his death at Elm Cottage in 1859, he had collected over ten thousand specimens for his "dear museum", as he once described it.

One of Professor Wilson's innumerable interests was the use of anaesthesia in surgery, prompted by a personal ordeal during an operation before Sir James Simpson's revolutionary discovery of chloroform as an anaesthetic. Wilson also urged the use of oxygen in resuscitation. He was, in addition, the first in Britain to prepare colour-blindness tests for railwaymen and sailors.

His many years of crippling ill-health before his early death led him to seek the reputedly beneficial climate and peace of Morningside. After lodging in the district, he spent his last days at Elm Cottage. His elder brother Daniel joined him there for a short time before leaving to accept a professorship in Toronto, where he died in 1892.

Returning from Elm Cottage to Churchhill by way of Clinton Road, it may be recalled that this was the route taken by early horse-drawn buses and trams which plied between Register House, at the east end of Princes Street, and, originally, Churchhill. Later they went as far as the Old Toll House beside the Jordan Burn at the foot of Morningside Road, and eventually to the Braid Hills terminus.

The history of the city's transport system has been well documented in D. L. G. Hunter's valuable book, *Edinburgh's Transport*. In this detailed study there are many references to the development of facilities between Princes Street and Morningside.

In 1879 a steam-operated bus was the pioneer in public transport but it proved unsuccessful. The Edinburgh Transport Act of 1871 authorised tramways "to be worked by animal power only". Local authorities were permitted to construct or own a tramway system though they were not allowed to operate it: this function was leased to private operators. Edinburgh's earliest companies were H. & A. Inglis, Lindsay & Paterson, Thomas Bouch (the engineer of the first Tay Bridge) and Croal.

Horse-drawn buses were introduced in 1871. Some such "buses" were old stage coaches; others, known as "brakes", consisted of rows of bench-style seats, with no sides, passengers clambering aboard by ladder. The horses had bells round their necks and the bus driver had a whistle to warn other traffic of his movements.

By 1872 the horse-drawn bus had been replaced by the more suitable horse-drawn tram. A journey cost 3d for passengers travelling inside and 2d for those perched, sometimes precariously, on the outside platform or on the roof.

One of the earliest horse-drawn tram services was that from Princes Street to Morningside. Trams on this route stopped at Glengyle Terrace, where, in front of Barclay Church, stood a team of horses, each held by a trace boy. Extra horses were yoked by the boys to the trams to double their horse power as they toiled up the steep hill to Leamington Terrace. Here the horse which had journeyed from Princes Street was unyoked and ridden by the trace boy back down to the stance at Glengyle Terrace. Often a boy would wait at Leamington Terrace until one of his friends arrived with the next tram, then they would race each other downhill on horseback. A similar system operated from Maxwell Street, at the foot of Morningside Road, where trace boys waited with extra horses to haul the trams up to Churchhill.

An albeit infrequent service was provided on the circular route from Register House via Salisbury Place to Churchhill (later to the Morningside Asylum gates) from the earliest days of the horse-drawn trams. The various city services were distinguished by buses or trams painted in different bright colours and this Morningside service was red. The old circular route was not the same as the bus route of today, which goes via the Grange Road, Strathearn Road and Strathearn Place, as prior to 1897 Strathearn Place was a *cul-de-sac*. The horse-drawn bus and tram route to Churchhill and Morningside went from Salisbury Place to Grange Road, turning left at the top of Marchmont Road into Kilgraston Road and right into Hope Terrace, then across Whitehouse Loan into Clinton Road and, finally, half-right and half-left from Clinton Road into Churchhill.

By an Act of 1897, provision was made for the acquisition of the villa at the west end of Strathearn Place, then, as mentioned, a *cul-de-sac*. Duly purchased, it was demolished, opening Strathearn Place, and, by the same Act, horse-drawn trams were permitted to proceed directly from Grange Road, through Strathearn Place, to Churchhill. In this year, the Morningside service was extended to the Braid Hills terminus, and, that summer, to Fairmilehead, with occasional runs to Lothianburn. A carmen's shelter was situated at Morningside Station.

The year 1897 also brought other fundamental changes. Cable-cars were permitted by another Transport Act. Two power stations were built, at Shrubhill and Tollcross; the latter was demolished in 1971. The experience of cable-car haulage in San Francisco, a city with steep hills like Edinburgh, was drawn upon. Edinburgh's first cable-cars set forth in 1897 and during this same year a tram line, partly single and partly double, was authorised to run from the top of Marchmont Road, through Strathearn Road and Strathearn Place, to Churchhill and the Braid Hills terminus. By 1899 this line was laid and in operation. It was agreed that the old horse-drawn tracks from the Clinton Road route be removed, though this was not in fact completed until 1900. The new single cable-car line in Strathearn Place was specially designed to avoid the noise then associated with the changing of points, which offended residents.

By 1902 Edinburgh's cable-car service was in full swing. Although a few horse-drawn trams remained in use, by 1907 these had been completely withdrawn. Morningside people, like most other Edinburgh citizens, were relieved when the horse-drawn transport services at last ended. Over the years, much concern had been expressed at the hardship suffered by horses on the city's steep hills. Icy roads in winter provided special hazards. One of the worst spots was the sharp turning from Whitehouse Loan into Clinton Road, apparently often the scene of horses slipping and falling.

Edinburgh's first tramcars operated by overhead electric pulleys were introduced in 1922. The last of these to run in the city was seen during "Last Tram Week" in 1956. The number 35 tram, the final one to operate in Edinburgh, is now in the city's Transport Museum.

We return from East Morningside to Churchhill, from which prominent vantage point the extensive panorama of modern Morningside stretches out before us. In this district past and present are so closely interwoven that our descent over the brow of Churchhill into the heart of Morningside must again be delayed — but for the last time — as echoes from earlier days detain us.

Jane Welsh Carlyle, whose association with Woodcroft in East

Jane Welsh Carlyle,
one-time resident
of Churchhill

129

Morningside has already been described, records in her published letters some interesting impressions of the Morningside she knew in 1856, and her distinguished husband Thomas Carlyle related, in that year: "My Jeannie has come across to Craigenvilla (fond reminiscences of Craigenputtock!) her aunts' new garden residence of their own in Edinburgh's Morningside quarter, some neat little place where the surviving two yet live."

Craigenvilla, apparently a substantial villa, stood in its spacious garden at the south-west corner of Churchhill and what was then Banner Place (now Morningside Road) extending from this corner downhill to Newbattle Terrace. *The Edinburgh and Leith Post Office Directory* of that year lists "The Misses Welsh, Craigenvilla, No. 2 Banner Place. " The house, under previous ownership, had been known as Grafden Villa. The site is now occupied by tenements and a large house-furnishing business owned by a former City Councillor.

Thomas Carlyle's reference to Craigenputtock is to the house in Dumfriesshire which Jane Welsh's grandfather, and later her father, had owned; a house with deeply sentimental associations often referred to in the Welsh family chronicles. Whether Jane Welsh's aunts changed the name of the house at Churchhill from Grafden Villa to Craigenvilla in order to commemorate the old family house in Dumfriesshire is now difficult to discover.

During Jane Welsh Carlyle's short stays at Craigenvilla, from which several of her published letters were written, she made interesting comments on the Morningside of 1856, especially its Free Kirk atmosphere. This was just over ten years after the Disruption, when a substantial portion of the congregation of Morningside Parish Church, not many yards downhill from Craigenvilla, had "come out" to found Morningside Free Kirk. The two Misses Welsh would appear to have been devout members of this new congregation.

Thomas Carlyle's reference to his wife's having gone to Craigenvilla continued: "They had all gone deep into conscious devotion, religious philanthropy, prayer meetings, etc., etc., but were felt to be intrinsically honest-minded women, with a true affection for their niece, however pagan!"

"They were so unexpectedly tender and glad over me", wrote Jane, that she forebore to make her usual acid remarks on the morning prayers, grace before meals and general "Free Church air" of the house. Just how great an effort of tolerance this demanded from her is made clear: "One of your letters", she wrote to Carlyle, "arriving as breakfast was served caused us all to fall quite unconsciously into *Sin*. Sin against 'T'olly Goast'. I was reading my letter, and had taken a sip or two of tea and bitten into my soda scone, and the others had done the same, when Grace suddenly shrieked out like 'a mad', 'Mercy! we have forgotten the Blessing'. I started on my chair, and (to such a pitch of compliance with

130

'Coostom in Part' have I already reached!) dropped *instinctively* the morsel *out of my mouth into my hand (!)* till I should see what steps were to be taken, for making our peace with Christ. But the case was judged past remedy — and the breakfast allowed to proceed unblessed." Why, she complained elsewhere to an old family friend, did her aunts live "in such a fuss of religion"? "My dear," explained the friend, "they were idle plenty to leeve on and nocht to do for't *they micht hae ta'en to waur!* So we maun *just thole them* and no compleen."

Jane Welsh Carlyle refers again to Morningside's strict observance of the Sabbath in a letter to her husband on August 24th, 1857, in which she also comments on more earthly aspects of the village. "Certainly it is a devil of a place for keeping the Sunday, this!" she writes. "Such preaching and fasting, and 'touting and praying' as I was never before concerned in." The weather was apparently warm. "75 F in the shade yesterday. But there is plenty of east wind to keep one from suffocating, provided one can get it without the dust. I used to fancy Piccadilly dusty; but oh my, if you saw Morningside Road!" If Mrs Carlyle found Morningside Road dusty, she also appears to have found it noisy, reporting in another letter to her husband that she lay awake in the early morning "amidst a tearing rumble of carts that seemed to drive over my brain."

While living at Craigenvilla, Jane paid several visits to her birthplace in Haddington, and complains of delays in train journeys back to Edinburgh via Longniddry. In her later years, when she described herself as "a living miracle", she suffered much pain and frequent sleepless nights. While at Craigenvilla in 1862, four years before her death, she recorded in her diary her need for morphia to induce sleep, adding on one occasion: "Am just going in an omnibus to Duncan Flockhart's for it." Duncan Flockhart's, the chemists, were in 1862 established at 52 North Bridge (they are referred to in a later chapter.)

Carlyle himself may well have resided in the villa at Churchhill — possibly in April 1866 when he was installed as Rector of Edinburgh University. Jane Carlyle, afraid of the climate in Edinburgh and the long journey north, remained in London on that occasion. After the Rectorial Address, she received a telegram from her husband's close friend Thomas Tyndall, which read: "A perfect triumph." Jane, who lived for her husband's success, was overjoyed and waited eagerly for his return. An injury to his ankle, however, forced him to remain in Edinburgh. He was, at this time, the guest of Professor James Syme at Millbank in Canaan Lane. Carlyle, in his condition, could not have been in better company, Syme being the leading surgeon in Europe. The Sage of Chelsea's triumphant stay in Edinburgh, during which he was unable to cope with the number of invitations extended to him and receptions held in his honour, ended with tragedy. Two days before his eagerly awaited return to London, Jane, during a drive round Hyde Park, died in the back of her carriage. She was sixty-five. Jane Welsh Carlyle was laid to rest in the churchyard of her beloved Haddington. "Her death", wrote Carlyle, "has shattered my whole existence into immeasurable ruin." He himself died fifteen years later.

Another echo from the past to claim our attention is from the "city trained bands and proper bands of musick" which led a great procession of city dignitaries and important citizens in Edinburgh's last official Riding of the Marches in 1717. Their lengthy route included Doo or Dove Loan (in more recent times re-named Albert Terrace in honour of the Prince Concort), one of the few streets in Morningside with a name not derived from local history. This narrow country lane, today still a secluded byway through a pleasant residential area with a fine row of Edwardian houses on the southward side, was known as Doo Loan because of the many pigeons which resorted here from the nearby large doo'cote at Merchiston Tower. It led to the old village of Tipperlinn, and formed the northern boundary between the lands of West Morningside and Merchiston. The eastern boundary of West Morningside estate was Morningside Road, and the old "wester hiegait" through the Burgh Muir, extending from Churchhill to the southern boundary, the Jordan Burn. The western boundary, Tipperlinn Load, ran uphill from the Jordan Burn, through the old village of Tipperlinn, to the Merchiston estate.

What is now Albert Terrace therefore formed an important "march line" or boundary between West Morningside and Merchiston, and hence was on the route of the great procession inspecting Edinburgh's internal boundaries for the last time in 1717.

The city records relate: "About 9 of the clock in the morning the cavalcade 'sumptuously apparelled' and on horse-back rode out from the Bristo Port, by the Windmill and Siens, turning westwards to Brownsfield House and Merchiston Tower. From Merchiston then through the lane on the south side of the house, through Tipperling Lane to Boroughmuirhead Lane, thence to the village of Egypt and eastward by the cemetery wall of St Roque, next proceeding to the Grange House through Cant's Loan to Cameron, Priestfield, passing on the eastern side of the gallows at Gibbet Toll Road, Bedford Hall, the Crackling House, the Pleasance, St Mary's Street, to Newhaven, and finally returning to the city."

This ceremony, "the Beating of the Bounds", is of great antiquity, being recorded in Roman and Hebrew days. It is still observed each year, even if purely ceremonially, in the Borders. It was never carried out frequently in Edinburgh. The traditional biennial occasions were on the Feast Days of the Holy Trinity and All Hallows. The object of the Riding was to check that landowners had not, since the last tour of inspection, encroached on their neighbours' property. Records indicate that, in the vicinity of Tipperlinn Loan, successive Lairds of Merchiston regularly edged their way into the precincts of West Morningside.

The nineteenth-century Edinburgh historians who described "the last Riding of the Marches in 1717" were not to know that this, in fact, was not to be the last. The ancient ceremony was revived, after nearly two and a half centuries, albeit symbolically and on a smaller scale, on June 8th, 1946. The occasion was the celebration of the Allied victory in the Second World War. The procession of that day may have been much diminished in number and less than "sumptuously apparelled", and its route may have been shorter than in earlier centuries, but the significance of the occasion had surely never been greater.

Leading the victory procession was the Captain of the Orange Colours, City Treasurer Andrew H. A. Murray, subsequently to become Lord Provost of Edinburgh. The Orange Colours, which have no religious significance, were originated in 1626 when the Companies of Burgesses were formed to serve the King's Army, especially when danger threatened from abroad. The eight companies, each of two hundred men drawn largely from the old Craftsmen's Guilds or Corporations, had separate distinctive colours. The company with the Orange Colours were given the honour of leading city processions in 1633. From 1677 the office of Captain of the Orange Colours was always held by a member of the Edinburgh Town Council nominated after Town Council elections.

CHAPTER 8

The Bore Stone · Morningside Parish Church

THE BORE STONE

As we take our last view from Churchhill before descending the steep hill into Morningside, we may recall those, prominent in the pageant of Scottish history, who, in varied circumstances, have traversed Morningside Road in successive centuries.

In early times Roman Legions marching up Watling Street from south of the Border reached the vantage point of Fairmilehead before descending by the old Braid road to what was to become Morningside and then climbing over Churchhill and Burghmuirhead on their way to the important settlement at Cramond. In 1298 Edward I of England, intent on suppressing the Scots, camped on the Braid Hills and from there, on July 15th of that year, marched with his well-equipped army along the route of what is today Morningside Road, then westwards to Falkirk, where he inflicted a serious defeat on William Wallace. A month later Edward returned by the same route to his base on the Braids.

In 1580 the Regent Morton, after his fall from power, was conveyed as a prisoner along Morningside Road on his way to Dumbarton. An unsuccessful rescue attempt was made by his friends, who leapt out from their hiding place amongst the rocky undercover of the Braid Hills. Just under a century later Oliver Cromwell, encamped with sixteen thousand men on Galachlaw, near Fairmilehead, sent foraging parties down into Morningside Road, where they met with stiff resistance from local residents.

Sixteen years after Cromwell's invasion, Morningside Road witnessed the spectacle of brave Covenanter prisoners, taken after the Battle of Rullion Green, being escorted to confinement in the city. On September 17th, 1745, Bonnie Prince Charlie and his Jacobite army entered Edinburgh from the north via Slateford and by way of the Braid Burn. Seeking to avoid the range of the Castle's artillery, they proceeded up Morningside Road nearly to Churchhill before turning right along Cant's Loan (now Newbattle Terrace) into Grange Loan. Here the Prince paid a visit to his loyal supporters, the Dicks of Grange House, before continuing eastwards to Holyrood.

Grant, in his *Old and New Edinburgh*, described the Morningside which one would have looked down upon from Churchhill in the mid-nineteenth century: "A secluded village consisting of little more than a row of thatched cottages, a line of trees and a blacksmith's forge still slumbered in rural solitude in 1850. There were a few large villas, some old, like East Morningside House and the Whitehouse, some comparatively new like Falcon Hall, but they and the nearby cottages were all in the country separated by fields of oats and barley from both Edinburgh and Newington until building began seriously in the 1850s."

The short stretch of Morningside Road between Churchhill Place and Newbattle Terrace was for long known as Banner Place, while the section on the other side of the road between Albert Terrace (the old Doo' Loan) and a point just opposite the Churchhill Theatre was known as Marmion Terrace. The old Waverley Terrace began just beyond this and extended as far as the Baptist Church. The villa at 65 Morningside Road which faces the entrance to Albert Terrace and Abbotsford Park still bears the name Flodden Lodge. All these names are derived from the tradition associated with the Bore Stone which stands high up on the northern boundary wall of Morningside Parish Church. The inscription on the metal plaque below the stone reads:

THE BORE STONE

In which the Royal Standard was last pitched for the muster of the Scottish Army on the Borough Muir before the Battle of Flodden

1513

It long lay in the adjoining field, was then built into the wall near this spot and finally placed here by Sir John Stuart Forbes of

Pitsligo, Bart.

1852

Highest and midmost was descried
The royal banner, floating wide;
The Staff, a pine tree strong and straight:
Pitched deeply in a massive stone
Which still in memory is shown,
Yet bent beneath the Standard's weight.

Marmion

Disenchanting as it may be to the many Morningside residents and visitors who stop to marvel at the stone, its authenticity and claim for an honoured place in Scottish history have been seriously challenged by Henry M. Paton in a lengthy and scholarly article in the *Book of the Old Edinburgh Club*, Vol. XXIV (1942). Paton's thesis is closely argued and well documented. The stone, he points out, exhibits no evidence of having been a bore stone: there is no bore, natural or man-made, in which the staff of a standard could have been implanted. It seems that the many writers who accepted the tradition established by Sir Walter Scott failed to seek for historical evidence to support it.

Prior to the publication of Sir Walter's romantic poem *Marmion* in 1808, there had been no suggestion of the stone's having held the Royal Standard. Several letters from Scott concerning *Marmion* and his other historical works make it clear that the great romantic novelist was not unduly concerned with historical accuracy. Nevertheless, it would appear

135

The name "Marmion Terrace" is seen to the left above the shop at the corner of Morningside Road and Abbotsford Park, Churchhill
By courtesy of Yerbury

from records that the Bore Stone did for long lie in "the adjoining field" further up Churchhill, opposite the entrance to the old Doo' Loan. In earlier centuries it had probably been one of several march stones (also known as har, hare or hoary stones) which stood in the vicinity of Tipperlinn Loan. In later years it was moved further down Churchhill, near to its present site, when the ground now occupied by 67 and 69 Morningside Road was about to be feued. The Bore Stone was, as the inscription indicates, placed on its present pedestal by Sir John Stuart Forbes of Pitsligo in 1852.

It is Paton's second principal argument which is probably the most telling. The Royal Standard of James IV was, he points out, never hoisted on the Burgh Muir before Flodden. The accounts of the Lord High Treasurer of Scotland for the year 1513 make this clear. They contain several entries concerning expenditure on banners and standards prior to Flodden, including "items for cloth to make the King's banner and the King's Standard, with fringes and cases", but, as Paton stresses, it is the following "items" which are significant: "4s for the making of them [the banners] in haist" and "10s to ane man to byde on the standards and to bring them in haist that nycht that the King's grace departit furth of Edinburgh." James IV in fact left Edinburgh on August 18th, 1513 — before his Standard and other banners were ready. These were "brocht in haist" after his departure and raised during the main muster of the Scottish army, which took place not on the Burgh Muir but at Ellem, a

The Bore Stone
Photograph by the late Mr W. Mair

137

small village on the southern fold of the Lammermuirs, close to Flodden and the English border. This information destroys Sir Walter Scott's tradition of the Royal Standard being hoisted in the Bore Stone and also discredits factually his colourful and eloquent description in *Marmion* of the vast assembly of the Scottish army on the Burgh Muir.

Mr Paton summarises his thesis thus: "If there were no muster, then there was no Standard; if no Standard, then there is nothing of special note to be recorded about the Bore Stone. At best it is 'just an old stone'." It is a coldly clinical dismissal of the romantic legends woven around Churchhill and its neighbourhood by the fertile imagination of Sir Walter Scott! The tradition of the Bore Stone will die hard, as will the association of this highest part of the Burgh Muir with the days preceding Flodden. Some writers have suggested that perhaps not a hundred thousand but possibly some thirty thousand men assembled there, on that part of the ancient Burgh Muir which today surrounds the Astley Ainslie Hospital in Canaan Lane.

MORNINGSIDE PARISH CHURCH

Morningside Parish Church, now simple Morningside Church, stands at the corner of Newbattle Terrace. Its steeple clock is one of the cherished landmarks of Morningside. The establishment of this little church was also an historical landmark in the development of the district, important not only in ecclesiastical annals but for the part it played in changing Morningside from "a secluded village consisting of little more than a row of thatched cottages" into a modern bustling suburb. The origin of the Parish Church was in a circular letter of June 19th, 1837, distributed to people residing in the great mansion-houses of the district and also to those dwelling more humbly in the "row of thatched cottages". The circular announced:

> Although a place of worship for the village of Morningside and its neighbourhood has for some time been felt to be highly desirable, in consequence of the gradually increasing population, no efforts have hitherto been made to supply the deficiency. It is now proposed to make an attempt to do so.
>
> While submitting a proposal for this purpose it is impossible to omit referring to the unspeakable obligations under which the whole district has been long laid to both the Clergymen of this large Parish [St Cuthbert's at the West End of Princes Street], Dr Dickson and Mr Paul, for their indefatigable and unwearied labours among them, amidst all the conflicting claims of so overwhelming a charge devolved upon them as the West Church Parish, and to which no language can possibly do justice. Among other labours there may be mentioned that for considerably upwards of twenty years Divine Service has been regularly performed once a week at one time on

Morningside Parish Church from the architect's plan, 1837

Thursday evenings, and latterly on the Sabbath evenings, in the School Room of the village. . .

It is proposed that the district to be connected with the new Church should extend from Buccleuch Parish on the east to the Parish of Colinton on the west, and from the Parish of Liberton on the south to St David's Parish on the north.

It was estimated that this first parish church for Morningside would cost £1,600, excluding the site. There would be seating, including a front gallery, to accommodate six hundred and thirty-four people. Side galleries, to provide for another one hundred and thirty people, were to be built later. It was soon possible to delete the estimated cost of a site, Sir John Stuart Forbes of Pitsligo, owner of Greenhill House, donating a third of an acre, valued at two hundred guineas, from his estate.

Subscribers to the church building fund came forward readily. A list of these, dated December 25th, 1837, was headed by Mr Alexander Falconar of Falcon Hall, followed by his five daughters. Other generous donors included Sir George Warrender of Bruntsfield House, the Rt. Hon. Lady Napier and the trustees of the late Lord Napier of Merchiston, the Governors of George Watson's Hospital, the Managers of the Royal Asylum (which had received its Charter in 1807 and which, with its recent acquisition of the village of Tipperlinn, occupied a large area of Wester Morningside estate), Charles Chalmers, Headmaster (brother of Dr Thomas Chalmers) "and the young gentlemen of Merchiston Academy", General Robertson of Canaan Bank and numerous others.

Many notable people who resided outwith Morningside but who had some connection or special interest in the district, perhaps because they chose to spend part of the summer in its pleasant sunny seclusion, also contributed. These included Lady Colquhoun of Luss, Benjamin Bell (the famous Edinburgh surgeon) and Dr John Abercrombie (a celebrated Edinburgh physician).

Within a very short period £2,075 16s was raised, and it was therefore decided to proceed with the building of the new church. John Henderson was engaged as architect. The General Assembly of the Church of Scotland enacted a Constitution on May 28th, 1838. The boundaries of the parish were defined more specifically as "That part of the Parish of St Cuthbert's bounded on the north by the Canal, running south in a line to Braidhill to a point where Colinton and St Cuthbert's Parishes meet, and then eastwards to the point where the Parishes of Liberton and St Cuthbert's meet, then north by the east end of Blackford Hill." This extensive area was to be disjoined from St Cuthbert's and created a new *quoad sacra* parish to be called "the Parish of Morningside".

Just nineteen months after the original subscription list had been issued, the opening service of the new Parish Church of Morningside took place, on Sunday, July 29th, 1838. Dr Thomas Chalmers preached at the morning inaugural service and the Rev. James Begg of Liberton in the afternoon. A newspaper report of the event read: "There was an overflow attendance and many went away unable to gain admission. Dr Chalmers preached with all his accustomed eloquence and power." That Dr Chalmers should have delivered the inaugural sermon was most appropriate: not only did he live within a few yards of the new church, but none had advocated the policy of church extension more vigorously and eloquently than he.

Services were conducted temporarily at the new church by the Rev. David Davidson and the Rev. Dr John Paul of St Cuthbert's, until the Rev.

George Smeaton, assistant at North Leith, was appointed the first minister on March 14th, 1839. Three years later he was succeeded by the Rev. Dr Thomas Addis, but this appointment was short-lived. Dr Addis resigned his charge in 1843 to join Dr Chalmers and his supporters at the Disruption, and was appointed minister of Morningside's first Free Church. Dr Addis's predecessor, the Rev. Smeaton, also "came out" at the Disruption while serving at Falkland, becoming a Professor in the Free Church College. A fund for the building of a manse had been established in 1841 but the Disruption again had its effect, this time financially: the fund suffered because of the large number of church members who left to join Morningside's Free Church. A permanent manse was not acquired until 1881 when Harlaw House, 52 Morningside Park, originally built by David Deuchar of Morningside House, was purchased for £3,230. The present-day manse is in Cluny Avenue.

The annals of Morningside Parish Church have been recorded in great detail by the late William Mair and published at length in the church's centenary booklet, in one of the volumes of the *Book of the Old Edinburgh Club* and, in summary, in Mair's *Historic Morningside*. In these publications and in an earlier booklet by John Stuart Gowans (1912) are many interesting facts not only about the history of the church but also the development of Morningside during the latter half of the nineteenth century. The church's steeple clock, a familiar landmark in Churchhill, must have attracted the glances of countless Morningside residents over the years on their way to work in the city. No clock is provided for in the original architect's drawings but in 1840 the church records list: "To school fund for clock including case, £19.12.5d" and "To Mr Clark, Clockmaker, £14.2 shillings". The "movement" or mechanism of the Old Schoolhouse clock was transferred to the steeple of the Parish Church, but it must have been replaced by the school's managers as photographs of the school in the latter half of the nineteenth century indicate that it was still functioning. When the school was eventually closed after the opening of South Morningside School in 1892, the clock stopped at twenty minutes to four and the hands have remained at this time ever since. When, some time ago, the clock face was repainted and the hands removed, many Morningside people waited anxiously to see what would happen. To their relief, the clock was restored to its original state, and the brightly painted gold hands replaced at their appointed hour. In 1929 a new clock was installed in the Parish Church steeple at a cost of £64, the original old school clock mechanism having become worn and erratic.

Within two years of its establishment in 1838, the congregation of the Parish Church were contributing to special funds for the poor of the village, especially for the provision of coal. In 1841 eighteen pounds of candles were required for lighting the church. Gas lighting was introduced eleven years later, in 1852. In 1862 a marked prosperity may be noted in

141

the congregation, indicated by the generous collections. Morningside itself was by this time already beginning to develop rapidly.

In about 1880 the Parish Church entered upon a period of great activity and it was felt that the Church building required to be enlarged. The alternative was to provide for the growing congregation by building a new church further south, slightly beyond the lower reaches of the village. After much debate this latter course was decided upon and an iron church costing £650 was built in 1884 at what is now 2 Cluny Avenue, a few yards from the present Parish Manse. This was in due course to become St Matthew's Parish Church in Cluny Gardens, now Cluny Parish Church.

Expansion of the congregation continued steadily and a plan for a proposed new steeple, put forward in 1887, was laid aside and, instead, the chancel was enlarged and the organ transferred to the east end of the church.

The fiftieth anniversary of the Church was celebrated on May 10th, 1888 by an evening meeting held in the Morningside Athenaeum at the north-west end of Chamberlain Road. Even the extended chancel failed to provide adequate accommodation and a letter to the congregation dated January 20th, 1914 made a revolutionary proposal: that the original church be demolished and replaced by a new and very much larger building. The First World War intervened, however, and this proposal was left indefinitely in abeyance.

An event of particular significance for Morningside was the reunion, in June 1960, of the Parish Church with Morningside High Church. The High Church (now the Churchhill Theatre) had been built in 1894 as the last home of Morningside Free Church, as already mentioned. The reunion with the original "Mother Church" of the parish in 1960, nearly a century and a quarter after the Disruption, brought the wheel of history full circle.

A living link between past and present at Morningside Parish Church is the devoted service, through four generations, of the Gilbert family as Church Officers. The Rev. Robert William Macgoun, who succeeded Dr Thomas Addis as minister in 1843, had a gifted daughter, Hannah C. Preston Macgoun, R.S.W. who was a regular exhibitor in the Royal Scottish Academy. Miss Macgoun illustrated two of Dr John Brown's classics, *Rab and His Friends* and *Pet Marjorie*. The Rev. Macgoun lived with his family in Banner Villa, immediately north of the Parish Church and now 69 Morningside Road.

The street now known as Newbattle Terrace, immediately beyond the Parish Church, has had a succession of names. Originally the southern boundary of the East Morningside estate, it used to be a country lane leading eastwards from Morningside Road, the old "wester hiegait", round the Burgh Muir and past the Grange of St Giles to the old Dalkeith Road, the "easter hiegait". From the early sixteenth century and for a period of nearly one hundred and thirty years, when the Grange of St

Giles was owned by the Cant family, it was known as Cant's Loan or Loaning. Soon after the Parish Church was built it became known, at its western entrance, as Church Lane. The architect's sketch of the church shows Cant's Loan and gives the impression that this part of Morningside Road was then less steep than it is today. Eventually the name Newbattle Terrace was given to commemorate the marriage between one of the Forbes family of Greenhill and a member of the Marquis of Lothian's family of Newbattle Abbey near Dalkeith.

Several of the villas in Newbattle Terrace are of relatively early date, being indicated in the first Ordnance Survey Map of 1852. One of these was named Banner Lodge in perpetuation of the legend of the nearby Bore Stone. Morningside Parish Church Hall was built in 1899. The villa opposite, Kirkbank, which stands next to the church, was built a decade later, with a view to the extension of the church.

A more recent terraced villa, 30 Newbattle Terrace, was from 1895 the home of Alexander Carlyle, M.A., and his wife Mary Carlyle Aitken, daughter of the famous Thomas Carlyle's sister Jean. Mary Aitken married her cousin, Alexander Carlyle, in 1877. His two sons, Edward and Oliver, attended George Watson's College when this was situated beside the Royal Infirmary, overlooking the Meadows. Alexander Carlyle presented to the National Library of Scotland a valuable collection of his uncle's manuscripts and gifted the Sage of Chelsea's industrious fountain-pen to Edinburgh's Central Public Library. Alexander Carlyle and his wife rest in Morningside Cemetery.

Pitsligo House, near the corner of Newbattle Terrace and Pitsligo Road, incorporates the former Newbattle House, in which lived, from 1868 until her death, the Dowager Lady Liston Foulis, wife of Sir James Foulis of Colinton and eldest daughter of Robert Cadell, successor to Constable as Sir Walter Scott's publisher. Lady Foulis possessed the original manuscripts of Sir Walter's *Pirate* and *Redgauntlet,* and five volumes of his correspondence. In 1947 Newbattle House was purchased by the owner of a well-known Edinburgh bakery and it became the Martin Benefaction, a pleasant residence for elderly ladies, administered by Dr John Martin. Pitsligo House was built in 1970 by the Merchant Company of Edinburgh Trust as a similar residence and it incorporated Newbattle House. Here between thirty to forty women enjoy tastefully designed and comfortable accommodation. The Edinburgh Merchant Company's crest adorns the entrance to Pitsligo House.

Returning to Morningside Road from Newbattle Terrace, one's attention is attracted by the quaint row of terraced shops on the opposite side of Morningside Road, extending from the southern boundary wall of Bank House to Morningside Place. Set in the wall beyond the last of these shops is an old milestone, now barely legible, indicating "One mile from Tollcross." This is one of three stones which marked the distance to Fairmilehead. The Fairmilehead stone still stands near the entrance to the water filtration works, three miles from Tollcross, but the intermediate second milestone, which should be located on the old Braid Road near the Braid Hills Hotel, has disappeared.

Bank House, from its high prominence at the south corner of Albert Terrace and Morningside Road, commands a magnificent view over Morningside to the Braid and Pentland Hills rising steadily on the horizon. The house has recently undergone effective exterior restoration. The conservatory at the top of the steep entrance steps in Morningside Road is something of a landmark, glimpsed over the twelve-foot-high wall (the height of which, incidentally, indicates the considerable earth-cutting which took place during the construction of the busy thoroughfare over Churchhill).

Originally named Morningside Bank, the house was built in 1790 on land feued by Lord Gardenstone, then owner of Morningside estate. This land was formerly part of the original West Morningside. Subdivision of the house into Middle Bank House and North Bank House was carried out about 1860.

Bank House is mentioned in the biography of Cosmo Gordon Lang, Archbishop of Canterbury from 1928 to 1942, by J. G. Lockhart. Archbishop Lang referred to the important childhood impressions absorbed in an "old world" garden. His family, including his younger brother Marshall, came to live at Bank House when Cosmo was four, during his father's five years of distinguished service as minister of Morningside Parish Church, just opposite the house, on the slope of Churchhill. While Cosmo, converted to the Church of England when at Cambridge, was to become the head of that church, his brother was, remarkably, to achieve the parallel distinction of being appointed Moderator of the Church of Scotland in 1935.

Born at Fyvie in Aberdeenshire in 1864, where his father, the Rev. John Marshall Lang, was parish minister, the future Archbishop of Canterbury was named Cosmo Gordon after the local Laird. In later years he vividly recalled his boyhood days in Morningside, "at that time a quaint country village, with villas and quiet lanes and no houses built beyond it. Real scene of my childhood was the garden of Bank House, Morningside. I suppose it was quite a small garden but it was my world from the age of four to nine. It was my *own* world where my imagination for once had its unclouded day. It was a world of make-believe—a bundle of sticks on which I stood enduring the fancied flames of a Christian martyr—the great black roaring cat who to me was the Devil, walking about seeking whom he might devour."

An amusing interlude which occurred during the General Assembly of 1935, over which as Moderator, the Very Rev. Marshall B. Lang presided, is recorded in the Assembly Proceedings of that year:

Professor Lamont drew the attention of the House to the fact that
Dr Cosmo Gordon Lang, brother of the Moderator Dr Marshall B.

Lang, was seated in the Gallery. It was with gratitude and joy, said Professor Lamont, that they had with them in the House the head of their great Sister Communion, the Archbishop of Canterbury. The Moderator, in welcoming him, said: "Your Grace. . ." (the remainder of the sentence was drowned in applause and laughter). "It is a very singular pleasure," he continued, "to welcome you to the floor of the Assembly, not only as one I have been familiar with in past years (renewed laughter) but as representing the great Sister Communion in England." (Applause.)

The venerable Archbishop said that he had not come prepared with an address worthy of the Assembly, or of its traditions. "I must content myself," he continued, "in the fewest possible words, in saying with what satisfaction I find that the choice of Moderator this year has rested upon one of whom at least I can say that he belongs to a highly respectable family, and that he has retained its traditions of respectability, orthodoxy and fidelity to the Church of his fathers more successfully than his elder brother. (Laughter.) With all my heart I pray that God's blessing may continually rest upon the Church of my Fathers." (Loud applause.)

The Moderator expressed the gratitude of the Assembly to the Archbishop for the words he had spoken and the blessing he had given to them as fathers and brethren of the Church of Scotland.

The father of these two eminent churchmen, the Very Rev. John Marshall Lang, C.V.O., D.D., Ll.D., had himself been Moderator of the Church of Scotland in 1893, and in 1909 he became Principal of Aberdeen University. His son, the Rev. Marshall B. Lang, who followed him as Moderator, was the author of *The Seven Ages of an East Lothian Parish,* and had at one time been Minister of Whittinghame in East Lothian. Cosmo Gordon Lang was Archbishop of Canterbury during the Abdication of Edward VIII. The brothers were cousins of the distinguished actor Matheson Lang.

CHAPTER 9

Morningside Village

The much-weathered milestone built into the wall immediately beyond the last of the quaint terraced shops which stretch downhill on the right-hand side of Morningside Road provides an appropriate place at which to pause before entering the heart of what was the original village of Morningside. Wester Morningside Estate, the fourth of the lots into which the Burgh Muir was divided and feued in 1586, comprised twenty-six acres. Its northern boundary was Albert Terrace (originally Doo'Loan), and it was bounded by Myreside to the west and Morningside Road to the east. The southern boundary was the Jordan Burn, running from Myreside to the Briggs o' Braid at the foot of Morningside Road, just before Maxwell Street and Braid Church. On this estate, over several centuries, three villages arose: Morningside, Myreside and Tipperlinn, the last being of greatest antiquity.

While the keeps, castles and mansion-houses surrounding the area on which Morningside was to develop were all sixteenth-century or earlier, the first map showing Morningside as a distinct location was Richard Cooper's Plan of the City of Edinburgh and Adjacent Grounds, 1759. The village of Morningside is indicated by three houses. In J. Adair's Map of Midlothian, 1735 various places surrounding Morningside are shown but the village itself is not. John Laurie's map of 1763 indicates two small groups of houses which may be assumed to be Morningside.

James Grant, in *Old and New Edinburgh,* described Morningside as "a row of thatched cottages, a line of trees and a blacksmith's forge" (to which description other writers have added: "and an alehouse"). The origins of this settlement may be traced to the steady growth of several farms in the district. The earliest of these, and the nearest to what was to become Morningside village, were the farms of Canaan, Egypt, and Plewlands. Of early origin, but more distant (yet no doubt providing work for the villagers of Morningside), were those of the Grange of St Giles, to the east, and Braid, Comiston, Oxgangs and, more remotely, Swanston, to the south. The village soon became an increasingly important first stopping place on the principal drove road into Edinburgh from the prosperous farmlands to the south on the Biggar Road.

Morningside, therefore, had its origins in agriculture, the development of which was later boosted when the Edinburgh Suburban and South Side Junction Railway—as it was originally named—was inaugurated in 1885. This permitted crops and cattle from surrounding farms to be transported to and from the busy goods depot at the end of Maxwell Street, next to Morningside Road Station.

The second important factor in the development of Morningside village was the movement of Edinburgh's wealthier citizens southwards to the sunny "morning side" of town. They built their villas and mansion-houses on the new, generously proportioned plots which resulted from the sub-division of the lands of Canaan and, later, neighbouring estates. In meeting the needs of the newly-resident gentry, the hamlet of Morningside became an important and bustling village. The systematic development of Morningside probably began very soon after the beginning of the nineteenth century, though existing records date only from 1812. In that year, James Knox's Map of Edinburghshire provides some indication of the layout of the village, its principal dwelling houses and streets. More comprehensive and valuable detail is given in Robert Kirkwood's map of 1817. This provides us with a good picture of the Morningside which had then become an early suburb of Edinburgh. It can be clearly distinguished, along with the estates derived from the 1508 and 1586 feuing of the Burgh Muir and the mansion-houses built within them by 1817.

By the time of the first Edinburgh Ordnance Survey Map of 1852 Morningside and its environs were well delineated and readily recognisable in relation to present-day houses and streets. As regards the demographic development of the district, *Gray's Annual Directory* for 1832-3, the first Edinburgh directory to group the city's residents into districts, lists under Morningside and Canaan a total of thirty-seven people, these, however, being only the gentry, professional people, tradesmen and shopkeepers. This selective listing of the local population in Edinburgh street directories continued until the late nineteenth century. In 1884 Morningside Road for the first time appears divided into a series of short individual sections, each with a different name. Commencing at Churchhill, these little streets, proceeding downhill, through the village to the Jordan Burn, the city boundary, were: Waverley Terrace, Marmion Terrace, Banner Place, Morningside Bank, Esplin Place, Blackford Place, Falcon Place, Reids' Buildings, Morningside Terrace and Morningside Village. The total population in 1884 listed in these various streets, the forerunners of Morningside Road, was seventy. Again, this figure is confined principally to professional people, tradesmen and shopkeepers. A year later, in the *Edinburgh and Leith Directory* for 1885-6, Morningside Road is no longer shown as a series of individual streets but as one major road which had absorbed its constituent sections, whose names were gradually to fade into obscurity. In this directory properties in Morningside Road are, for the first time, shown in numerical sequence from the corner of Colinton Road to Morningside Station, numbering from 1 to 276. In this new Morningside Road one hundred and fifty residents are listed. Such figures are, of course, no index of the growth of population, being exclusive of the increasing number of people by then residing in the various streets built on both sides of Morningside Road, and of the many people who did not qualify for inclusion in early street directories.

Morningside continued to develop. In addition to the earliest reasons for growth — farming and the building of large villas and mansion-houses which absorbed local labour and services — another more recent factor which contributed towards rapid development was transport. The year 1872 saw the provision of the first horse-drawn trams, and just over ten years later came the inauguration of the Edinburgh and South Side Suburban Railway and the opening of the passenger station, Morningside Road. With the advent of the horse-drawn and, later, cable tramcars, the growth of the village had still been gradual, but, with suburban railway services, the village atmosphere changed almost overnight as Morningside suddenly developed into a desirable and rapidly spreading residential suburb. Many old village cottages which had once straddled the ancient Wester Hiegait were swept away, despite the protests of their occupants. Those which survived had, by the beginning of the twentieth century, become museum pieces, dwarfed by the serried rows of tenements which towered above the busy new highway to the south.

In the Braid, Cluny and Morningside Drive districts "villadom" was steadily established. Morningside Public Library was opened in 1904. A cinema and ballroom followed. It was not until the decade prior to the Second World War, however, that the Greenbank district to the south witnessed a vast building programme of bungalows. In the midst of all this development, the venerable mansion-houses of the old Morningside estates, dating back to the original feuing of the Burgh Muir, remained pleasantly surrounded by their ample gardens and orchards, still apparently as remote as when their first owners built them as summer residences in the country.

We must now proceed beyond the milestone at the corner of Morningside Place. From existing printed records and recollections, or memories passed down by generations of Morningside residents, a reconstruction may be attempted of the principal features of the village towards the close of the eighteenth century and their gradual alteration or disappearance amidst the final massive building programme completed by the beginning of the present century. This reconstruction is made in terms of present-day street numbers.

On the right, immediately beyond the milestone and opposite Newbattle Terrace, is Morningside Place, originally named Deuchar Street after the family who for so long owned Morningside House and its surrounding lands, which included this ground. The first villas were built here in the 1820s. At 2 Morningside Place Dr Thomas Chalmers resided for a year while awaiting the completion of his new villa at Churchhill. Opposite this little bungalow, the substantial villa, 1 Morningside Place,

Milestone at north corner of Morningside Place and Morningside Road

Photograph by Mr W. R. Smith

was for a short period the Morningside Free Church manse. No. 4 was for long the home of the Cowieson family. In 1895 Peter Cowieson acquired the Old Schoolhouse of Morningside when the new South Morningside School was opened in 1892. At 6 Morningside Place resided the Misses Balfours, aunts of Robert Louis Stevenson, who, as a boy, was a frequent visitor to this house, where he carved his initials on a cupboard door. On one occasion, while seated on the garden wall with his air-pistol, he accidentally shot a pellet into the arm of young Miss Cowieson of No. 4. The incident was revealed only many years later when this lady, then in her nineties, was admitted to hospital, where she explained the small scar on her arm, for so long romantically concealed and, perhaps, secretly treasured. Trafalgar House, 3 Morningside Place, is believed to have been built by a close relative of Lord Nelson, who named it after the great naval victory. At No. 7 resided the sisters of Dr John Brown, author of *Rab and His Friends* and assistant to the distinguished Edinburgh surgeon Professor Syme of Millbank in Canaan.

While most of the original houses of Morningside village have long since disappeared, fortunately one of its oldest buildings remains largely unchanged. This is the Old Schoolhouse (a few yards downhill on the right, beyond Morningside Place), where the hands of the old clock have remained permanently at twenty minutes to four since the little school was closed and South Morningside School opened in 1892. The tower of the Old Schoolhouse still clearly proclaims the date of its foundation, 1823. It thus pre-dated the Parish Church by fifteen years and, as already

149

mentioned, some of the earliest meetings of the congregation were held in the Old Schoolhouse, where Dr Thomas Chalmers on occasion preached.

The origins of the old school have been hitherto unknown. Some references to it are to be found in the archives of St Cuthbert's Parish Church in Lothian Road, now kept in Register House. Morningside was, in early times, within the extensive parish of St Cuthbert's. Other references are found in the minutes of the meetings of the School Board of St Cuthberts and Dean, filed in the Edinburgh Room in the Central Public Library. None of these sources, however, goes back as far as 1823. Fortunately, the original deeds of conveyance of the ground on which the school was built and the names of people involved in its establishment were eventually discovered among the papers in an Edinburgh solicitor's office. These refer to a Morningside resident, George Ross, who was to become so closely identified with the school that for many years it was to bear his name.

The origins of the school are identified with another notable Scottish personage of the early nineteenth century, Lady Maxwell of Pollock, a generous benefactress of Scottish education and other social needs of her day. D'Arcy, Lady Maxwell of Pollock, as she was known, was a remarkable woman, of legendary beauty and refinement, and compelling personality. The youngest daughter of Thomas Brisbane of Brisbane, Largs, she married Sir Walter Maxwell of Pollock at the age of seventeen. Two years after her marriage her husband died, leaving her with a child who also died soon afterwards. Lady Maxwell, in the midst of such sorrows, exhibited a deep religious faith and she devoted her life, talents and considerable means to charitable works. She was a close friend of Lady Glenorchy and, although they were very different in personality and religious attitudes, they collaborated closely in church enterprises, especially the early ecumenical services held in St Mary's Chapel in Niddry's Wynd, off the High Street. Lady Maxwell also enjoyed a close friendship with John Wesley, with whom she conducted an extensive correspondence. Wesley visited her at her home, Saughton House, then on the outskirts of Edinburgh, during his visits to the city in 1782 and 1784, Lady Maxwell, while remaining a devout member of the Church of Scotland, joined Wesley's Methodist Society, but her friend Lady Glenorchy was far more critical of the famous evangelist and did not embrace Methodism. Indeed, she eventually precluded Methodist preachers from participation in her interdenominational services in Niddry's Wynd.

Some years before her death in 1810, Lady Maxwell established an Industrial School for Poor Children in Rose Street, which was later transferred to Horse Wynd, off the Canongate. John Wesley visited the Rose Street school on several occasions and was much impressed. One of the trustees of the Rose Street Industrial School in 1810 was George Ross, an Advocate of distinction and later a Judge of the Commissary Court of

The Wee School, Morningside

The original Morningside Schoolhouse, opened 1823, closed 1892 and still standing

Scotland, who resided in the stately and pleasantly situated mansion, Woodburn House, in Canaan Lane, Morningside. In the charter of March 27th, 1823 by which James Robertson, factor of William Deuchar, owner of Morningside estate, conveys a small portion of land for the building of Morningside's village school, George Ross of Woodburn is the first-named of four men involved in the establishment of the school. The others were Alexander Falconar of Falcon Hall, James Evans of Canaan Park and Henry Hare of Newgrange. By 1849 James Hare had moved to London and the Rev. Dr John Paul and the Rev. James Veitch of St Cuthbert's Parish Church had been invited to assist in the management of the school. Later that year many other prominent local people became shareholders (at £10 each), thus helping to support the school. These included Sir George Warrender of Bruntsfield House, Sir John Stuart Forbes of Pitsligo (owner of Greenhill Estate) and Mrs Henry Craigie, formerly Miss Jessie Pigou Falconar of Falcon Hall. A portion of the substantial legacy left by Lady Maxwell for the continuation of her educational benefactions was apparently to be used in support of the school, which, by 1856, had been in operation for just over thirty years. In that year George Ross noted: "I have settled the sum of £1,300, £1,200 of which is at present in City Bonds having 4% interest, on Morningside School of which from the interest, (say £48), £25 per annum is to be paid to the teacher of Morningside School and £12 per annum to the female teacher of the sewing school. I retain for the present the management of Morningside

151

Andrew Cockburn, once "Maister" of the Old Schoolhouse, c. 1890

School." In a postscript he added: "The two ministers of the parish, namely the Rev. Dr Paul and Dr Veitch of St Cuthbert's, are trustees of both schools." From the middle of the nineteenth century it would appear from records that George Ross managed the school largely unaided. It became known simply as the "Ross School", and later as the "Subscription School".

Articles and letters, which have appeared in Edinburgh newspapers over many years, about the personal recollections of those elderly Morningside residents who once attended the school, give us some insight into its life in various periods. Information about early teachers is sparse, but a Mr Galgour appears to have been "the maister" in 1837. In 1873 the *Edinburgh Post Office Directory* tells us that this position was held by a man whose name was well-remembered by all who attended the school during his long period in charge, Andrew Myrtle Cockburn. He was known to his pupils, and to Morningside villagers generally, as "Cocky Cockburn". A Moray House graduate, he came from the village of

Redding near Polmont. After twenty years service as "maister" of the village school, Cockburn was appointed First Assistant at South Morningside School in Comiston Road when this much-needed new primary school opened in 1892. His two colleagues at the old school, Miss Margaret Cameron and Miss Campbell, referred to in the records as "from the Ross School", also served on the staff of South Morningside School for some time, as did Miss McAllister, former pupil-teacher at the Ross School, who, soon after being transferred to South Morningside, left to undertake further studies, presumably at Moray House Training College.

Andrew Cockburn's daughter, who continues to live in Morningside, has many memories of the Old Schoolhouse, which, she recalled, was for some time known as the "Subscription School". School fees were apparently levied on those parents considered able to contribute towards their children's education, and she remembered one parent, whose several children attended the school, who paid fees in kind. The man was an artist and over several years he presented the "maister" with a series of water-colours of various aspects of Morningside and district. These paintings were sold some years ago and unfortunately cannot now be traced.

Pupils came to the old school from the village itself and also from places as far distant as Lothianburn and Swanston. Just how many children attended is not on record, but judging from the large enrolment at South Morningside School when it was opened in 1892, attendances at the village school just prior to that must have stretched the two small classrooms to full capacity. Pupils who lived some distance from the old school would have come on foot or horseback, or riding on farm carts. This use of horses may have accounted for the school's becoming known as "the cuddy school". The horses were tethered in the little lane beside the school (still there today with its two pillars to prevent entry by traffic) which leads to Springvalley Terrace. This lane became known as "Cuddy Lane", though on old maps it is named Rosewood Place.

The great event in the old school's year was the annual prizegiving ceremony attended by most of the villagers attired in their "Sunday best" clothes. For many years the prizes were donated and presented by the Misses Falconar of nearby Falcon Hall, and the closing vote of thanks to the "maister" was proposed by John Johnstone, factor to the Deuchar family, the owners of Morningside estate. He was a man, with fiery red hair and long beard, greatly revered by the people of the village. The schoolhouse, for long a popular social or community centre, was the meeting place of the Marmion Lodge of the Independent Order of Good Templars. This organisation enjoyed strong support and provided two annual social highlights, a winter soiree and a summer outing to Habbie's Howe at Nine Mile Burn.

Following the Disruption in 1843, many parents who "came out" in support of Dr Chalmers and his colleagues and left the Parish Church

Children at the Old Schoolhouse

withdrew their children from the village school and sent them to the Free Church School, housed in a little building just beyond the village smiddy, where the Public Library now stands. As several contributors to the press recounted some years ago, many former pupils of the old village school achieved distinction in various walks of life, some in far-off parts of the world. One became a wealthy merchant in India and eventually received a knighthood.

Sixteen years after Ross's memorandum of 1856, by the Education (Scotland) Act of 1872, education became compulsory. In Scotland it came under the Scotch Education Department, administration being in the hands of local School Boards until 1919. They were then succeeded in the city by the Edinburgh Education Authority and, in 1930, by the Edinburgh Corporation Education Committee. More recently, with the advent of new systems of local government, Lothian Regional Council took over. While no records survive describing how the Act of 1872 affected the old village school, fortunately there are papers relevant to the school which have been discovered so that it is possible to trace the various stages in its latter years when, as the result of the Act of 1872, it passed from private ownership. Ten years afterwards, the Educational Endowments (Scotland) Act of 1882 led to a body of Commissioners being appointed to supervise and administer the country's

154

many small schools founded by charitable benefactors. By 1889 the Commissioners were administering the Ross School in Morningside, along with several other such schools in Edinburgh known as Dr Bell's schools. These included Lady Glenorchy's School, Wightman's School, the Canongate Burgh School and the Lochend Burgh School. The minutes of a meeting of the Commissioners in 1889 indicate their power, twelve months thereafter, to close the Ross School in Morningside, but it would appear that this step was not taken and that the little school continued to operate under the administration of the Edinburgh Educational Trust, established in 1882. This body, it seems, kept the old schoolhouse open until the early 1890s. The next reference to the school occurs in the Register of Sasines for 1895. In that year, three years after South Morningside School in Comiston Road had been opened, the old schoolhouse and its small surrounding area of land were sold to Peter Cowieson, owner of the villa at 4 Morningside Place, by the Edinburgh Educational Trust. He appears to have let the premises for various uses. In 1946 the little building was sold by the Cowieson family to the Brethren, a religious group who still find the well-preserved simplicity of the old school particularly well suited to their weekly services. This little religious community has done much to restore and preserve the old schoolhouse and its clock, now brightly repainted and proclaiming distinctly the date of the village's earliest educational establishment. Consideration has been given to the installation of a new clock mechanism so that the hands, for so long set at twenty to four, may move again, but it seems unlikely that this will happen.

Morningside village was centred on the small area now occupied by the Public Library and the "Merlin". On this, the west side of Morningside Road, cottages stretched at irregular intervals from just beyond the schoolhouse, downhill to what is now Morningside Park. On the east side of the road cottages extended, again rather sparsely, from the present-day south-west corner of Falcon Avenue to the Briggs O'Braid over the Jordan Burn, the ancient city boundary running along the back of Maxwell Street and under Morningside Road, past the north side of the lawn surrounding Braid Church. The west side of the village, the more populous, in which were situated certain important institutions, formed part of the eastern boundary wall of Morningside Estate, while the cottages on the east side of Morningside Road lay on the western boundary of the extensive lands of Canaan. The Parish Church, further up the hill at the corner of Newbattle Terrace, was thus somewhat removed from the centre of the village, but, as already related, it was built on this site as a result of the free gift of land by Sir John Stuart Forbes of Greenhill. Before 1885 separately numbered "streets" had, as already mentioned, formed the village High Street. After this date, they were combined and renumbered to form part of Morningside Road.

We have already noted the little lane (once known as Rosewood Place)

155

immediately beyond the school, leading to Springvalley House, or Spring Villa as it is named in one old map of the area. This fine mansion-house, set amidst pleasant gardens and some acres of farmland, was demolished in 1907. A stone plaque set in the tenement wall above 43 and 45 Springvalley Terrace commemorates the house which gave its name to this part of Morningside. Springvalley House was for some years the residence of James Grant, celebrated author of *Old and New Edinburgh,* that classic and monumental work on the history of the city which was first published in parts by Cassells in 1880. Grant, an Edinburgh-born historian and military expert, wrote fifty-six novels. His other works included *The Romance of War, Memoirs of an Aide-de-Camp* and *Memoirs of Kirkcaldy of Grange and Montrose.*

We return to Morningside Road by the former Rosewood Place, now Springvalley Terrace. This little lane retains some of its original character, three old stone cottages of the village still being occupied. Viewhill Cottage is amongst the very few Morningside houses listed in Gray's *Annual Directory of Edinburgh, Leith and the Suburbs* for 1832-3. This cottage, with the adjacent Rosewood Cottage and the third, now named Pentire, are indicated on the first Edinburgh Ordnance Survey Map of 1852. Pentire Cottage is still numbered 142 Morningside Road although it is some distance from the main road.

Immediately beyond what was Rosewood Place was an area of open ground on which the present small block of tenements was eventually built. The south gable-end of these was built against the end of the little row of two-storey shops and houses which appear on early maps. The ground-floor shops were among the earliest in the village and included a dairy. The shopkeepers lived in their back shops and on the floors above. At the rear of the row, reached through a little pend and now numbered 160 Morningside Road, is a group of original two-storey houses, still occupied and retaining something of the atmosphere of the old village. One of these houses indeed still has its outside stone staircase.

Beyond the last of the shops in Morningside Road was an open area, on the front edge of which there stood, until it was demolished to provide a fore-court for the Merlin a few years ago, a large rectangular two-storey building. The front of this was hard against the pavement, which was thus at this point made dangerously narrow. Originally occupying the ground floor of this inelegant building was one of the earliest and most important institutions of the village, Dick Wright's smiddy. In 1955 a writer to the press, recalling the main features of Morningside in about 1880, wrote of this: "It was a recognised howff for gossip between the villagers and the ploughmen who brought in their horses from the farms to be shod, and there were always horses there and always a pile of 'singed sheip's heids', for in these days 'sheip's heids' were not skinned but were sent by the butchers to the smiddies to be singed, thus preserving the juiciest parts. But for the absence of the spreading

DENHOLM'S SMIDDY.
MORNINGSIDE

The principal village smiddy in Morningside, Denholm's smiddy

chestnut tree, Dick's might have been the smithy of the poem. Children on the way to and from school (almost next door) looked in at the open door. We loved to see the flaming forge, to hear the bellows roar, and to catch the burning sparks that flew like chaff from a threshing floor. All that belongs to a bygone day. Dick Wright was the beadle of Morningside Free Church."

After the closure of Dick Wright's smiddy in about 1900, the ground floor of this old building was occupied by a sculptor whose yard extended some distance to the rear, this land now being occupied by the Merlin and its car park. The upper floor became a joiner's workshop. At one time part of the premises was occupied by a printer and the building was known for a period as the Blackford Press, the name probably being derived from the fact that this short stretch of Morningside Road — no longer than the Merlin's frontage — was once called Blackford Place.

While it may have been a popular howff, a centre of village gossip and a source of fascination to pupils of the old schoolhouse — all of which tended to give it a somewhat romantic atmosphere — Dick Wright's was not Morningside's oldest smiddy. When Grant described the village as "a row of thatched cottages, a line of trees and a blacksmith's forge", the reference would appear from records to have been to Denholm's smiddy. In Gray's *Annual Directory* of 1832-3, the first Edinburgh directory to have a separate heading for Morningside, "J. and W. Denholm, smiths" are listed alongside a total of seven shops. (There is no reference to Dick Wright's smiddy at this period.) Denholm's smiddy occupied the site on which Morningside Public Library was built in 1904.

Just beyond the Merlin is a little lane with, at its end, a group of small cottages, one of which is numbered 174 Morningside Road although

157

it is a considerable distance from the main road. This anomaly arose because of the difficulty experienced, during the first complete numbering of Morningside Road in 1885, in labelling such scattered dwellings. This group of cottages is the last and oldest survivor of the heart of the original Morningside village. Some of these quaint little houses, tastefully renovated, are still occupied.

Pictures published with such captions as "Morningside Smiddy" (as, for example, that in Mair's *Historic Morningside)* would appear not to portray either Denholm's or Dick Wright's but a third smiddy which, according to the Edinburgh Ordnance Survey Map of 1894, stood somewhere amidst the little cottages just described. Three blacksmiths are shown on this map.

Denholm's smiddy and its adjoining cottage, described in the early Post Office Directories as being in Falcon Place, were, after 1885, allocated the numbers 186 and 188 Morningside Road. Both were demolished in 1903 to make way for the building of the library. The Edinburgh Public Library Report for 1905 states that, "Three years ago, representation was made by the inhabitants of the district of Morningside in favour of a Branch Library in that part of the town." The wishes of the inhabitants were granted and Denholm's smiddy, one of the village's oldest institutions, second in antiquity only to the schoolhouse, having stood for over seventy years, made way for the establishment of the fast-growing suburb's newest institution.

Morningside Public Library was opened on November 9th, 1904 by John Harrison, second son of Lord Provost George Harrison, who became Edinburgh's City Treasurer. The Harrison family had close connections with Morningside, having lived for many years in Rockville, the controversial Pagoda house in Napier Road, described in an earlier chapter.

When the library was opened, six thousand volumes were considered an adequate initial stock. Ten years later this number was closer to ten thousand. In 1929 the library building was extended. Today the stock of books held has, compared with the year of opening, increased ten-fold, and the annual issue is now seven hundred thousand. On the site of the old village smiddy there now operates one of the busiest libraries in Scotland.

Adjacent to Denholm's smiddy, at the corner of what is now Springvalley Gardens, was the Free Church School. Its site is now covered by the shops and tenements at 190 to 196 Morningside Road. Immediately beyond the old Free Church School was Reid's Lane (leading to Reid's Cottages or Buildings) and then an extensive dairy farm, long owned by John Reid. The cottages, today well preserved and still occupied, once housed the workers of Reid's farm. Among those who at various times resided here was James Gavine, the builder responsible for the construction of the Midmar district of Morningside. Immediately beyond

Morningside House, left, the original manor house of Morningside village, built c. 1780 (now the Co-operative supermarket stands on its site), and, right, the old smiddy

By courtesy of the late Miss C. E. Evans

the cottages, a pend runs past what was once a dance-hall and later the Springvalley Cinema into an open area now occupied by car lock-ups. On the left, just before the lock-ups, is an old two-storey building, the upper floor of which has a very old door, possibly a relic of one of the byres of Reid's Dairy. Just beyond this building may be seen, built into a boundary wall, a number of interesting and apparently very old ecclesiastical stones of varied motifs. Local tradition has it that these stones were set here by the owner of the nearby sculptor's yard. This sculptor, it is said, was on occasion engaged in the alteration or demolition of old churches, from which the stones originated. They are much older than any that would have been obtained from local Morningside churches, but they may have been brought here from some much older church in the city.

From about the middle of the nineteenth century there were several dairy farms in the Morningside district, but Reid's byres and outbuildings extended over such a wide area in the vicinity of Springvalley Gardens and Terrace as to make this undoubtedly the principal farm of its kind in the old village of Morningside. Elderly residents will remember it as Springvalley Farm. The press article quoted below describes the dairy farm in its heyday: "The cows were all numbered with big black figures painted on their flanks. Each morning they used to proceed in stately single file on their own to pasture in 'The Shooting Field' next to the Hermitage, and equally stately was their procession back home for the evening milking. I have counted up to 130. Milk for the villagers was delivered by the milkmaids picturesquely dressed. The milk pails and cream pitchers were hung on a large hoop which the milkmaid carried with both hands, she being in the middle."

This colourful era of rural Morningside came to an end when Reid's byres were demolished in 1899 to make way for Springvalley Gardens and Terrace, built soon after. Immediately beyond Reid's Lane, now Springvalley Gardens, and on what is now the site of the Morningside Branch of the Edinburgh Savings Bank and the short row of tenements extending to the great modern supermarket at the corner of Morningside Park, stood the principal manor-house of the old village, Morningside House. Of modest proportions and simple style, it stood a short distance back from Morningside Road, behind a pleasant front garden. There were extensive grounds and an orchard to the rear, now forming the back gardens of several houses on the north side of Morningside Park. A large pear tree still flourishes in the back garden of 8 Morningside Park, a last relic of the orchard of Morningside House. When Morningside Road was numbered in 1885, Morningside House became 200, now the number of the Savings Bank.

When Morningside House was built and by whom is difficult to determine. The lands of Morningside passed through a long succession of owners, the early "lairds of the village". This area, originally known as Wester Morningside and then simply as Morningside Estate, was one of the lots into which the Burgh Muir was divided for feuing by Edinburgh Town Council in 1586. The original feu was obtained by Edinburgh Merchant Andrew Napier, brother of Sir Archibald Napier of Edenbellie, then "Laird of Merchingstoun". Andrew Napier's ownership was short-lived. In 1587 the lands of Morningside passed to his nephew and thereafter to John Cant of Morton Estate. Cant for some time owned the Grange of St Giles, while his son Andrew became the owner of Comiston House. Newbattle Terrace, as already noted, was originally known as Cant's Loan, leading as it did from Morningside to Grange House. From John Cant's other son, Ludovic, Morningside Estate passed to Thomas Beg, an Edinburgh merchant, and then to William Menzies, owner of the neighbouring lands of East Morningside. Morningside remained the property of successive owners of East Morningside Estate for just over one hundred years — until 1764. Among later owners was John Orr, an army surgeon, and John Mosman, a merchant who had previously acquired the extensive adjacent lands of Canaan. Mosman, at his other estate at Auchtyfardle in Lanarkshire, had welcomed to his home, with much-appreciated kindness, Mrs Maclehose (Robert Burns' "Clarinda"). She enjoyed there rural peace and hospitality "such as makes one forget the past."

Mosman's nephew Hugh Mosman sold Morningside Estate in 1789 to Francis Garden of Troup, the eccentric and benevolent Lord Gardenstone, Senator of the College of Justice. A considerable amount of information has come down to us about this owner of Morningside House, who was perhaps also its builder. Lord Gardenstone, who chose as his legal title the name of his birthplace in Banffshire, was raised to the Bench in 1764. He came to live in Morningside House just four years before his death there in 1793.

Kay's portrait of Lord Gardenstone highlights one of his many eccentricities: he is shown entering the city on horseback, on an animal somewhat mild and aged to compensate for his Lordship's apparent lack of horsemanship, while alongside runs a little boy in Highland dress. The boy accompanied Lord Gardenstone all the way from Morningside House to the courts in Parliament Square and there looked after the horse till the day's proceedings were over, when he commenced his return journey to Morningside, again trotting attentively behind his master.

A great lover of pigs, the noted judge developed a special friendship with one of them, which in winter served a useful purpose before the era of electric blankets: the small creature would be placed in his noble master's bed to heat it and would then complete his duties by sleeping all night on his master's clothes to ensure that these were comfortably warm in the morning!

While living at Morningside House, Lord Gardenstone regularly, and apparently to his benefit, partook of the mineral waters of St Bernard's Well beside the Water of Leith at Stockbridge. During the first year of his

Lord Gardenstone, former owner of Morningside House, from Kay's "Portraits"

161

residence at Morningside, 1789, he erected over the well a little Doric temple and dome designed by Nasmyth and modelled on Sybil's Temple at Tivoli. A statue of Hygeia, the work of Sir John Steell, was later placed beneath the canopy and the well with its surrounding enclosure presented to the city by William Nelson, the publisher, in 1884.

Lord Gardenstone is the first person referred to in the records as having resided at Morningside House and it is thus possible that it was he who built this simple mansion-house in the midst of Morningside village. Work may have been completed before he took up residence in Morningside Estate, purchased in 1789. Contemporary maps of Edinburgh either do not include the outlying village of Morningside, or, if they do, do not indicate Morningside House by name or show its exact location. The earliest Edinburgh directories do not list Morningside House, the first to do so being that of 1836-7.

The statement by Grant, in *Old and New Edinburgh,* that "in the year 1758 there was no other mansion-house of any importance in this area except Falcon Hall and Morningside House itself" is confusing, as is a further statement: "There died in Morningside House, in the year 1758, William Lockhart of Carstairs who was thrown from his horse at the Boroughmuirhead." Elsewhere Grant refers to Morningside House and Morningside Lodge as being the same house and he says that in Morningside Lodge Lord Provost William Coulter died in 1810. However, there is no supporting evidence that either Lockhart or Coulter ever resided in Morningside House. Furthermore, Morningside Lodge, which according to Grant was synonymous with Morningside House, was clearly another house altogether. This was probably the original name given by Coulter to the mansion-house he built on the Canaan estate in 1780 and which was named Falcon Hall by its next owner. Again, there is no evidence to support Grant's statement that Morningside House existed in 1758. It seems very probable that this house was built by Lord Gardenstone in about 1789, shortly after his purchase of Morningside Estate.

Lord Gardenstone was known to be extremely generous to his household staff and tenants in the various estates he owned earlier, and it may be assumed that such benevolence was also shown towards the people of Morningside Village during the distinguished judge's few years as "the laird".

David Deuchar, who purchased Morningside Estate and its mansion-house in 1795 from Lord Gardenstone's nephew, was of note in his own right, and even more so on account of his having "discovered" a young man who was to become one of Scotland's, and indeed the world's, greatest portrait painters — Henry Raeburn. Deuchar was an etcher and engraver of some distinction whose studio is listed in Williamson's *Edinburgh Directory: 1790-92.* The entry reads, "D. and A. Deuchar, seal engravers to the Prince of Wales [afterwards George IV] opposite the

Cross, South Side." The Cross was the Mercat Cross in the High Street, Deuchar's premises being on the south side of the High Street, near Parliament Square. Near Deuchar's studio was the shop of his close friend "James Gilliland, jeweller, Parliament Close". Almost daily the two met to exchange news and discuss business of mutual interest involving both their skills. During one such visit by Deuchar to Gilliland's shop, his friend drew his attention to the remarkable talent of his new apprentice, Henry Raeburn. Deuchar was shown some of young Raeburn's work and was immediately and deeply impressed. He himself gave this young protege his first formal tuition in drawing, then introduced him to David Martin, one of Edinburgh's notable painters and engravers, who had studied under Allan Ramsay. Raeburn became Martin's dedicated pupil.

The young apprentice jeweller whose genius was first recognised by Deuchar, and who was knighted by George IV at Hopetoun House in 1822, was a former Heriot's foundationer, born in a small slated cottage at the side of a mill lade of the Water of Leith at Stockbridge. His father was a yarn boiler, but both Raeburn's parents were dead by the time he was six years old. After six years as a pupil at Heriot's Hospital, as the school in Lauriston Place was originally known, he began his apprenticeship with Gilliland, which was to lead to his discovery by Deuchar. To mark the happy accident of their first meeting in 1773, young Henry Raeburn soon afterwards produced a miniature portrait of Deuchar. The latter reciprocated with a pen and wash drawing of the young apprentice then aged seventeen. Both relics of this friendship, so fortuitous for the world of art, were acquired in 1931 by the National Gallery of Scotland from the Deuchar family.

David Deuchar's own work has been overshadowed by his association with Raeburn, but it was in fact of fine quality and much in demand. Of special note were his seal engravings commissioned by George IV. In addition to engraving, the lapidary etching which he originally took up as a hobby earned him considerable distinction. In 1788 he published a series of forty-six copper-plate etchings of the "Dance of Death" paintings by Hans Holbein the younger, which portrays all classes of men, from Pope to beggar, terrorised by death. In the Fine Art Room of the Edinburgh Central Public Library may be seen "A Collection of Etchings after the most eminent masters of the Dutch and Flemish Schools, particularly Rembrandt, Ostade, Cornelius Bega and Van Vhet; accompanied with sundry miscellaneous pieces and a few original designs, by David Deuchar, Seal Engraver, Edinburgh." Miss E. Ethel Evans, for long resident in Morningside before her death some years ago, possessed a rare collection of Deuchar's original works. The whereabouts of this collection is not now known.

Following Deuchar's death at Morningside House in 1808, his estate was inherited by his four sons, in unusual sequence: ownership passed first to the youngest, then progressively to eldest. While the eldest son

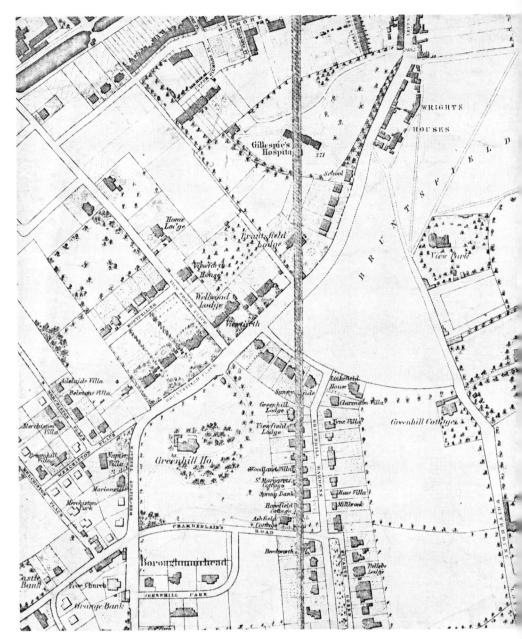

Johnston's Plan of Edinburgh, 1861

For continuation south see following pages

164

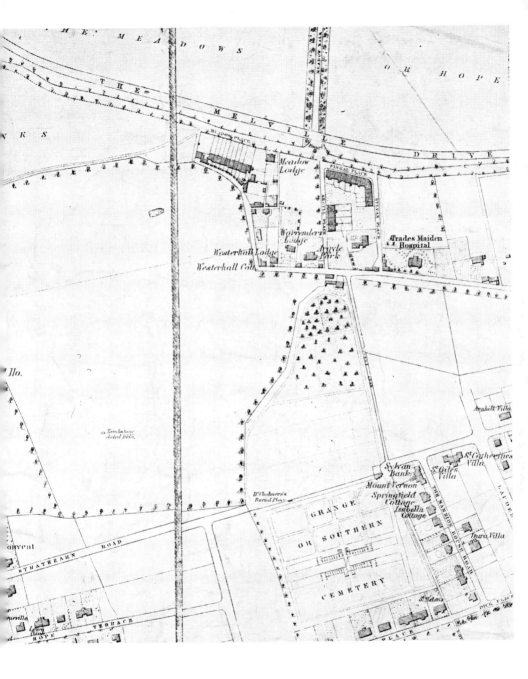

Johnston's Plan of Edinburgh, 1861

For continuation north see previous pages
By courtesy of Edinburgh City Libraries

166

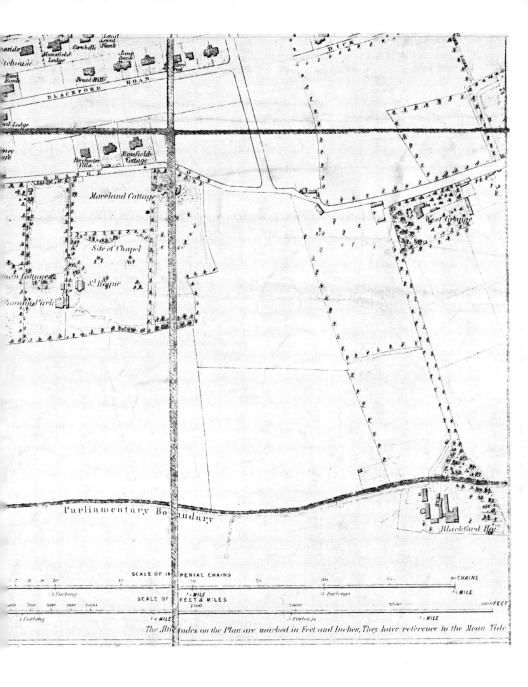

SCALE OF IMPERIAL CHAINS

1 Furlong

SCALE OF FEET & MILES

The Altitudes on the Plan are marked in Feet and Inches. They have reference to the Mean Tide

Alexander followed his father as a seal engraver, his youngest brother John entered the world of science, becoming a lecturer in chemistry at the University of Glasgow and, later, at Edinburgh University, where he was the first to lecture in his subject to female students. At this time the chemistry classroom and laboratory were in Lothian Street.

Finally, the property in Morningside, including Morningside House, passed to David Deuchar, F.R.S.E., manager of the Caledonian Insurance Company. By 1871 he appears to have moved from Morningside House, for in that year the *Edinburgh Post Office Directory* lists John Reid, dairyman, as occupying the old village mansion-house. In fact, the last of the Deuchar family to reside in Morningside House had vacated it for the substantial villa, Harlaw Lodge, which he built at 24 Morningside Park, just a short distance west of Morningside House, in 1874. Here he resided until 1881, when he sold it for £3,230 to Morningside Parish Church as its first permanent manse. They in turn sold it some years ago and the manse is now at 5 Cluny Avenue. The large villa in Morningside Park today recalls its long Parish Church association by its name, Mansewood. Morningside Place, which passes the top of Morningside Park, was for long known as Deuchar Street.

The Reid family remained in Morningside House until it was demolished in about 1895. High up on the wall of the tenement block built on the site of the front garden is a carved stone plaque commemorating the Diamond Jubilee of Queen Victoria in 1897. The plaque is deeply embedded, almost flush with the surface stonework of the tenement, suggesting that it was inserted when the tenement was built, probably late in 1897. It is directly above the Savings Bank at 200 Morningside Road, once, as already noted, the number of Morningside House.

Immediately beyond the southern end of this row of tenements, the stables of the old house remained for many years after Morningside House itself had disappeared. They were owned by a well-known Morningside doctor who resided in the corner villa at 2 Morningside Park, later demolished to make way for the supermarket. At 3 Morningside Park are the premises of the enterprising Morningside Club, which has its origins in the Morningside Liberal Club established on November 30th, 1889 in a two-storey house at what was then 247 Morningside Road (where the annual rent was, initially, £23). That house, the property of a Mr Johnston, was, along with a number of similar adjoining houses, demolished in about 1889 to make way for the tenement between Canaan Lane and Jordan Lane. The inaugural meeting of the Morningside Liberal Club, the membership of which numbered one hundred and fifty, was attended by several Morningside Town Councillors and prominent residents. Subsequent meetings of the Club discussed many topical issues of concern to the people of Morningside: the need for a new and larger school to supersede the old schoolhouse; the state of footpaths; the removal of the lunatic asylum, established in 1813 in Morningside Park,

168

to the outskirts of the city; the need for improved suburban railway services, and the construction of a skating pond at Braid Hills. In November 1890 the Club considered purchasing the Morningside Halls at Morningside Drive (later the Dunedin Hall), but their offer was not accepted and the premises were acquired instead by the Morningside Unionist Club. In May 1899 the Morningside Liberal Club purchased 3 Morningside Park, where it continued to function until 1950, when it became a social club. In the 1960s the premises were altered to provide the excellent facilities now enjoyed. Morningside Club's strong sense of pride in the history and traditions of the district from which it takes its name is signified by its membership badge which combines an Egyptian falcon, symbolising the land of Canaan, the falcons of Falcon Hall and the rays of the morning sun.

At the beginning of the nineteenth century anyone proceeding down the west side of the old high street would, once he passed the whitewashed garden wall of Morningside House, have found himself in open country "of pastures green, waving corn and sweet-smelling hawthorn hedges all the way to Fairmilehead". There were no other houses on this west side of the road until the other side of the Jordan Burn, in the districts of Braid to the left and Plewlands to the right. Morningside Park was not built till nearly a century later. After 1813, in the area between what is now Morningside Park and Maxwell Street, "the pastures green" would no longer have been quite so visible. In that year there was built, at long last, "an asylum for the cure or relief of mental derangement". This was originally the East House, forerunner of today's Royal Edinburgh Hospital. Its high enclosing wall extended from just beyond the garden of Morningside House to the Jordan Burn at the Briggs o' Braid near Braid Church. The large gates and little cottage-type lodge at the entrance to the new hospital stood almost opposite Jordan Lane. The southern boundary wall of the hospital extended westwards along what is now the back of Maxwell Street, on the north bank of the Jordan Burn. On reaching the Jordan Burn with its little bridge, one had reached the boundary of old Morningside Village, which was also, for centuries until 1882, the southern boundary of Edinburgh itself.

Where the lawn surrounding Braid Church borders on Morningside Road there once stood the old toll-house. While not shown on Kirkwood's map of 1817 or on the Ordnance Survey Map of 1852, it does appear on the Johnston-Lancefield map of 1861, located on the south bank of the Jordan Burn, just beyond the city boundary.

On January 20th, 1852 a meeting of the Commissioners of Supply and Road Trustees for Midlothian had before it a petition, signed by one hundred and twenty Morningside families, about a lively and heated topic of village conversation — their objection to having to pay a toll at Wright's Houses (near the present-day Barclay Church) which they had to pass on visits to and from the city. "We unfortunates of Morningside," they

169

protested, "cannot even visit a friend in Gilmore Place without incurring this extraction." There was no possibility of avoiding the toll by taking a route via Viewforth, since a check bar had been erected there too, while to make the even longer diversion along Cant's Loan (Newbattle Terrace), Grange Loan and Newington resulted in being caught at the Grange Loan toll.

One of Morningside's nearby "lairds", Sir John Stuart Forbes of Greenhill House, supported the Morningside villagers on the grounds that "those who go in by omnibus to their businesses in the City in the morning and return in the afternoon have each to pay twopence extra for toll charges — they have to pay one shilling extra on every railway parcel delivered beyond the toll at Wright's Houses, their coals are also charged proportionately higher and so likewise every other article, the parties making the charge in allocating the price of the toll in most cases imposing besides a large margin for their own profit."

Another neighbouring "laird", Sir James Forrest of Comiston, a former Lord Provost, commented, when it was pointed out that the Wright's Houses toll-bar had operated for fifty or sixty years, that, while this was true, there had been "no Morningside at all at that time". Sir James was opposed to all of the city's toll-bars being moved outside its boundaries on the grounds that this would lead to suburban housing development, to the detriment of rents for those flats in the city vacated by tenants moving to the outskirts, but he did nevertheless support the petition for the removal of the Wright's Houses toll-bar southwards.

The Morningside villagers won their case. Soon afterwards the new toll-house was built on the south bank of the Jordan Burn, just outside the city boundary, where it remained for nearly thirty years until the abolition of road tolls throughout Scotland in 1883.

In 1888 Sir John Skelton, owner of the Hermitage of Braid, obtained permission to have the then obsolete Morningside toll-house carefully dismantled and re-built as the gatehouse at the entrance to his drive. On a lintel at the rear of the house the number 259, the original number of the old toll-house in Morningside Road, may still be seen, very faintly now, above the built-up doorway at which the tolls were once collected. The toll-gate was operated from within the adjacent bay window.

In about 1880 the keeper of the old Morningside toll-house had been Mrs Mark, a forbidding lady of German or Dutch origin who struck terror into the hearts of Morningside children who enjoyed trying to slip beyond the toll-bar unnoticed.

Opposite the old toll-house, horses which had drawn the old buses, and later tramcars, from the city were tethered in the then open area beside the high enclosing wall of the asylum at the back of Maxwell Street. Suitably refreshed, they later resumed their arduous haul up the steep brae to Churchhill. While these horse-drawn buses and trams which plied from the city to Morningside were fairly well patronised, the old coaches or cabs were not so popular, colourful as they were, trotting down Morningside Road to the warning blasts of the driver's coaching horn. In summer, however, business improved.

In the summer of 1859 there was a great invasion of tourists and it was recorded that, "One day one might see five hundred new faces in Edinburgh." (The Edinburgh International Festival, with its immense increase in the number of "new faces", was still a long way off!) During this mid-nineteenth-century tourist boom, one of the well-advertised mystery tours by "coach and pair" was a visit to Morningside. When they reached the toll-house, the cabbies suggested to their passengers that they might wish to stretch their legs and enjoy a pleasant stroll along the lane which now leads to a social club and which in those days ran along the bank of the Jordan Burn. Some distance along the lane, the visitors were met by a group of well-dressed gentlemen who invited them to relax in a game of "thimble and pea" or be entertained with card tricks. Many visitors returned to the city with much less in their purses than when they arrived at Morningside.

There is a reference to Morningside's old toll-house in Robert Louis Stevenson's *Edinburgh: Picturesque Notes* (1879). The author proclaims, in no uncertain terms, his views upon the development of Morningside: "Just beyond the old toll-house at the foot of Morningside Road, the

The old Toll-House which stood at the Briggs o' Braid in Morningside Road and was rebuilt as the gate-lodge at the Hermitage of Braid

171

chisels are tinkling on a new row of houses. The builders at length have adventured beyond the toll, which had held them in respect so long, and proceed to career in these fresh pastures like a herd of colts turned loose. It seems as if it must come to an open fight at last to preserve a corner of free country unbedevilled.''

Joseph Laing Waugh, the author of several novels which have become classics of their kind, resided in Comiston Drive. He too refers to the old toll-house at Morningside, and the nearby low stone wall, overhung by a large and pleasant hawthorn tree, is also mentioned in his *Robbie Doo*. The broad wall was once a favourite haunt of schoolboys. Under its slabbed top were a series of little cellars, formerly pigsties.

Proceeding uphill from the site of the old toll-house, we pass Jordan Lane on the east side of the old village high street. The short row of high tenements on the south side at the entrance to this street were the first to be built in Morningside, in about 1857. The stretch of Morningside Road extending from Jordan Lane to Canaan Lane was originally known as Jordan Place.

Grant's description of old Morningside might have included, ''and the village inn''. At the corner of Canaan Lane from at least 1800 onwards, and probably earlier, there stood one of Morningside's earliest institutions, an inn which came to be named The Volunteers' Rest, but

An early horse-tram to Morningside, standing at Tollcross

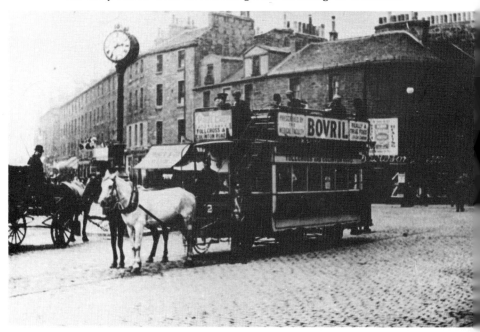

which was known to many villagers as The Rifleman or, in later years, as The Volunteer Arms or The Canny Man's. Until relatively modern times this was Morningside's only hostelry. Some writers have claimed that there were at one time as many as seven public houses in Morningside but this is difficult to substantiate, though there were a number of licensed grocers in the early days, on whose premises drink might on occasion have been available.

At the south corner of Canaan Lane and Morningside Road a cottage-type inn existed towards the end of the eighteenth century. This, the original village inn, was purchased by Mr James Kerr in 1871. He was the "Canny Man", having earned this title because of his steadying influence on the carters who patronised his premises and tended to consume their drinks rather quickly. "Ca' canny man," was the advice offered by Mr Kerr to such customers. His name stuck, and it also became the name by which the inn was commonly known during his ownership.

James Kerr was a native of Biggar, where his father was a blacksmith. He had first come to Edinburgh to take charge of Ushers the brewers' team of horses which pulled the old dray carts to various hostelries in the city. Successful in this job, he saved enough money to be able to purchase the little inn at the corner of Canaan Lane. The Volunteers' Rest, as he named it, became a popular rendezvous for the many carters coming to Morningside with produce from outlying farms at Comiston, Hunter's Tryst and Braid. Here they would not only obtain refreshment and exchange the news of the day but also, if required, have an expert eye cast over their horses by Mr Kerr.

One of the great annual events in Morningside Village in the early nineteenth century was the Carters' Parade which took place on the first Friday in April. This was a lively affair: there were stalls selling sweets and spelderns in Morningside Road, which was decked with coloured flags. The day ended with a dinner, which may have been held in the Volunteers' Rest.

While it was the patronage of the carters which was important to the village inn, it was from its popularity with a quite different class of clientele that its name originated. These were the men of the Edinburgh Volunteers. Not far from the village hostelry, a short distance up Braid Road, then the main road to Biggar and the south, a path led from a break in the hawthorn hedge on the east side to a large field (still unbuilt upon) on the south side of what became Hermitage Drive, facing the steep slopes of Blackford Hill. This was known as "the shooting field" and was used by the Edinburgh Volunteers and, latterly, the Edinburgh and Midlothian Rifle Association. The targets were on the slope of the west side of Blackford Hill. In the interests of accurate marksmanship, it may be assumed that visits to the village inn were more fitting after than before practice at the butts. At any rate, the inn's signboard "The Volunteers' Rest" was obviously appropriate.

Two water-colour artist's impressions of the old inn at Canaan Lane may still be seen in the public bar. A caption on each reads: "The Golden Drop was first blended and sold here in the year 1871." The initials F. D. O. on these paintings are interesting. The *Edinburgh and Leith Post Office Directory* for 1883 lists a "Mr F. D. Ogilvie, artist, No. 1 Belhaven Terrace", who is presumably the painter of these pictures.

It is possible, though of course mere conjecture, that Mr Ogilvie was also the artist referred to earlier in connection with the old schoolhouse, who paid the fees of his several children in kind, with a series of paintings of Morningside and district.

In addition to the water-colours of the original Volunteers' Rest, the present-day premises, built in about 1890, house many interesting relics of bygone days. These include a complete range of copper whisky-blending jugs and measures, ranging from the minute to those holding several gallons, used in the production of the "golden drop". There is also an interesting collection of decorative bridles (perhaps preserved from the original owner Mr Kerr's dray horses), a selection of coaching horns, and a quite fascinating old accounts book for 1892-3 in which regular customers were each allocated their own page, or several pages. The page headings reveal how the owner of the old inn knew each "regular" personally, often simply by his Christian name or occupation. We find recorded such customers as, "Old John, Shepherd with Falconhall", "George the joiner", "Hughy, mason at the asylum", "Soldier Jock", "Tom, labourer" and "the gasman", and there are entries such as, "Four quarts of beer during hay-making at Falconhall". The prices of drinks in 1892 — for instance "glass of whisky, 4d" — are such as to spark off the now frequent argument over the relationship between such prices and their modern equivalents.

In the old accounts book of 1892, most debts are shown as having eventually been "squared". Had a similar book been kept twenty years earlier it would, it seems, have revealed at least one customer whose debts were not so regularly paid — a fortunate occurrence, as it happens, because as a result the Volunteer Arms possesses its two most valuable treasures. The customer in question was the distinguished Scottish landscape painter Sam Bough, R.S.A., who resided at the end of nearby Jordan Lane and who is given further attention in a later chapter. Whether to repay his debts, demonstrate his versatility, or simply as a commercial arrangement, the great and prodigious painter of landscapes presented to James Kerr in 1871, as the inn's signboard, a two-sided oil painting of a kneeling rifleman of the Edinburgh Volunteers, painted on a large oak panel and signed by the artist. Earlier Sam Bough had presented a picture of the same subject painted on canvas. These works would now bring a price large enough to settle a thousand-fold any debts incurred.

The eastern section of Morningside Road extending from Canaan Lane to Falcon Road West was once known as Morningside Terrace, now

The original Volunteers' Rest (now the Volunteer Arms) at the corner of Canaan Lane and Morningside Road, c. 1800

the name of the street branching off from the south side of Morningside Park. When Morningside was still a village what is now Steel's Place was called Steelies' Close or Steelies' Slip. Here there was once a cemetery for cats and dogs. Almost midway between Steel's Place and Falcon Road West were the main gates at the head of the drive leading to Falcon Hall.

From the Falcon Hall gates a row of low terraced cottages extended to a point almost opposite the old village schoolhouse, running the length of the short high street on the east side. Opposite were Esplin Place and Blackford Place. In the last cottage in this row, Falcon Cottage, which was larger than the others, lived the village doctor, Dr George T. Beilby, M.D. This house stood on the site of what is now 161 Morningside Road. Here was born, in 1850, (Sir) George T. Beilby, Ll.D., F.R.S., a distinguished pioneer in physical and industrial chemistry. Another early village doctor was Dr John Airth.

Beyond these cottages, which stood on the west boundary of Canaan, lay open ground as far as the Parish Church at the corner of Newbattle Terrace. The tenements on the north side of Falcon Avenue were not completed until 1915, and the modern flats opposite much more recently. The last short section of Morningside Road, from the Parish Church to Churchhill, originally named Banner Place, has already been described. At this point the northern boundary of the village was reached.

The features and institutions of old Morningside Village which I have

The stone-pillared gateway leading to Falcon Hall to be seen on the east side of Morningside Road, before the beginning of the old cottages

By courtesy of Miss Jean Campbell

176

described appeared, flourished and, in most cases, disappeared over a period of some two hundred years. In the chronological sequence of smiddy, inn, village school and Parish Church can be traced the development of the community. Until the mid-nineteenth century Morningside remained remote from the city. It was the transport explosion which transformed the accessible village into a suburb.

Among many recorded statistics concerning Morningside's development, two are important in showing the type of suburb it became. Despite the wide variety of houses built from the middle of the nineteenth century onwards, no instance has ever been recorded of housing, even in the most humble dwellings, becoming unfit for occupancy. Even today, in the heart of the old village, two of the earliest cottages remain comfortably occupied. Morningside's record is apparently unique in the history of Edinburgh's housing.

As a result of the vast growth of "villadom" from about 1870 onwards, steadily effected by the chisels which tinkled beyond the old toll-house, much to Robert Louis Stevenson's regret, came Morningside's second distinction. In the pleasant residential districts of Cluny, Hermitage and Braid almost every villa originally had resident "servants", usually spinster ladies with their own "purpose-built" quarters. Thus the proportion of women in Morningside was considerably higher than in any other part of Edinburgh.

The village of Morningside, unlike its neighbour and one-time rival, the now non-existent village of Tipperlinn, did not merit a place on the earliest maps of Edinburgh and environs. Today, however, it covers a wider area and has a larger population than many small Scottish towns.

Old cottages in Morningside village facing Denholm's smiddy, c. 1880
By courtesy of Mr Gilmour Main

CHAPTER 10

Tipperlinn · The Royal Edinburgh Hospital

TIPPERLIN

Braidburn towlies
Morningside swine;
Tipperlinn's the bonnie place,
Where a' the ladies dine.

So ran the jingle chanted, probably during their playtime games, by some of the children attending Morningside's old schoolhouse — presumably those from what was then considered a rival and much superior place to Morningside, the ancient neighbouring village of Tipperlinn.

Tipperlinn is indicated on very early maps (such as that of Timothy Pont of 1660) some considerable time before Morningside village merits a place. Consisting of two facing rows of double-storey cottages, perhaps no more than twelve in number, the village of Tipperlinn appears to have existed prior to 1586, as when, in that year, Edinburgh Town Council feued out the Burgh Muir in lots, one of these was defined as Wester Morningside. The boundary of this portion was "frae Merchistounnis Butts to the Tipperlynn quill it cam to the hiegaitt besyde the Brighous called Browns of the Briggs." The "Brighous called Browns of the Briggs" would appear to be the Briggs o' Braid, the little bridge spanning the Jordan (then the Pow) Burn at the foot of what is now Morningside Road.

The name Tipperlinn is thought to have been derived from the Gaelic *tober* or *toper,* meaning a well, and *linn,* a pool or river. The well which gave rise to the first part of the name, though now covered over, is still in the back garden of Viewfield House in Tipperlinn Road, built about 1830. The pool or river was the Pow or Jordan Burn which, much diminished, still flows past what were the southern fringes of the village. A well referred to as the "Tipperwell" was noted by Thomas Telford in 1813, during his survey of possible new water supplies, but it was not drawn upon.

Long before Telford turned his attention to it, the well at Tipperlinn had served a purpose other than simply providing drinking water. The Tipperlinn of the schoolhouse jingle, a "place where a' the ladies dine," was of a later era, when the village had become a summer resort for Edinburgh's wealthier citizens. Yet this was not Tipperlinn's "finest hour": centuries earlier it had enjoyed a still greater distinction.

In its earliest days, the principal feature of Tipperlinn was its community of weavers, whose artistic skill achieved recognition in the reign of George III. The master-weavers had their looms on the ground-floors of their cottages, their families living on the upper floors, reached by outside forestairs of simple style, like those once common in Edinburgh's Lawnmarket and High Street and in the village of Newhaven near Leith. The other operatives lived in small thatched cottages adjacent to the houses of the master-weavers. The village well provided the water essential for dyeing and other processes.

While this ancient village and its prosperous industry have long since disappeared, fortunately some details of the principal weavers have been recorded. The father of the weaving community of Tipperlinn was Ebenezer Gairdner. Some accidental good fortune had a hand in Ebenezer's talented career, helping to earn him a "By Royal Appointment" warrant — though as the result of another person's misfortune. This other person was the young nineteenth Countess of Sutherland, tragically orphaned while still a small child. Her claim to the Sutherland title was contested in the House of Lords and decided in her favour in 1771. In delicate health, she returned to her birthplace, Leven Lodge, which stood in what is now Valleyfield Street on the fringe of Bruntsfield Links. Possibly the child's guardians favoured Leven Lodge on account of its proximity to the Links, for long considered a healthy locality and for this reason treated as a protected area. Part of the Links was reserved for the grazing of goats and ewes, kept for the production of whey, thought to be a most beneficial tonic. Wealthy citizens of Edinburgh in poor health rented houses beside Bruntsfield Links during the few weeks of the whey season. It was during this season in 1772 that the young Countess was here in residence.

While playing one day with some young friends on the Links, the child was hailed by the Sutherland family weaver, Ebenezer Gairdner of Tipperlinn, who was on his way to deliver a supply of damask tea towels to Leven Lodge. In the Edinburgh of the late eighteenth century, such artistic weaving was an important decorative feature for afternoon tea parties in the house of the gentry, each hostess taking great pride in the family crest or distinctive pattern woven specially for her household. So fascinated, it is said, was the young Countess by the intricacy of Gairdner's work that she herself enthusiastically took up hand-spinning. She did not forget her introduction to this art and some years later, when Gairdner produced a special tablecloth designed to portray the "Triumphs of Britannia", this and some of his other work was, as a result of the good offices of the now influential Countess of Sutherland, shown to Queen Charlotte. The royal response was immediate and highly favourable: Gairdner was awarded the title of "Damask Manufacturer to Her Majesty" and a promptly dispatched order from the Queen called for two hundred and thirty patriotic tablecloths.

Linen damask and cotton woven in floral designs, and damask of the

179

"dambrod" pattern in blue-and-white or pink-and-white squares, in the form of tea and table-cloths, were the characteristic products of the Tipperlinn looms. Some years ago there was an elderly lady in Morningside who still cherished in her possession a well-preserved large tablecloth with the date "1754" woven into it. It was a product of Ebenezer Gairdner's day. Unfortunately, the whereabouts of this and other examples of Tipperlinn workmanship are now not known.

Gairdner's yarn-boiling premises, which employed many workers, were located in the Vennel, that quaint little passageway which still leads from Lauriston Place, past the remains of the old Flodden Wall and George Heriot's School, to the West Port and Grassmarket. In his day, this was within the ancient district of Wester Portsburgh, and here Gairdner's apprentices took part in a once popular street game. The apprentices of Samuel Gilmore's "roperie" in the Grassmarket (this was the Gilmore after whom Gilmore Place was named) would make a large ball of tow and rags, encased in wire and with a long wire handle, known as "the Grassmarket Ball". This was soaked in turpentine, set alight and thrown into the air, to land somewhere in the broad expanse of the Grassmarket. The apprentices of Gairdner's nearby premises made their own type of missile known as "the West Port Ball" and sent it likewise aflame high in the air. Where the balls landed, still alight, a dangerous game of football was played, the balls being kicked about until extinguished. The boys of Heriot's Hospital were enthusiastic spectators and often participated in these contests.

As Gairdner's weaving business at Tipperlinn prospered, he opened a warehouse in the then new and fashionable South Bridge, this being registered as "Ebenezer Gairdner and Son". Gairdner died in 1797. His son, also Ebenezer, continued the well-established family business and became Deacon of Edinburgh's Incorporation of Weavers (or Websters) in 1798. The weaver's motto, *Sine me nudus,* and their insignia, a representation of Adam before the Fall, were once to be seen above the doorways of several old houses in the West Port.

While weaving (which ceased in 1856) still prospered at Tipperlinn another very different industry, foreshadowing the coming scientific age, was established just to the north-west of the village, on an acre of ground feued from John Orr, who farmed at Granthill and Morningside. This was a chemical plant for the manufacture of sulphuric acid, established in 1770 by the surgeon Dr Thomas Steel of Grangebank House in Burghmuirhead, in partnership with Walter Neilson of Bothwellshields and Thomas Gladstanes of Leith. The firm, Steel, Gladstanes & Company, was commonly known as the Tipperlinn Chemical Works. The Thomas Gladstanes of this enterprise was the grandfather of the famous Victorian Prime Minister.

The chemical plant at Tipperlinn appears to have been surrounded by a certain air of mystery in the minds of villagers and boys attending

Morningside's old schoolhouse, being referred to as "the black works". Eventually it was transferred to Glasgow and absorbed into the growing Imperial Chemical Industries.

The third industry at Tipperlinn was pioneer "tourism". From about the mid-eighteenth century the village became a summer health resort for wealthy Edinburgh citizens drawn by its relative remoteness and beneficial climate. It was this attraction of the city's "best people" that gave use to the taunting rhyme of the village children, "Tipperlinn's the bonnie place, Where a' the ladies dine."

When Dr Thomas Chalmers came to live in Morningside in 1840 he joined the Kirk Session, and Tipperlinn, along with Merchiston and Burghmuirhead, was allocated to him as his district for visitation as an elder. In 1891 his nephew, David Chalmers of Redhall in Colinton, wrote to the Rev. Dr Thomas Addis, the minister of the Parish Church who had "come out" at the Disruption and become the first minister of Morningside's Free Church: "I formed a kindly acquaintanceship with that now extinct and rural hamlet Tipperlinn . . . James Knox who had been an eminent land surveyor occupied the largest and principal house at the south end of the row . . . My youngest brother James took lessons from Knox in land surveying and I recollect we occupied many an early summer's morning in a trigonometrical and geodetical survey of the proposed new parish, which was afterwards adopted and confirmed at a

Morningside - aerial view
By courtesy of Aerofilms, London

181

meeting of the presbytery in the new church . . . I cannot part from the hamlet of Tipperlinn without recalling the spare figure of its patriarch in those days, William Munnoch, a handloom weaver."

The David Chalmers who wrote this letter was the son of Charles Chalmers, the first headmaster of Merchiston Castle School and brother of Dr. Thomas Chalmers. James Knox the surveyor was well known for his plans of Edinburgh in about 1820. While these, including one of 1812 which shows both Morningside and Tipperlinn, may still be seen, the survey referred to in the letter, which Knox carried out for Morningside Parish Church, opened in 1838, cannot now be found. About half a century later, Sir James Steel, Lord Provost of Edinburgh (1900-03) was responsible for much housing development in the Tipperlinn district and other parts of Edinburgh. This was the Lord Provost under whose "reign" cable tramcars were introduced into Edinburgh and who was responsible for supervising the establishment of the City Fever Hospital at Greenbank Drive. It was at the opening ceremony of this hospital performed by King Edward VII, that Sir James Steel was created a baronet.

James Goodfellow of Newington United Presbyterian Church, who carried out devoted missionary work in the south side, describes, in his interesting book *The Print of His Shoe* (1906), his labours in Newington, Grange and Causewayside. "One fine type of an old Scottish grandmother," he wrote, "born and brought up in the picturesque hamlet of Tipperlinn, carried with her to the Court [Grange Court] the traditions of the weaving industry of the village and of the famed patriotic tablecloths which Yeben [Ebenezer] Gairdner designed for Queen Charlotte and which gained for him the title of 'Damask Weaver to Her Majesty'. She was much respected by her new neighbours. When a girl, she walked from Tipperlinn to 'Burghmuirhead Schule' and had a lively recollection of examination days when Mr Henshaw, the schoolmaster would march his pupils in procession from the foot of Canaan Lane to the schoolroom, his brother leading the way with the bagpipes, doing his best to stir their young hearts with patriotic enthusiasm by the enlivening music of the pibroch, greatly to the admiration of the onlookers." Whether the "Burghmuirhead Schule" referred to is the old Morningside village school or some other institution is difficult to discover.

When David Chalmers wrote to Dr Addis in 1891 and James Goodfellow compiled his book a little later, the picturesque village of Tipperlinn to which both refer had long since disappeared in the wake of the laudable new enterprise, the "asylum for the cure or relief of mental derangement".

Today nothing remains of the ancient village except the old draw-well in the garden of Viewfield House and a stone, one foot high and with a semi-circular head, bearing the date "1660". It stands on the right-hand side of the roadway leading from Tipperlinn Road to the Royal Edinburgh Hospital, against the garden wall of Tipperlinn House, now a special unit

182

Restoration of the Monarchy stone, 1660. This relic of the old village of Tipperlinn still stands to the west of the roadway leading past Tipperlinn House to the Royal Edinburgh Hospital

By courtesy of Mr Brian Smith

for adolescent patients. This stone is believed to commemorate the restoration of the monarchy after the death of Cromwell. A number of similar stones are to be found in other places in Scotland. Perhaps this one, in what was once the high street of old Tipperlinn, was first erected somewhere near its present site by the weavers who here plied their craft a century before Ebenezer Gairdner, who inherited from them and expressed in his work his community's patriotism and loyalty.

THE ROYAL EDINBURGH HOSPITAL

It was a stroke of good fortune which brought fame to Gairdner and to Tipperlinn as a community of weavers, and it was another man's sad misfortune which was to sweep away this ancient village and establish on its site a great and beneficial institution. Whereas Gairdner wove patterns in cloth, the man whose tragic fate brought a new era for Tipperlinn wove words and ideas: he was Robert Fergusson, one of Scotland's greatest poets, to whom the much more feted Robert Burns expressed deep gratitude for inspiration received. Fergusson was a poet of such genius that Robert Louis Stevenson was proud to call himself his reincarnation.

The story of the Royal Edinburgh Hospital is so rooted in the history of Edinburgh in the latter half of the eighteenth century that the period merits description in some detail. This was "Edinburgh's Golden Age", which one contemporary writer described as "a hotbed of genius". An English visitor in 1769 wrote: "Here I stand at what is called the Cross of Edinburgh and can, in a few minutes, take fifty men of genius and learning by the hands." Edinburgh's famous men, philosophers, artists, architects and economists, included such immortals as David Hume, Adam Smith, Allan Ramsay and Robert Adam. For over half a century the Scottish capital rivalled and perhaps even outshone London and Paris as a centre of learning.

If the Edinburgh of the late eighteenth century pulsed with intellectual vigour and achievement, it was also, and perhaps because of this, a city of great gaiety and colourful social life for the wealthy. In the many taverns and inns which enlivened the honeycomb of famous closes in the Old Town over a score of clubs flourished. In these the city's merchants, writers, artists, lawyers and other professional men foregathered in the evenings. Among the clubs were such famous institutions as the Friday Club (the membership of which included Sir Walter Scott, Lord Cockburn, Professor John Playfair, Sydney Smith and the Rev. John Thomson of Duddingston, a distinguished landscape painter), the Poker Club (of which David Hume, Adam Smith and Fletcher of Saltoun were members) and the Cape Club (graced by the celebrated painter Runciman, John Rennie, a civil engineer of distinction, James Watt, the pioneer of the steam engine, and the renowned portrait painter Henry Raeburn). Other clubs, each with its own distinctive ritual of procedure, included the Spendthrift, the Hellfire and the Crochallan Fencibles.

Most celebrated of the many taverns in which clubs met was Johnny Dowie's in Libberton's Wynd, a little back from the south side of the High Street on the site of the present-day George IV Bridge. It was in this tavern that Robert Burns wrote much of his work. Here "mine host", in cocked hat and with buckles on knees and shoes, supervised the varied and liberal fare until the stroke of midnight was heard from the many nearby clocktowers. A special delicacy on Johnny Dowie's menu was Nor' Loch trout—washed down with the specially potent heavy beer for which Edinburgh brewers were at that time famed far beyond Scotland.

Nor' Loch trout was but one of many special delicacies available in Edinburgh's social circles in the eighteenth century. By 1729, the English custom of morning and afternoon tea had been adopted by the Edinburgh gentry. Food of all kinds was plentiful and wines from the Continent such as claret and hock were cheap. Lunch or dinner might include crab, mussels, shrimps or oysters, all "fresh drawn frae the Forth" and available at reasonable prices. So abundant were lobsters that they provided a highly profitable export trade. While fish were not always of good size or quality, due, according to certain writers of the time, to the laziness of local fishermen who were unwilling to venture into the deeper waters of the Forth, meat of many kinds was plentiful. Vast quantities of strawberries and cherries seem to have been available, and even home-grown pineapples. The quality of butter and cheese was, however, poor. So interesting was the variety and abundance of food and wine available that several historians have chosen to record the most fascinating statistics in great detail. In the midst of such abundance, however, the poor of the city, who were many, existed largely on potatoes and cheap drink.

Nearly a score of newspapers and reviews were published, daily or weekly. Industry prospered, supported by an impressive network of trade and craft incorporations and guilds. Intellectual vigour and achievement flourished too. Good food and wine was plentiful, and night-life was throbbing and convivial. This was the Edinburgh into which Robert Fergusson was born on September 5th, 1750, in Cap and Feather Close off Halkerstone's Wynd in the High Street. Fergusson's parents were working class but financial assistance through the award of a bursary enabled their son to be sent to the High School, where he showed promise in Classics which encouraged the hope that he might enter the ministry. He was awarded a bursary to Dundee Grammar School and later gained entrance to St Andrew's University.

Robert Fergusson

By courtesy of the Scottish National Portrait Gallery

Young Robert Fergusson's performance at St Andrew's was average. One of his tutors wrote of him: "Lighthearted — his poetry ran away with him." He had not been long at St Andrew's when his father died and soon afterwards he was obliged to leave without taking his degree. He was sent by his mother to live with an uncle at Old Meldrum in Aberdeenshire. His uncle was a man of confused attitudes and strict religious outlook who treated his nephew unkindly. Young Robert, unable to endure the situation, left, walking the whole distance back to Edinburgh. This marathon journey seemed to undermine his health which was never good thereafter.

Living once again with his mother and sister in Warriston Close, opposite St Giles, Fergusson obtained a post as a copy-writer in the Commissary's Office in the city — and well may we imagine the former university student of some promise whose "poetry ran away with him" struggling against daily boredom and frustration.

Nevertheless, like so many creative artists who have triumphed over the most uncongenial circumstances, young Robert Fergusson persevered and continued to write — and as a result Scotland's cultural heritage became immeasurably richer. On January 2nd, 1772, when he was twenty-two, his first major poem was published in the important and widely read *Ruddiman's Magazine*. This was "The Daft Days", and, in the readily receptive literary circles of eighteenth-century Edinburgh, its appearance brought Fergusson fame overnight.

> Now mirk December's dowie face
> Glowers our the rigs wi' sour grimace,
> While thro' his minimum of space
> The bleer ey'd sun
> Wi' blinkin' light and stealin' pace
> His race doth run.

Other works of obvious genius quickly followed: "Caller Oysters", "Hallow Fair", "The Tron Kirk Bell" and "Braid Claith", each capturing the atmosphere and spirit of the Edinburgh of that time. Scotland's "newly arrived" poet became the toast of the Capital's cultural circles and, especially, of the clubs of the Old Town, and his company and readings were eagerly sought.

The famous Cape Club, which met in various "Cape halls", notably the Isle of Man Arms in Craigs' Close near the Royal Exchange, was privileged to add Fergusson's name to its long and celebrated membership roll (which included Raeburn, Runciman and Watt — and the notorious Deacon Brodie, who was to inspire Robert Louis Stevenson's *Dr Jekyll and Mr Hyde*). The Cape's membership, unlike that of most other such clubs, was of varied social and professional background. Each member was styled a Knight of the Cape and given a mock title such as "Sir

186

Brunstone", "Sir Macaroni", or "Sir Discovery". Robert Fergusson, the club's poet laureate, became "Sir Precentor". The club's stated object expressed the spirit of Edinburgh's intellectual night-life: "After the business of the day is over, to pass the evening socially with a set of select companions in an agreeable but at the same time rational and frugal manner." Beer and porter were the traditional drinks, and conversation and song — and, after Fergusson's admission, poetry — were the principal entertainments of the evening.

As the young poet's reputation spread one can imagine his having enjoyed almost nightly acclaim, either at the Cape Club or at private social gatherings in the homes of many of Edinburgh's most influential people. Of most likeable personality, with a lively sense of humour and a fine singing voice, one can imagine, further, that, as an evening wore on and the beer and wine flowed, Fergusson would be called upon again and again to entertain the company. In such stimulating and appreciative surroundings his imagination soared. The daily boredom of the Commissary's Office would then seem far away, and would later be endured for the sake of another night of poetry, song and conviviality to follow.

For nearly a year Fergusson enjoyed the euphoria of success. Then the first reactions set in. As yet another evening of intellectual ecstasy ended at the Cape Club and his fellow Knights of the Cape took leave of him and made their way to comfortable homes in the city, the effects of the night's heavy drinking gradually wore off and reality slowly seeped back into Fergusson's mind like the gradual dispersal of a haar over the Firth of Forth. As he turned into his own rather less well-appointed home in Warriston Close he might have shared the emotion of loneliness so well expressed by Gray in his *Elegy* when he wrote the line: "And leaves the world to darkness and to me." Fergusson was increasingly encountering a mental darkness: the heaviness of depression, the deadening effect of melancholia. He now wrote his "Tavern Elegy":

> Now the short taper warns me to depart
> 'Ere darkness shall assume his dreary sway,
> 'Ere solitude fall heavy on my heart
> That lingers for the far approach of day.
> Who would not vindicate the happy doom
> To be forever numbered with the dead
> Rather than bear the miserable gloom
> When all his comfort, all his friends are fled.
> Bear me, ye Gods, where I may calmly rest
> From all the follies of the night secure,
> The balmy blessings of repose to taste,
> Nor hear the tongue of outrage at the door.

The inner struggle deepened. He became withdrawn and haunted by

187

despair. In the autumn of 1773 "he retired to the country to seek the peace of mind he had in vain sought for in the town", but the same restlessness soon drove him back to Edinburgh. He continued to write for *Ruddiman's Magazine* but his poetry was now tinged with melancholy and his anticipation of death. He withdrew from company and suffered feelings of guilt and remorse for what he considered to be his dissipated and idle life. He was unable to sleep; he burned his manuscripts and wrote no more.

Early in 1774 Fergusson seemed to show slight improvement. By way of diversion he took part in a political election campaign, but this led to renewed drinking bouts and his sense of despair returned. The Cape Club minutes record "Sir Precentor as persistently absent", and on 2nd July, 1774 they note a decision "to devote the remainder of the fines of the absentees of this meeting for the benefit and assistance of a young gentleman, a member of the Cape, who has been a considerable time past in distress."

On July 28th, 1774 the *Caledonian Mercury* reported that the poet had "been seized with a very serious sickness", and on September 3rd the Cape Club minutes regretted "Sir Precentor's continued absence because he has been very ill". One evening later that month the poet's gloom appeared to lift; he went out with some friends and, writes his first biographer, Sommers: "He was taking a glass of wine . . . when he had the misfortune to fall from a staircase by which he received a violent concussion of the head." Recovering, he murmured his favourite song, composed in earlier days, "The Birks of Invermay", rendering it with a pathos unsurpassed in the happy moments of his convivial brilliance.

Fergusson soon refused all food and drink, becoming violent "so that three men could hardly restrain him". Eventually, now beyond the pathetic attempts of his mother and sister to look after him, "he was removed raving to the madhouse amidst their lamentations". Early in October 1774 the minute book of the Old Edinburgh Charity Workhouse has this chilling entry: "Mr Fergusson in the cells."

The Charity Workhouse had been built by Edinburgh Town Council in 1698. Its site is described by Grant in *Old and New Edinburgh:* "Those who see Forrest Road now . . . can form no conception of the features of the locality for more than a hundred years before 1850. A great archway [in the Telfer Wall] led from Bristo Port by a winding pathway a hundred yards along [now Forrest Road] . . . to a wicket, or klicket-gate in the city wall opposite the centre walk of the Meadows. On the west side rose the enormous mass of the old Charity Workhouse . . . on its east side were the ancient offices of the Darien Company, the Correction House and the Bedlam. . ." James Skene of Rubislaw's valuable collection of pen-and-wash and water-colour drawings now housed in the city's Central Public Library includes a view of the Bedlam behind the old city wall. An inscription high on the wall of the tenement at the south-west end of

The Edinburgh Bedlam behind the old city wall. Long since demolished, its site is marked today within the triangle formed by Bristo Port, Teviot Place and Forrest Road. Here Fergusson spent the last weeks of his life
Water-colour by James Skene from the Edinburgh Room collection of the Edinburgh Central Public Library

Bristo Port commemorates the site of the Darien Building built in 1698.

Comrie, in his *History of Scottish Medicine,* also describes the Bedlam as being attached to the Charity Workhouse. Smith, in his biography of Fergusson, notes that it was annexed to Darien House, was known as "the Schelles" and was situated in the south-east corner of the triangle made by Teviot Place, Bristo Port and Forrest Road (laid out in 1842), inside the old city wall which ran opposite the present Medical School.

It was to the Bedlam that Fergusson was taken. "A dreary and sequestered mansion", his biographer Sommers called it. First attempts to take the poet there had been strongly resisted. Sommers continues: "On pretence of taking him in the evening to visit a friend, he was put into a sedan chair and carried to the place. When the sedan chair was set down in the narrow lobby, Fergusson instantly detected the decoy and fraud — showing restored sanity — and gave a great cry. This was answered by shrieks from the other wretched captives in the house." After his first sleepless night of confinement, when "he paced his cell in sullen sadness", he inquired of the keeper who had brought him there. Being told, "Friends," Fergusson replied: "Yes, friends indeed. They think I am too

189

wicked to live, but you will see me a burning and a shining light." "You have been so already," responded the kindly keeper. "You mistake me," said Fergusson. "I mean you shall see me and hear of me as a bright minister of the gospel."

The name Bedlam was applied to many primitive asylums for the insane in Britain; the Edinburgh one, established in 1698, was amongst the first. The original Bedlam was in the Hospital of St Mary of Bethlehem in London, opened in 1545 and administered, as was common in pre-Reformation days, by an order of nuns dedicated to Our Lady of Bethlehem. In the course of time the name Bethlehem became vulgarised to "Bedlam". While as early as the fourteenth century, in Robert II's reign, records refer to houses set aside for "the keeping of the furious", the Edinburgh Bedlam was the first of its kind in Scotland. The Old Royal Infirmary of Edinburgh, opened in 1738, had, however, made provision, under ground level, for the insane.

Comrie also provides some detail of the conditions endured by Fergusson in the Edinburgh Bedlam: "Twenty cells on the ground floor are damp, where the patients in winter must suffer severely from the cold. Part of these attached to the old city wall have no fireplaces or other means of heating, nor any other building above or below them. They are lighted and aired solely by openings in the doors by which they are entered and which doors open on to a courtyard in which the patients walk. The noise and cries which issue from these cells must thus be dreadfully distressing to the other patients. Keeping patients in bed or in chains so that they cannot injure other patients is considered the sole object of the duties of the keepers."

Fergusson's final sufferings in such conditions were mercifully brief. Even in his anguish and confusion his early study of the classics was not forgotten, as one recorded incident revealed. One evening when a cloud passed over the moon, the poet cried out: "Great Jupiter, snuff the moon!" As the darkness increased he exclaimed, in a tone of great vehemence and with gesticulation: "Thou Great God hath heard me!"

During his short confinement in the Bedlam Fergusson was visited regularly by his mother and sister, when many pathetic scenes occurred. Dr John Aitken, a prominent Edinburgh doctor of the time, recorded the hapless poet's situation as "a bed of straw on a stone floor and surrounded by inmates of criminal background." The cultured and sophisticated surroundings of the poet's heyday in the Cape Club were long past. Even the visits of some of his distinguished friends of those days brought no relief. During what was to be the last visit by his mother and sister he begged them not to leave him, but they were not permitted to stay. Early the next day, October 16th, 1774, Robert Fergusson died, at the age of twenty-four.

Robert Burns on many occasions acknowledged his unqualified indebtedness to Fergusson and attributed to him a decisive influence on the future of Scottish poetry. Indeed Burns revealed that at one point he had "given up rhyming altogether until meeting with Fergusson's Scottish poems, when I strung anew my wildly sounding lyre." The Ayrshire bard, in his "Epistle to William Simpson", expressed his bitter reaction to the manner in which, he alleged, Fergusson was latterly neglected:

> O Fergusson! thy glorious pairts
> Ill suited law's dry, musty airts!
> My curse upon your whunstane hearts
> Ye E'nburgh Gentry!
> The tythe o' what ye waste at cartes
> Wad stow'd his pantry!

During his stay in Edinburgh nearly twelve years after Fergusson's death, Burns was again indignant when he witnessed the neglected state of the Edinburgh poet's grave in the churchyard of Canongate Kirk. In 1789, at his own expense, Burns erected the plain but dignified headstone which now marks Fergusson's resting place, and composed the inscription:

> Here lies Robert Fergusson, Poet
> Born Septr. 5th. 1751
> Died Octr. 16th. 1774
> No sculptured marble here, nor pompous lay,
> No storied urn, nor animated Bust;
> This simple Stone directs Pale Scotia's way,
> To pour her Sorrows o'er her Poet's Dust.

The date of Fergusson's birth is stated wrongly, the year being 1750 not 1751. On the back of the stone is engraved: "By special grant of the Managers to Robert Burns, who erected this stone, this burial place is to remain forever sacred to the memory of Robert Fergusson."

Another man who had valued Fergusson's friendship and admired his genius, erected a more lasting and living memorial to his name. In addition to Dr John Aitken, the ill-fated poet's medical attendant during the last stages of his mental illness, two other Edinburgh doctors witnessed Fergusson's sufferings. One was Dr Alexander ("Lang Sandie") Wood, one of the city's most distinguished and much-loved physicians. The other was his young "apprentice", Dr Andrew Duncan.

Duncan had known Fergusson before his illness and may well have attended some of the meetings of the Cape Club during the height of the young poet's success. So appalled and saddened was he when he observed Fergusson's last agonising days, standing by helplessly, that he resolved to dedicate himself to the establishment in Edinburgh of an asylum for the more humane and enlightened treatment of the insane. Duncan's resolve and perseverance were to be rewarded: he was to see the opening of what is now the Royal Edinburgh Hospital in Morningside. Such were the obstacles, however, that this was not to come about until nearly forty years after Fergusson's death.

The long delay was not due to any lack of effort on Dr Andrew Duncan's part. Although many other prominent Edinburgh citizens had also been deeply disturbed by the circumstances of Fergusson's demise, it was not easy to persuade them or the authorities to translate regret into, financial support for his proposals. The young doctor had to wait patiently until he had achieved a position of influence.

His ability soon became apparent. Indeed, a year before Fergusson's death, Dr Andrew Duncan had established a quarterly medical journal which became the *Annals of Medicine,* of which his gifted son, also Dr Andrew Duncan, was to succeed him as editor. The founding of Edinburgh's first public medical dispensary in West Richmond Street in 1776 was another of Dr. Andrew Duncan's early achievements, and this was followed by an important series of lectures on the theory of medicine. In 1790 he was elected President of the Royal College of Physicians of Edinburgh and in the same year was appointed to the Chair of the Institutes of Medicine, succeeding a distinguished Morningside resident, Professor James Gregory of Canaan Lodge.

In 1791, having now achieved a position of considerable eminence not only in medical circles but also in the life of the city, Dr Duncan renewed his campaign for the establishment of an asylum. His personal appeals for funds, however, still drew little response. He persuaded Edinburgh's Lord Provost and other citizens of note to issue a public appeal but again this met with a poor response. Yet a further plea to Lord Provost Neil MacVicar proved fruitless. This appeal recommended that an application be made to Parliament for the appropriation of the considerable amount of money bequeathed by John Watson for pious and charitable purposes in Edinburgh. John Watson, who died in 1762, had left £4,721 for the establishment of a school for the education of children of professional gentlemen who had died prematurely or suffered misfortune. Watson's trustees, by careful investment, had increased his bequest to over £90,000 by 1823. This money was, however, used instead to found the John Watson Institution in the Dean district at Belford Road.

In 1807 the University Principal, George Baird, came to Dr Duncan's aid, and his public appeal was more effective. Through the influence of the Lord Advocate, Henry Erskine, and Sir John Sinclair, Parliament then agreed to contribute £2,000 from funds obtained from the sale of Highland estates forfeited by landowners who had supported Bonnie Prince Charlie in the '45 Rebellion. Thus, as one official account of its history comments: "The Royal Edinburgh Hospital owes its origin not only to the tragic death of Robert Fergusson, but also to the tragic destiny of Bonnie Prince Charlie." Fergusson, incidentally, had been a Jacobite. In commemoration of the efforts of Henry Erskine and John Sinclair, two wards in the present-day hospital are named after them.

192

The money obtained permitted the purchase of four acres of land on the Morningside Estate from Catherine Burnett, wife of Alexander Forbes of Shivas, for the sum of £1,420. A second substantial contribution, £1,700, came from a group of Scotsmen in India.

Dr Duncan's unrelenting perseverance had at last been rewarded. In 1807 he was granted a Royal Charter for the establishment of the Asylum and two years later, on June 8th, 1809, he had the satisfaction of seeing its foundation stone laid by William Coulter, then Lord Provost of Edinburgh, the man who, thirty years earlier, had built the mansion-house on the nearby Falcon estate which was subsequently to become Falcon Hall. The inscription on the foundation stone read, "An asylum for the cure and relief of mental derangement." When it came to designing the building, Robert Reid, the King's Architect for Scotland, who designed St George's Church in Charlotte Square, offered his services without charge.

The new asylum, known as the East House and described as "a grim grey building", was ready by July 1813, its site being the area now bounded by Millar Crescent, Morningside Terrace, Maxwell Street and Morningside Road. The grounds were enclosed by a high stone wall extending from what is now Morningside Park, down Morningside Road, turning right along the back of what is now Maxwell Street, where part of it remains. The entrance to the asylum was by a large wooden gate nearly opposite what is now Jordan Lane. The little entrance lodge, which remained on the west side of Morningside Road until about 1900, was rebuilt as the gardener's cottage and is still to be seen on the right, just inside the entrance to the Royal Edinburgh Hospital from Morningside Terrace.

On July 19th, 1813 the first five private fee-paying patients were admitted. Thirteen years later, the records state that all patients from the old city Bedlam, where Fergusson had died, had been transferred to the East House at Morningside.

At the date of its opening, just over £7,500 had been contributed, from the sources already mentioned and from private donations. The new Edinburgh Asylum was not the first to be established in Scotland. A number of Scottish doctors had pioneered a new approach, a more humane attitude, to those suffering from mental illness. As a result of their efforts beneficial institutions had been opened at Montrose in 1782 and in Aberdeen in 1800. In England in 1796 William Tuke, the Yorkshire Quaker, had founded his Retreat at York, while in Paris four years earlier Philipe Pinel had dramatically pioneered in Europe a new "humane era" in the treatment of the insane by undoing the chains which bound fifty-three of his patients in the Bicetre Hospital, a bold step which was severely criticised by many of his medical colleagues. In Pinel's hospital the new era meant comfortable wards, warm clothing, good food and other personal comforts for patients.

A portrait by Raeburn of Dr Andrew Duncan, founder of Edinburgh's first asylum for the insane. On the right is a framed picture of the original asylum building, the East House

The original Edinburgh asylum building, the East House, between Morningside Park and Maxwell Street

From the outset, the directors of the new Edinburgh Asylum at Morningside, including Dr Duncan and his son, closely studied Pinel's work, and two young Edinburgh doctors, Robert Christison and Andrew Combe, went to Paris to train under Pinel, later becoming managers of the Morningside Hospital. Dr Robert Christison was to become Professor of Forensic Medicine and later of Pharmacology, and was the leading figure of his day in the Edinburgh Medical School. His autobiography gives a vivid picture of his life and times. Fittingly, on September 26th, 1930, the centenary of Pinel's death, a bust of the great French psychiatrist was unveiled by the French Ambassador to Britain. This was placed above the entrance of the old West House, now McKinnon House. As the original entrance door is now at the rear of the building, the bust of Pinel was re-sited in a special walled section in front of the entrance to McKinnon House. Pinel is now surrounded by the sculpted heads of several other

194

pioneers and supporters of advancement in the treatment of mental illness. These are William Tuke, Dr Andrew Duncan, Florence Nightingale, Dorothea Lydia Dix, Robert Gardiner Hill and Campbell Clark. The original bust of Pinel was erected in Morningside before any such tribute to him in France.

At first the new Edinburgh Asylum of 1813 was supervised by two visiting physicians, Dr Thomas Spens and Dr Andrew Duncan the younger. The first superintendent was Mr Hughes from St Luke's Hospital, London, whose wife acted as matron. Mr and Mrs Hughes, who were not qualified in medicine, were succeeded by Mr and Mrs Radley who had some experience working in London and Dundee. The three-storey house in which they lived still stands at Churchhill on the north side of the entrance to Abbotsford Park. It is an austere, tall villa, the ground floor of which now comprises two shops, 102 and 104 Morningside Road, the upper floors being residential.

From its establishment, admission to the new Edinburgh Asylum was restricted to private patients who, or whose families, could afford to pay £56 per annum in fees. This was the subject of much public controversy over the years. A full account of this, and of the changes resulting from successive Parliamentary Lunacy Acts from 1815 onwards, is contained in an important Memorandum by Dr Arthur Mitchell, M.D., one of Her Majesty's Commissioners in Lunacy for Scotland, published in 1882. In Dr Mitchell's Memorandum, reference is made to Dr Andrew Duncan's concern to establish an asylum. "In my opinion", Dr Duncan had stated, "it is impossible to conceive a more interesting object of charity than the man of genius when a pauper lunatic." Dr Duncan's initial concern had been for those of ability and distinction who developed mental illness. Nevertheless, he did advocate better treatment for all sufferers. Yet, despite this wider consideration, in 1882, over a century after Robert Fergusson had died, controversy still raged over what should be done for those "of humbler origin".

By July 1840 the East House building had been finally completed at a total cost of £27,000. Three years earlier, the asylum Management Board had decided to build an extension to the original premises, and this became known as the Western Department or West House. This new building was opened in 1842.

In 1841 Queen Victoria, who had contributed to the cost of the extension, agreed to become patron of the hospital and the title "Royal Edinburgh Asylum" was thus adopted. With the opening of the West House it became possible to admit patients unable to pay fees. Fees demanded were now in fact reduced to £15 per annum, though "pauper patients" were frequently not required to pay, being maintained by their Parish Councils. By 1882 the Royal Edinburgh Asylum decided to restrict the number of pauper patients to four hundred. However, the substantial income received from private patients eventually made it possible to admit more and more pauper patients. From the outset the Edinburgh Asylum admitted patients from any part of Scotland and this remained its policy, but when Rosslynlee Asylum was opened in 1874, the Royal Edinburgh Asylum was able to restrict admission to patients residing in Edinburgh.

For fifteen years after the opening, in 1813, of the asylum for which he had so long and so unrelentingly campaigned, Dr Andrew Duncan was closely associated with it. On July 5th, 1828 he died in his eighty-fourth year, and the Town Council accorded him the tribute of a public funeral. He was buried in the little Buccleuch Cemetery now overshadowed by the great Appleton and Hume Towers of Edinburgh University in George Square. The walls surrounding his grave bear commemorative plaques to young medical students and doctors whom he had specially befriended and who pre-deceased him. He had requested that they be interred close to where he himself would finally be laid to rest. On the south wall of the enclosure is a plaque to Charles Darwin, uncle of the famous author of *The Origin of Species* and a biologist of some note.

A feature of Dr Andrew Duncan's life seems to have been his remarkable capacity for getting things done, and always with great tact and good humour. The spirit of comradeship and conviviality which he infused into the medical profession of his day was one of the outstanding achievements of his life — and indeed his achievements were many, extending far beyond the establishment of the Edinburgh Asylum. He founded also the Royal Dispensary in West Richmond Street, the first such establishment in the city for the medical care of people in poor circumstances. For his public services, the freedom of the City was conferred on Dr Duncan in 1808. He obtained royal charters for the dispensary and the asylum, and also for the Royal Medical Society of Edinburgh and the Royal Caledonian Horticultural Society, both of which he was instrumental in founding. His versatility and range of interests was extremely wide. The Aesculapian Club, the Harveian Society, the Medico-Chirurgical Society and a gymnastic club were also results of his practical enthusiasm. Such labours did not diminish his physical stamina: in his eighty-fourth year he climbed Arthur's Seat on May Day morning, a practice he had begun fifty years before. A portrait of Dr Andrew Duncan by his close friend Henry Raeburn, whom he greatly encouraged, is treasured still in the premises of the Edinburgh Royal College of Physicians in Queen Street, while another hangs in the National Portrait Gallery in Queen Street. Yet another, by a pupil of Raeburn, may be seen in the old banqueting hall of the Royal Edinburgh Hospital at Craighouse.

A fitting tribute to the hospital's founder is the Andrew Duncan Clinic, an important unit in a modern extension of the Royal Edinburgh Hospital, opened by Queen Elizabeth, the Queen Mother, in 1965. In the entrance hall to the clinic a display cabinet contains many documents and maps illustrating the history of the hospital. Included is the original charter granted to Dr Andrew Duncan in 1807.

When, in 1837, the Management Board of the Edinburgh Asylum decided to build the new extension to be known as the Western Department or West House, Dr William Mackinnon of Aberdeen was, in anticipation of the development, appointed its first Physician Superintendent. When he took up his appointment in 1839 there was a great influx of pauper patients.

The proposed West House revived a problem for people still living in the adjacent village of Tipperlinn. Ever since the feuing out of the Wester Burgh Muir in 1586, the residents of Tipperlinn had enjoyed a right-of-way from the village down to the Pow (later the Jordan) Burn, where, in time-honoured fashion, the women did their washing in this once strongly-flowing stream. In 1701, during the Riding of the Marches, the Town Council noted that the Laird of Merchiston had planted trees along the right-of-way, and some of these which tended to cause an obstruction were ordered to be removed. Over a century later the managers of the asylum, wishing to extend East House westwards across the right-of-way to the Pow Burn, readily obtained permission from the Governors of George Watson's Hospital who owned the land but were blocked by protests from the villagers of Tipperlinn insisting on their time-honoured rights. Although the firm attitude of the Tipperlinn people was considered "unreasonable and based on absurd whims", the asylum managers were forced to revise their plans and build new premises further to the west of East House. Even so, the villagers objected to "the discomforts and dangers of passing so close to a mental hospital", and the hospital managers were compelled to link East House and West House by an underground passageway and to erect two very high walls. The original wall of West House still remains in Morningside Terrace.

The route of the ancient right-of-way may still be traced. From the roadway at the corner of Tipperlinn Road and Morningside Place (now the northern entrance to the Royal Edinburgh Hospital), it passed Tipperlinn House on the right (now the Young People's Unit) and the gardener's cottage on the left, and ran into Morningside Terrace to the right and down the little steep lane (now inaccesible) which ran eastwards along the boundary fence of what, until some years ago, was the coal depot of the railway goods yard. This lane then turned right past the west gable end of Maxwell Street and crossed Maxwell Street, continuing to the present-day railway footbridge and into Balcarres Street. Just to the right, beyond the railway footbridge as one emerges into Balcarres Street, the substantial burn from Comiston, which still joins the Jordan Burn at the back of Maxwell Street, may once have formed a number of pools and it is possible that it was here that the women of Tipperlinn came to wash their clothes. Another reason for the right-of-way continuing beyond the Jordan Burn into what is now Balcarres Street was that, in earlier times, it led into open fields from which the Tipperlinn villagers were able to dig peat.

Some forty years after the dispute between the villagers of Tipperlinn and the asylum managers over the preservation of the right-of-way, the issue again arose. In 1883 the hospital authorities and the newly formed Edinburgh and South Side Suburban Junction Railway Company were entering into an agreement which would permit the railway company to close the old pathway skirting the northern and western boundaries of its newly acquired land. The Bill then before Parliament, which contained certain clauses granting the Railway Company the right to close part of the right-of-way, was opposed by two of the feudal superiors across whose land the pathway ran. When the House of Commons passed the Bill, one of these local feu-owners challenged it when it came before the House of Lords. The Lords decreed that the Tipperlinn right-of-way did not fall within the jurisdiction of Parliament but was the responsibility of the Edinburgh City Police. The clause in favour of the railway company was therefore rejected, although by this time the last of the cottages at Tipperlinn had long since been swept away. The railway authorities were forced to build the footbridge leading to Balcarres Street. Thus, after

A small ivory medallion with, on one side, a miniature portrait of Dr Andrew Duncan by Sir Henry Raeburn and, on the reverse, an enclosed lock of Robert Fergusson's hair.

several centuries, the ancient right-of-way from the old village was still upheld by the highest authority in the land.

About twenty-five years ago, however, the little pathway from the south end of Morningside Terrace to the back of Maxwell Street was at last closed—as the result of a fire in the adjacent stonemason's which rendered a section of the original East House boundary wall skirting the yard and pathway unsafe. More recently, the building of a new telephone exchange in the former coal depot has led to the final disappearance of the ancient pathway.

Soon after West House was opened, further land was purchased which surrounded the old village of Myreside and included Myreside Cottage. For long this last remainder of the village was used as a hospital annexe, but it was destroyed by fire some years ago.

Dr Mackinnon, whose term as Physician Superintendent lasted seven years, introduced many innovations. These included dormitories to replace the original solitary "cells". The stay of patients was made more congenial by the introduction of such recreational pursuits as music,

Medallion with lock of Robert Fergusson's hair and a dedication to Dr Andrew Duncan

199

literary lectures, gardening and excursions into the country. Religious services became a prominent feature of hospital life. A library and museum were also established and Dr Mackinnon encouraged all patients capable of doing so to pursue the occupation they had followed before their admission, and as a result the hospital community became to a large degree self-supporting. Carpentry, tailoring, shoemaking, basketry, bookbinding and printing, along with sewing, knitting, embroidery and domestic work for female patients, were among the activities encouraged. Those qualified as teachers were persuaded to educate illiterate patients.

A particularly enterprising step was the installation of a printing press on September 15th, 1845. By drawing upon the literary talents — often of a high order — of several patients, a most interesting hospital magazine *The Morningside Mirror* was published, and this continues to be produced today, over one hundred and thirty years later.

Among sporting activities encouraged at the hospital, cricket was one of the first to be taken up with enthusiasm, the earliest match taking place in 1845. In the archives of the Royal Edinburgh Hospital, now preserved in the Edinburgh University Library, is a water-colour painted by a patient in 1878 and entitled "The Great Irrational Cricket Match". It portrays a match between the staff and patients of Morningside and those of the asylum at Larbert, played on the fine lawn at the rear of the original Larbert Asylum, now Bellsdyke Hospital. The picture's caption identifies many of the players.

Following the interest stimulated in patients by their participation in the bonspiels on the large skating pond which once existed at the Braid Hills, a curling pond was constructed in the hospital grounds, a little south of West House near the boundary wall beside the railway line. This pond was later stocked with trout. Today it is part of the pleasant gardens of Mackinnon House.

Dr Mackinnon was a man of enlightened approach, with many ideas far in advance of his time. His concept of a mental hospital as a therapeutic community is now firmly established in modern policy. In tribute to his labours, the original West House which he established was re-named McKinnon House in 1967.

Dr Mackinnon's successor, Dr David Skae, initiated further developments, particularly as regards the clinical classification of patients. There was at this time a gradual evolution in the teaching of mental diseases to Edinburgh medical students, originating with Dr (later Sir) Alexander Morrison, who had been apprenticed to Dr Alexander Wood ("Lang Sandie Wood"), the physician who attended Robert Fergusson during his confinement in the Edinburgh Bedlam. Dr Morrison was employed for some time as the private physician to a wealthy lady in London and while there he conceived the idea of establishing Edinburgh's first professorial chair in mental diseases, with himself as its first occupant, but his proposal met with no support.

Dr Morrison did, however, in 1823 inaugurate a course of lectures in London and Edinburgh simultaneously. Six students attended his Edinburgh lectures, the first course in mental diseases in Britain. Dr Morrison continued to give these lectures for thirty years. When he retired in 1852, his course in Edinburgh was continued by Dr Skae, Physician Superintendent at the Royal Edinburgh Asylum, who lectured until his death twenty years later in 1872. The lectures were conducted under the auspices of the Edinburgh University Extra-Mural School sponsored by the Royal College of Physicians, with clinical teaching being conducted at the Royal Edinburgh Asylum. As a consequence, this hospital became an important postgraduate training centre in psychiatry and many doctors who advanced their knowledge and practical experience at the Morningside hospital later took up important posts in other parts of Britain and beyond.

Dr Skae's lectures, however, were regarded askance by Professor Thomas Laycock, Professor of Medicine at Edinburgh University, who considered it his prerogative to lecture on mental diseases as part of general medicine. Professor Laycock had, in fact, also assumed the title of Lecturer in Psychology and Mental Diseases. He was a distinguished doctor and, following a number of early treatises on nervous diseases, his monumental work *Mind and Brain* was published in 1860.

Professor Laycock asked Dr Skae for clinical teaching and demonstration facilities at the Royal Edinburgh Asylum but the latter, jealous of his own status, refused to cooperate. Dr Skae's courses ended with his death in 1872 and his successor as Physician Superintendent at Morningside, Dr Thomas Clouston, ended the rivalry. Clouston, who had been an admiring pupil of Professor Laycock, was very willing to provide him with the facilities required. Professor Laycock died in 1876 and three years later Dr Clouston was himself appointed lecturer in mental diseases at Edinburgh University. This was the first such official separate lectureship established by the University. With this development, it could be said that "psychiatry had now come into its own and was no longer an insignificant part of general medicine". Dr Clouston held his new teaching post for over thirty years.

During Dr Skae's period of office further extensions to the asylum had become necessary. The managers obtained from Isabella Steel the ground at Tipperlinn on which had stood Dr Thomas Steel's chemical factory, and from 1853-6 they bought up the remaining portions of the old village. In 1856, the last of the weavers, Henry and George Murray and Alexander Munnoch, sold their houses to the asylum. Thus came to an end the ancient weaving community of Tipperlinn.

Asylum staff and their relatives moved into the former weavers' houses, but in 1861 these were considered unsafe and were soon afterwards demolished. On the site of the high street of the old village, Tipperlinn House was built in 1861 as the residence of the Physician

Superintendents. Soon after the death of Dr T. A. Munro in 1967, this substantial villa became, after alterations, the Young People's Unit, opened by Viscount Younger of Leekie on November 8th, 1968.

Dr Thomas Clouston, successor to Dr Skae in 1873, was a brilliant clinician, writer and teacher. He published what became a standard text-book on mental diseases. It was Dr Clouston who, as a result of increasing demands for additional hospital accommodation, for private patients of means, persuaded the asylum managers to purchase the adjacent mansion-house of Craighouse on Craiglockhart Hill. In 1894 Craighouse Hospital, with a particularly attractive situation and panoramic view over Edinburgh, was opened by the Duke of Buccleuch. Prior to the establishment of this important extension to the asylum, Dr Clouston had travelled widely in many countries to study the most advanced approaches in the treatment of mental illness.

No expense was spared in the building of Craighouse and its separate villas, South Craig, Bevan House and Queen's Craig. Sketch plans prepared by a patient were used by the architect, Sydney Mitchell. The total cost was £150,000. Dr Clouston, commenting on the desirability of providing every possible amenity which might be helpful to patients, perhaps had the tragic fate of Robert Fergusson in mind: "Nothing we can do for the comfort of our patients", he said, "is too much to atone for the cruelty of past ages." Certainly the facilities provided for them here were of the highest order. Established primarily for fee-paying patients, many of those admitted to Craighouse were wealthy, and every endeavour was made to ensure that they might enjoy the standard of life to which they were accustomed.

Dr Clouston was concerned especially with the prevention of mental illness and the teaching of "mental hygiene". "Men's conduct", he wrote, "must be largely determined by their knowledge and by their vivid conviction of consequences . . . without mental hygiene in the shape of moral laws, education, social observances and religion, mankind could not possibly have undergone evolution from a lower to a higher stage at all..." It may be of contemporary interest that, when Dr Coulston wrote in 1894, a high proportion of his patients, both male and female, were ad-mitted as a result of alcoholic problems. Soon after the opening of Craighouse, the original East House building was demolished and the land purchased by James Millar, a builder, who erected Millar Crescent, Millar Place, Morningside Terrace and part of Morningside Park.

After thirty-five years of devoted service, which earned him the reward of a knighthood, Dr Clouston was succeeded by Dr George Robertson who was to achieve a very high reputation not only as a distinguished psychiatrist but also as an administrator and a pioneer in widening the scope of mental health services outwith hospital treatment. When, in 1918, the Hospital Board of Managers endowed a Chair of Psychiatry at Edinburgh University, he became the first incumbent. He was also responsible for establishing the Jordanburn Hospital in 1929, within the complex of what, by a new charter seven years earlier, had become The Royal Edinburgh Hospital for Nervous and Mental Disorders.

Professor Robertson, as consultant psychiatrist to the Edinburgh Royal Infirmary, instituted the "Tuesdays at Two" out-patient clinic at the Infirmary, and his arrangement for the informal admission of patients to the Royal Edinburgh Hospital in 1929 anticipated by thirty years such provisions initiated by the Mental Health Act of 1959. The out-patient department at the Jordanburn Hospital was built with an adjacent large lecture theatre capable of accommodating two hundred people.

Dr David Kennedy Henderson, who began his career as a junior member of Dr Thomas Clouston's staff, succeeded Professor Robertson in the Chair of Psychiatry following the latter's death in 1932. "D.K.", as he came to be familiarly known, had studied in the United States under the famous Dr Adolph Meyer, America's leading psychiatrist, and was for some time his first assistant at the Phipps Clinic in the Johns Hopkins Hospital, Baltimore. This clinic trained psychiatrists who later took up leading posts all over the world. After a further period as Physician Superintendent at the Glasgow Royal Mental Hospital, Dr Henderson took up the Edinburgh Chair. His text-book, written jointly in 1927 with one of his early pupils, Dr R. D. Gillespie, brought world renown. Professor Henderson became acknowledged as the leading authority on his subject in Great Britain. His personal distinction enhanced the already high international reputation of the Royal Edinburgh Hospital. For his services to psychiatry he was knighted in 1947. His *Evolution of Psychiatry in Scotland* is a valuable historical work.

Henderson had combined the posts of Professor of Psychiatry and Physician Superintendent of the Royal Edinburgh Hospital. After his retirement in 1954, these twin responsibilities were separated. The late Dr T. A. Munro was then appointed Physician Superintendent and the late Dr Alexander Kennedy became Professor of Psychiatry. It was the latter who planned the University Department of Psychiatry at the Royal Edinburgh Hospital in "The Tower".

After 1954 the staffs of both the University Department of Psychiatry and the Royal Edinburgh Hospital were steadily increased. Today the former has three professorial chairs, two of psychiatry and one of forensic psychiatry, this number exceeding that at any other British university. Now under the provisions of the National Health Service, the hospital has ten clinical teams, each with its specialised function, including the treatment of acute cases.

In the Royal Edinburgh Hospital of today, with its modern approach to the treatment of mental illness and its attempt to dispel from patients' minds the sense of being members of a closed, isolated community, the wheel has turned full circle since the days of Dr Mackinnon, who.

working in a very different era, regarded his patients as belonging to "a little world in itself". Today this "little world" is integrated in every way possible with the world outside.

Two principal aspects of the present-day hospital contrast strikingly with the appallingly dreary, prison-like conditions in which, two centuries ago, Robert Fergusson died during his confinement in "the cells" of the old city Bedlam under the charge of his "keepers". The facilities today provided for patients at Mackinnon House and Craighouse compare favourably with those of a modern hotel. Infinitely improved and enlightened environmental conditions are matched by a revolution in attitude over the last two centuries to the mentally ill, and research into new methods proceeds steadily.

The office of the Hospital Management Board preserves a valuable relic of the past, a reminder of how the long journey towards hope and advancement began. This is a little medallion of ivory, on one side of which is what is believed to be a miniature portrait by Raeburn of Dr Andrew Duncan, and, on the reverse side, a lock of Robert Fergusson's hair.

CHAPTER 11

The Land of Canaan

The high street of old Morningside village was bounded on its west side by Morningside Estate, stretching from Doo Loan (now Albert Terrace), at the brow of Churchhill, downhill to the Jordan Burn, the southern boundary of the village and of Edinburgh. On the opposite side of the street the boundary wall of the Canaan Estate extended from Cant's Loan (now Newbattle Terrace) to the Jordan Burn.

During the centuries following the feuing out of the western Burgh Muir in 1586, "the land of Canaan", as it came to be picturesquely known, eventually enclosed an area of sixty-five acres. Its boundaries extended from Newbattle Terrace and Grange Loan in the north to the Jordan Burn in the south, and from Morningside Road in the west to Blackford Park and Blackford Brae in the east. It was thus by far the largest of the estates which had once formed part of the ancient "Common Mure" and the most extensive of the various lands on which Morningside was gradually to develop. From its rural spacious meadows, orchards and gardens arose many fine villas, but Canaan has also remained the most pleasant of the Morningside lands.

Describing the varied features of Canaan involves reference to names such as Goshen, Eden, Hebron and Jordan, and the question of how such names originated in this district, described by a Scottish writer as "Edinburgh's Bible belt", immediately arises. Several explanations have been advanced. Henry Mackenzie, "the Man of Feeling", who for some time resided in Canaan Lodge, wrote: "At the distance of less than a mile from Edinburgh, there are places with Jewish names — Canaan, the river or brook called Jordan, Egypt — a place called Transylvania, a little to the east of Egypt. There are two traditions of the way in which they got their names: one, that there was a considerable eruption of gypsies into the county of Edinburgh who got a grant of these lands, then chiefly a moor; the other, which I have heard from rather better authority, that some rich Jews happened to migrate into Scotland and got from one of the Kings (James I, I think it was said) a grant of these lands in consideration of a sum of money which they advanced him."

Another suggestion is that Morningside's Biblical names may be traced to Oliver Cromwell's occupation of Galachlaw Hill near Fairmilehead in 1650. Others claim to find an association with the farm of Egypt just south of the Jordan Burn. Such explanations have some element of probability but they must be looked at in relation to known historical events.

In the Edinburgh Burgh Records for 1585, an entry for September 22nd states that Robert Fairlie, "Laird of the Braids", had granted the city the use of his "houssis callit Littil Egypt besyde the commoun mure for brewing thairin of the drink for the seik folkis in the mure and sic necessar usis as the toun hes found good to employ on the samyn". This seems to be the earliest reference in the records to the existence in the district which was to become Morningside of a Biblical or eastern place name. The "seik folkis in the mure" for whom Robert Fairlie was brewing beer were the unfortunate victims of the devastating plague of 1585 who were quarantined in wooden huts surrounding the little chapel of St Roque, which stood in the midst of what today are the pleasant tree-shaded grounds of the Astley Ainslie Hospital, a short distance from the original district of Littil Egypt.

The name Canaan first appears in the city records in 1661. The Edinburgh Town Council Minutes of that year record that on August 28th the Council agreed to set on lease to Mart (Margaret) Whilleis these "aikers of the wester commoun mure commounlie called Canaan" for a period of eleven years. On the death of Margaret Whilleis in 1667 the land passed to James Russell, described as an "indweller in Canaan". Canaan is described as "lyand betwixt the land of Braid on the south with a little stream [the Jordan Burn] the lands of Mr William Livingston some time".

Egypt, then, is first mentioned in 1585, but Canaan only much later, in 1661. Neither reference, however, provides any indication of the origin of these names. In tracing this, probability must take the place of documented fact. The search must begin not in the district of Canaan but a short distance to the south, in the neighbouring estate of Braid.

In the mid-sixteenth century, Edinburgh's magistrates were hard put to it to deal effectively with the increasing crimes of theft, assault and vagrancy within the city. In 1566 a gibbet or gallows was erected at the eastern end of the Burgh Muir, on the site of what is now Preston Street Primary School. One particular group of people caused the authorities considerable trouble. These were the gypsies or "vagabondis". In earlier days, the gypsies claimed, their forefathers were Christian pilgrims expelled from Egypt and forced to wander through India and, later, Europe. They had come to be regarded as exiled Egyptians, and this name was eventually abbreviated to "gypsies".

The gypsies first appeared in large numbers in Scotland in the early sixteenth century. At first they seem to have been accepted wherever they established their communities. Indeed, their colourful dress and way of life and their gifts of music and dancing attracted the attention, perhaps not surprisingly, of James IV, who in 1505 received some of their community at Holyrood, presenting them with ten French Crowns. Likewise, the Lord High Treasurer's accounts reveal that on May 25th, 1529 James IV's somewhat Bohemian son (later James V) also made a gift to the "Egiptianis that dansit before the King in Holyrudhous". In 1540 James V granted to "Johnne Faw, Lord and Erle of Egypt and to his sons and successors power to hang and punish all Egyptians within the Kingdom of Scotland".

Their fortunes were, however, soon to change. Perhaps Johnne Faw and his successors failed to maintain law and order within their communities, for in 1541 the Lords of Council issued an order for their expulsion from Scotland on account of "the gret thiftis and scaithis done be the saidis Egyptians upon our soverance lordis liegis and quhair thai cum or resortis". In accordance with the decree Edinburgh's magistrates forbade all gypsies residence within the city's limits. It was probably as a consequence of this that the first of Morningside's Biblical names arose. The principal Edinburgh gypsy community may very well have been established on the southern slopes of the Burgh Muir, in the future Morningside district, still within the city boundaries. To obey the magistrates' decree it would have been a simple step for the gypsies to have moved their encampment from the northern bank of "the little strand" (the Jordan Burn) to the southern bank. They would then have been within the Braid Estate. If this is what did in fact happen, they must have been squatters, as in the records of the period there is no reference to the Laird of Braid granting them asylum within his lands.

The above-mentioned entry in the Burgh Records relates that in 1585 Robert Fairlie, "Laird of the Braids", granted the City use of his "houssis callit Littil Egypt *besyde* the commoun mure" — *beside* and not *on* it. The word "Littil" preceding Egypt may be of significance in supporting the above suggestion as in gypsy communities established in Britain their leaders were given the titles of Kings or Erles of "Littil Egypt". This was a peculiarly gypsy term and it therefore seems probably that the "Littil Egypt" in which Fairlie's "houssis" were located was or had been the site of a gypsy community. It is also interesting to note that the "Lord and Erle of Egypt" to whom James V granted privileges in 1540 is recalled in S. R. Crockett's novel *The Raiders,* which is subtitled "Some Passages in the Life of John Faa, Lord and Earl of Little Egypt". There would certainly seem to be a strong probability that an "Egyptian" community existed on the fringes of the Braid Estate.

Littil Egypt, then, was in 1585 a distinct location in the future Morningside district and the first of its Biblical names. Though Canaan does not appear on record until 1661, the name might well have been in use for some years before this date as the 1661 reference is to "aikers of the wester commoun mure *commounlie* called Canaan," implying that the use of the name was already well established.

The suggestion that the name Canaan was first applied to the lands adjacent to Littil Egypt a decade before 1661 had the support of William Moir Bryce, the authority on the history of the Burgh Muir, who submitted that "there can be no question that the name Canaan was first

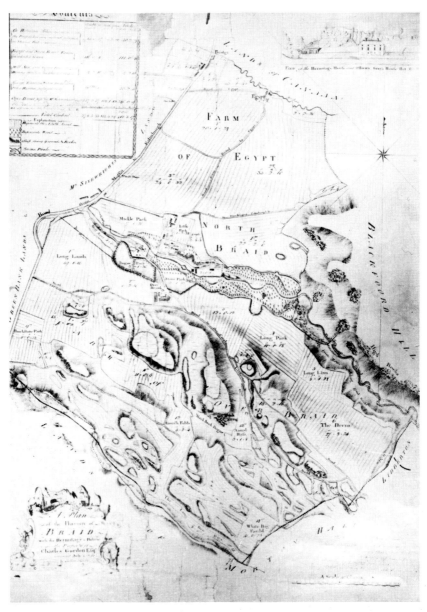

Plan of the Barony of Braid, drawn for Charles Gordon of the Hermitage of Braid in 1772 and showing Egypt Farm

applied during the Covenanting period and in particular during Cromwell's occupation of Edinburgh".

In 1650, prior to the Battle of Dunbar, Cromwell, with an army of 16,000 men, camped on Galachlaw, a hill which rises above the present-day Princess Margaret Rose Hospital in Frogston Road. It has been suggested that, during this encampment and his several fruitless invasions of Edinburgh, small bands of Cromwell's soldiers conducted forages in the vicinity of Littil Egypt, then a small community. Here they met with such stiff resistance from the local people that the Puritan troops, who frequently had Biblical phrases on their lips, likened these encounters to "Joshua against the Canaanites". This is one theory. Another is simply that Cromwell's men, passing through what they were told was the district of Littil Egypt and being Bible conscious, came to call the adjacent lands by the name of Canaan.

The district of Egypt (the "Littil" was eventually dropped) remained a distinct location for nearly three centuries. The route taken during the last Riding of the Marches on the Burgh Muir in 1717 included the village of Egypt. Charles Gordon's *Plan of the Barony of Braid,* drawn from a survey made in 1772, shows Egypt Farm occupying a considerable area of land and substantial farm buildings. The site of this farm was the junction of what are now Woodburn Terrace and Nile Grove, just a few yards south of the Jordan Burn. Gordon's plan names various places near the farm and indicates the "Road to Egypt", now Cluny Avenue. Other maps show Cluny Drive as "Egypt Avenue".

In later times it appears that the farmhouse was let to summer visitors, often people from Edinburgh who wished to enjoy a pleasantly rural holiday. Mrs Fletcher, wife of an Edinburgh advocate, records such a stay in 1799: "Mr Fletcher's health as well as my own seeming to require a change of air, we repaired with our children to a very inexpensive cottage in the Morningside district, to the south of Edinburgh, called Egypt, so named in memory of a gypsy colony who, as tradition says, had their headquarters in the immediate neighbourhood."

According to the *Edinburgh Almanack* for 1800, one of the hackney coaches which provided transport to places on the outskirts of the city such as Gorgie, Coltbridge and Canaan also stopped at Egypt, the fare from the Tron Church being two shillings. Egypt is mentioned as a place *en route* until 1802.

In a poem about Carlops written by Robert D. C. Brown in 1793, an interesting description is given of that village. Amongst those who attended the Carlops fairs was, we are told, "Israel, a man who lived at Canaan, Morningside, near the lands of Egypt and River Jordan in 1792, and whose children were known as 'the children of Israel'."

By the 1890s Egypt farmhouse was finally demolished and swept away to permit the building on its site and adjoining lands of the villas of

Nile Grove, Braid Avenue and Cluny. Among the last of the farmers of Egypt was a Mr Begbie.

We now recross the Jordan Burn from the Braid Estate, into which it was necessary to proceed to trace the origins of Morningside's Biblical names. The extensiveness of the land of Canaan, from which we set out, and its many interesting and distinguished people make this chapter the most comprehensive and varied of the chronicles which constitute the history of Morningside.

To the successive owners of Canaan since its earliest disposition to Margaret Whilleis in 1661, little interest attaches. By 1762 the owner of the estate had acquired a further twelve acres of the adjoining Whitehouse lands, and he later added a further twelve acres from the adjacent Wester Grange and a small portion of the lands of Blackford. In 1779 the now extensive land of Canaan was acquired by John Mosman, a successful Edinburgh merchant who, nine years later, also obtained ownership of Wester Morningside. This later passed into other hands but the Mosman family retained possession of Canaan for well over a century.

To continue the chronicles of Canaan, we turn to the south-western corner of the large rectangle formed by these lands, where Morningside Road crossed the Jordan Burn at the Briggs o' Braid, beside which the old Toll House stood. The little row of houses known as the Jordan Burn Cottages, just east of the toll, were razed to permit the building of a modern supermarket, but the original lane from which wicket gates led to the cottages remains, for long giving access to the Morningside Family Laundry, vacated in 1975 and now restored to house "The Angle Club", which provides billiards and snooker facilities for its members. This house is shown on the 1852 Ordnance Survey Map as "Elizabethan Cottage".

On the right as one enters Jordan Lane stands the first tenement block built in Morningside in 1857, replacing the old cottages on this site. When it was built the street which had been called Jordan Bank was re-named Jordan Lane and its houses were re-numbered. Continuing along Jordan Lane, we come to Ainslie Cottage on the right, indicated by a name-plate above the entrance. This pleasant little house was one of the original cottages of Morningside village. It takes its name from the Ainslie family, originally farmers and notable sheep-breeders at Oastly near Roslin, the first of whom took possession of the cottage in 1827 and whose successors remained here for nearly sixty years.

Some confusion exists over the possible residence in Ainslie Cottage of George Meikle Kemp, architect of the Scott Monument in Princes Street. A number of writers of booklets on Morningside have stated that the public funeral of Kemp took place from the cottage on March 22nd, 1844. William Mair in *Historic Morningside* however states that the celebrated architect's funeral took place from his home at 1 Jordan Bank, and that in the *Edinburgh and Leith Post Office Directory* for 1843-4 he is entered as "G. M. Kemp, 1 Jordan Lane", his cottage at this address eventually being demolished and replaced by the first Morningside tenements, referred to above. In fact, the directory which Mair mentions does not give Kemp as residing at "1 Jordan Lane" but simply as at "Jordan 1" the "1" being an abbreviation for "Lane". There is now no evidence of Kemp's precise address. Though the title deeds of Ainslie Cottage bear no reference to him, he might possibly have been a tenant there. He did in fact live for some time at Bloomsberry Cottage in nearby Canaan Lane. Some writers who have stated that he resided in Ainslie Cottage, and in particular Robert Cochrane, were close enough to him in time to have had some traditional, if not recorded, evidence of this.

George Meikle Kemp's life, though relatively short, had certainly been varied before he came to Morningside and died tragically in 1844. He was born in the small village of Moorfoot near Gladhouse Loch, on the border of Midlothian and Peeblesshire. His father was a shepherd who had to move about the district frequently to find employment. Thus young George attended many schools, including West Linton Primary School when he was eight years old, in which a commemorative plaque is treasured. He later went to Penicuik School when his parents moved to Newhall near Carlops. It was while living at Newhall that he was sent on an errand to Edinburgh, returning home by Roslin. There he visited the famous chapel and was overwhelmed by its beauty. This early experience inspired him to become an architect. At the age of fourteen he became an apprentice carpenter at Redscaurhead village, between Peebles and Eddleston. After five years' training, when he was proficient in making sketch plans and drawings, he moved to Galashiels to work as a millwright.

An enthusiastic walker, Kemp set out for Galashiels on foot. *En route* he met for the first time the man whose monument he was to design. As he reached Elibank, a carriage drew up and its occupant offered him a lift, which was gratefully accepted, though he did not recognise his distinguished companion, Sir Walter Scott.

After a year in the border town, Kemp returned to Edinburgh, obtaining a post as a carpenter with John Cousin of Greenhill Gardens, who undertook extensive tenement building in Edinburgh. Kemp's work amounted to ten hours labour daily, including Saturdays. The potential architect became restless. He left Edinburgh after two years, once again on foot, journeying this time through England, where he was specially impressed by York Minster, and to Europe, where the many famous cathedrals he visited profoundly influenced him. He returned after some time to Glasgow, and then finally to Edinburgh, where he married Elizabeth Bonnar. He found employment with the distinguished architect, William Burn. At this time, Kemp, though not a professional architect, began submitting plans for various restorations, including that of Glasgow Cathedral. For this his plans were seriously considered though not accepted.

In 1836 the committee charged with the erection of a fitting memorial to Sir Walter Scott invited designs, and Kemp's attention was drawn to the advertisement offering a fifty-guinea prize. He submitted his design under the *nom-de-plume* "John Morvo" a name he had seen inscribed by one of the original stonemasons on Melrose Abbey. His Gothic design was, in fact, the result of a close study of Melrose Abbey, from which, he admitted, "it was in all its details derived" and not from Antwerp tower as several critics later accused. Indeed, it was while he was making sketches of Melrose Abbey that his second meeting with Sir Walter Scott took place, Sir Walter looking over Kemp's shoulder to observe and comment upon his work. Neither could then know how their names would eventually be associated. The great novelist could not have imagined that the architectural detail Kemp was so carefully noting would find its place in his memorial.

Kemp's submission, one of fifty entries, was awarded third prize, and he was given fifty guineas, as were the first and second placed entrants. The Scott Monument Committee were, however, not satisfied with the designs and invited further contributions. Kemp, after making some revisions, again submitted his design. This time, on March 28th, 1838, the committee adopted his plan. The minute describes it "as an imposing structure 135 feet in height, its beautiful proportions in strict conformity with the purity of taste and style of Melrose Abbey. . ." He was awarded an initial fee of £100.

For nearly six years, while living at Bloomsberry Cottage in Canaan Lane and, finally, in Jordan Lane, Kemp concentrated on making his architectural dream a reality. Many proposals were made for its site, East Princes Gardens eventually being chosen. The foundations were laid on rock fifty-two feet below ground level and the height of the monument was increased to two hundred feet and six inches, with two hundred and eighty-seven steps. The sandstone used was from Binny Quarry. On August 15th, 1840 the foundation stone was laid by another Morningside resident, Lord Provost Sir James Forrest of Comiston, then Grand Master Mason of Scotland.

The monument's creator was not to witness its completion. For nearly four years he had been laboriously involved in its progress and in discussions over complications concerning costs and the realisation of his design. At the end of one such busy day, Kemp called at the office of the building contractor on the north side of the Union Canal basin near Fountainbridge. His business at last over, he set out on foot for Jordan Lane. Alas, the night was dark: he lost his way and stumbled into the deep water of the canal. Next day his cape and cane were seen floating on the surface, and later his body was recovered. Vast crowds lined the route as the *cortege* of his public funeral proceeded to St Cuthbert's Church burial ground at the west end of Princes Street. His gravestone, within distant

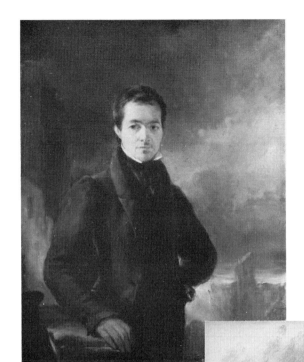

*George Meikle
Kemp, architect
of the Scott
Monument, who
resided in
Jordan Lane
c. 1838-40*

*Sam Bough, R.S.A., the famous
Scottish landscape painter who
lived in Jordan Lane*

sight of the towering pinnacle he designed, is inscribed with lines from the dirge composed by his friend James Ballantyne:

> Art is wrapped in weeds of woe,
> Nature mourns in accent low,
> Scotland sheds a heart-wrung tear
> O'er her son's untimely bier.
> The flowers that blush by mountain rill,
> The flowers that bloom on lonely hill,
> All drooping low their loss deplore
> Alas, their lover comes no more.
> Castled keep and sacred pile,
> Buttressed tower and fretted aisle,
> Wrapt in gloom are left alone,
> Now their worshipper is gone.
> Yet hope still cheers us while we mourn,
> And fame strews laurel o'er his urn.
> Behold that structure cleave the sky!
> And dream not genius e'er can die.

The Scott Monument was completed under the direction of Kemp's brother-in-law, William Bonnar, R.S.A., on October 26th, 1844. His son Thomas Kemp was accorded the honour of placing the final coping-stone at the top of his father's masterpiece.

Memorials to Kemp abound, notably at the little village of Redscaurhead where he served his apprenticeship as a joiner, and in the several primary schools in Peeblesshire and Midlothian which he attended. Many interesting relics also remain: some of Kemp's pencil sketchbooks are preserved in the Fine Art Room of Edinburgh's Central Public Library; a large handsome chair which he made for the Grand Master of the St Andrew Masonic Lodge in Edinburgh is still in the Freemasons' Hall in George Street; a fourteen-foot-high model of the Scott Monument is in Edinburgh's Huntly House Museum. Preeminently, of course, there is the Scott Monument itself.

Another Morningside resident is also prominently associated with the monument. The statue, at its base, of Sir Walter Scott and his favourite dog Maida was carved from a block of Carrara marble by Sir John Steell of Greenhill Gardens. This was the first marble statue to be commissioned in Scotland.

Kemp's famous monument cost just over £15,000 to build. Reactions to it were mixed; indeed much controversy reigned in which Kemp was accused of plagiarism and of being "an obscure man". Lord Cockburn — not one of Sir Walter Scott's admirers — criticised it strongly. Kemp would, however, have been consoled by the praise of William Burn (the most distinguished Scottish architect of his time), Sir John Britton (the great authority on English cathedrals) and Edinburgh's Town Council and

Magistrates whose booklet proclaimed that, "The Scott Monument is perhaps the finest, as it certainly is the most appropriate, monumental edifice in the Kingdom." Certainly Edinburgh's Princes Street skyline would be poorer without it.

Another of Morningside's Biblical names was, until recently, to be seen on the gate of 7 Jordan Lane. The originally large villa, of which this is just a part, was known as Salem. Unfortunately, during recent alterations the name-plate was removed. Immediately beyond this house, garage premises now occupy what was once the byre of a "dry dairy" — the cows were never put out to pasture but were always kept indoors.

A few yards further on, at No. 15, is Jordan Bank Villa: the name is now barely decipherable. This semi-detached house, along with the adjacent Nos 14 and 16, was purchased by the notable landscape painter Sam Bough, R.S.A., in 1867. Born in Carlisle, Bough was the son of a shoemaker. He worked for some time as a theatrical scenery painter in Manchester, and similarly for seven years in Glasgow. This experience is reflected in the dramatic style of his landscapes, which abound in minute detail.

Sam Bough moved to Edinburgh from Glasgow in 1866, and lived for some time at 5 Malta Terrace before coming to Jordan Lane. The apparent confusion concerning his Morningside address, at first recorded as 7 Jordan Bank, is due to the fact that, when the latter was incorporated into the newly created Jordan Lane, the houses were re-numbered, 7 Jordan Bank becoming 15 Jordan Lane.

In February 1867, Bough wrote hastily to a friend: "Getting newly acquired house in order — place in a mess — plasterers, masons, carpenters, plumbers making house habitable." A connecting door was made between Nos 14 and 15 and, in the former, an ornate plaster ceiling was created for the drawing-room and a large glass-enclosed studio built on the stone verandah at the rear. Bough also had studios at 2 Hill Street and 2a George Street.

A reference to the nearby Egypt farm is provided by a neighbour of Bough's. The artist, he recounted, was very fond of mushrooms. When these were in season, the two of them had an arrangement whereby whoever wakened first in the morning knocked at the other's window. Together, the friends then jumped the wall at the foot of their gardens, forded the Jordan Burn, crossed the Egypt Road (now Cluny Avenue) and entered Begbie's, the farmer of Egypt's field, which extended to the boundary of the Hermitage of Braid. Here, apparently, mushrooms abounded.

A man of Bohemian appearance and temperament, capable of great frivolity but also of deep seriousness, Sam Bough was a well-known figure in the still village-like Morningside of his day, especially in the original Volunteer's Rest at the corner of Canaan Lane. As mentioned earlier, the

215

two wooden inn signs he painted are preserved in the present-day Volunteer Arms.

Robert Louis Stevenson in *Edinburgh: Picturesque Notes* describes watching passengers coming aboard the steamer *Clansman* at Portree harbour in 1870. Among them was his friend Sam Bough. It is possible that R.L.S. visited Bough at his house in Jordan Lane. Elected an Associate Member of the Royal Scottish Academy in 1856, while working in Glasgow, but not a full member until 1875, when he was at the peak of his career, Bough exhibited at the Academy and in various other parts of Britain. His prolific landscapes were mainly of Scottish and North of England scenes. Bustling harbours held a special fascination for him.

The English artist, born in Carlisle, who became a great lover of Scotland and one of the most distinguished painters of his day, died at Jordan Bank Villa on November 19th, 1878, aged fifty-six. He was buried in Dean Cemetery and a special medallion portrait by William Brodie, R.S.A., is on his gravestone. Sixteen coaches conveyed the principal mourners, including many members of the Royal Scottish Academy, along crowd-lined streets. A contingent of Glasgow artists joined the funeral procession in Lothian Road.

While most of Sam Bough's works are now in private collections, several are in the Glasgow Art Gallery. Two small statues of the artist are in the Scottish National Portait Gallery.

The predecessor of Sam Bough at 14 Jordan Lane was David Ramsay Hay, a decorative artist and author. Hay, who was responsible for the interior decoration of Holyrood Palace during the reign of George IV was also engaged by Sir Walter Scott at Abbotsford. Since they were friends, Scott may have visited Hay at his Jordan Lane home.

No. 14 Jordan Lane, originally united with Jordan Bank Villa, is now the home of Wilfred Taylor, the author and columnist, whose *Scot Easy* refers to earlier occupants of this house and provides an interesting account of Jordan Lane in modern times.

At 17 Jordan Lane lived Charles D'Orville Pilkington Jackson (1887-1973), whose sculptures include the Robert the Bruce figure at the Bannockburn National Trust Memorial. The house at No. 20, for long named Braid Hill Cottage, is shown on the Ordnance Survey Map of 1852 as "Helen's Place". Returning from the end of Jordan Lane, the secluded modern villa on the right, No. 24, is named Bethel, the most recent Biblical name to continue the centuries-old tradition

The site of Morningside's original Cooperative Society Store is now occupied by a fish-and-chip shop at 239 Morningside Road, adjacent to the Volunteer Arms. Entering Canaan Lane, the little area on the right behind the original village inn, between Canaan Lane and Jordan Lane, was known as "Paradise". The "Paradisers", as they were called, with their small cottages and "Kailyards" ("the Kailyards of Paradise") formed a small community of their own. Some few yards further along on the right, a small drive leads to the substantial villa built as Morningside's original Police Station. A little beyond this, a small cottage up to very recently bore a metal plaque on its west gable-end with the name "Goshen". The immediate vicinity is indicated on the earliest Ordnance Survey Map as the district of Goshen, while the large villa standing a short distance back on the right, entered by a little lane, was named Goshen House or Goshen Bank. Here in 1868 resided, for a short time, Henry Kingsley, brother of Charles Kingsley, while editing the *Edinburgh Daily Review*. Before coming to Edinburgh, Henry Kingsley had written many novels and worked as a journalist in Australia. The *Edinburgh Daily Review* was a nonconformist publication most unsuited, one critic felt, to the editorship of Kingsley, who was, he wrote, "a round man in a square hole, knowing little or nothing about Scottish ecclesiastical history and even less about Edinburgh municipal affairs." There was considerable consternation over some of his "rollicking leaders", especially in northern manses, and Henry Kingsley resigned his post after eighteen months.

We pass the first block of tenements on the right and see yet another Biblical name on the door of No. 32: Hebron. Here for some time resided William Ritchie, co-founder with Charles McLaren of *The Scotsman* in 1817. McLaren was also a "Canaanite", living at Morelands, a large villa which is now a part of the Astley Ainslie Hospital. Almost opposite Hebron and immediately beyond the entrance to the modern block of flats, Falcon Court, is a small villa called Stonefield, which has associations with the Misses Balfours, aunts of Robert Louis Stevenson.

The feuing plan of Canaan for 1803 indicates a division into twenty-two lots. Many of the original purchasers of these built villas in this pleasant rural district, but there were several provisos, one being that villas were not to cost less than £300 to build (in the early nineteenth century this was a fairly sunstantial sum). When William Mosman had, in 1797, feued one of the lots to Thomas Steel (whose chemical plant at Tipperlinn has previously been mentioned) for the building of a small magnesia factory, he laid down the condition: "So far as the same shall not be a nuisance to the neighbourhood." Later purchasers of land in Canaan were allowed to build but "not to establish any trade or manufacture a nuisance to the neighbourhood". This later proviso seems more restricting than Dr Steel's. Perhaps the magnesia factory, built in what is now Steel's Place, on the western edge of Canaan, was not too popular with local residents. Mosman, in his feuing regulations, also reserved to himself "the right to the coal mines" on his land. Whether such mines did in fact exist and, if they did, where they were located is now impossible to determine. The original Edinburgh Town Council Charter governing Canaan decrees that, in the event of a brewery being established in the lands, the owner must have the malts and grains milled at the town's mill on the Water of Leith.

The villa which is now 11 Canaan Lane, is shown on Kirkwood's Map of 1817 as Canaan House, but by 1864 the name had been changed to Streatham House. In 1930 the Roman Catholic Benedictine Order acquired this house and established a day-school for boys, the first enrolment totalling five. Eventually the Priory School, as it was known, took boarding pupils and, by the time that the outbreak of the Second World War forced evacuation to the Abbey School at Fort Augustus, the roll at the Canaan Lane school had reached three figures. In 1945 Streatham House was compulsorily purchased by Edinburgh Corporation for use as a Children's Home and the Benedictine school re-opened as Carl Kemp's School at North Berwick. The celebrated broadcasting personality Gilbert Harding had been one of the schoolmasters at Canaan Lane.

Canaan Lodge, the third of the villas which are now owned by the Social Work Department of the Lothian Regional Council, and used for child care, was rebuilt in 1907, the original house of this name having been built on the same site in 1800. Of its many owners, the most distinguished and celebrated was Professor James Gregory, M.D., who purchased the house in 1814. The last of "the Academic Gregories", a remarkable Aberdeenshire family of whom fourteen held university professorial chairs over a period of two centuries, Professor James Gregory graduated from the Edinburgh Medical School in 1774.

Professor James Gregory,
M.D. of Canaan Lodge,
by Sir Henry Raeburn

218

He then studied further at Leyden with which Edinburgh for a period had close links. When appointed Professor of Medicine at Edinburgh in 1778, he was the fifth member of his family to occupy an Edinburgh University Chair. A brilliant teacher, his personal notes on his classes are still extant and indicate the greatly increased number of students attracted by his lectures.

He was Scotland's leading consultant at a time when, as Professor Christison wrote, "The Gregorian physic was free blood letting, the cold affusion, tartar emetic and the famous mixture which bears his name." This last for long made Gregory a household name in Scotland, and the means of its manufacture merits a place in the chronicles of Morningside. The prescription required large amounts of magnesia powder, along with pulverised rhubarb and ginger. Dr Thomas Steel had provided the magnesia from his works, and the rhubarb required for Gregory's mixture was, as previously mentioned, grown by Sir Alexander Dick of Prestonfield House. President of the Edinburgh Royal College of Physicians, Dick was an enthusiastic advocate of the health-promoting qualities of rhubarb, and was perhaps the first to cultivate it in Scotland. It is possible that Professor Gregory and Sir Alexander Dick jointly conceived the composition of the famous mixture, which was in universal demand after its inclusion in the Edinburgh Pharmacopia in 1839. It was added to the British Pharmacopia in 1885 and may still be obtained.

Professor Gregory was a man of wide cultural interests and one of Scotland's leading Latin scholars of his day. He moved in Edinburgh's

PRESCRIPTION FOR GREGORY'S POWDER, IN THE HANDWRITING OF JAMES GREGORY

From "History of Scottish Medicine" by Dr John Cowrie

highest social circles. He was a deep admirer of "Fair Burnett", the eccentric judge Lord Monboddo's attractive daughter to whom Robert Burns devoted an elegy. Any hopes Gregory may have had of marrying Elizabeth Burnett were, however, sadly dashed when she died of tuberculosis while still in her early twenties, and while staying at Upper or Nether Braid Farm where it was hoped that rest and fresh air might have brought restored health.

While residing at Canaan Lodge, Professor Gregory's eldest son John, an advocate, built up a large collection of birds. The site of his aviary and eagles' cage in the garden is indicated on the Ordnance Survey Map of 1852. Henry Mackenzie, one of Edinburgh's celebrated literary figures in Gregory's day, was a close friend of the Professor and stayed for some time at Canaan Lodge. Later residents have included Macdonnell of Glengarry. The last occupant of the house before its acquisition by Edinburgh Corporation in 1937 was Dr Thomas G. Nasmyth of the then Scottish Board of Health. After its rebuilding in 1907, however, no traces of the original house remain. Professor Gregory's extensive library, incidentally, was presented to Aberdeen University, while his portrait by Sir Henry Raeburn was bequeathed to Fyvie Castle.

On the wall immediately beyond the gateway to Canaan Lodge are two rectangular stones bearing the numbers "5" and "7". The first denotes the diameter in inches of the pipe laid from Comiston springs in 1681, bringing the "sweet waters", underground at this point, to the reservoir at Castlehill. This was Edinburgh's first piped water supply. The "7" refers to the diameter of the pipe from Swanston, laid in 1790 alongside the original five-inch one. Similarly marked stones, indicating the continuation of the pipes' course, are to be seen on the inside of the south boundary wall of nearby Woodville and on the east wall of Whitehouse Loan, opposite the end of Clinton Road. The notes to the Canaan feuing plan of 1803 assert Edinburgh Town Council's "liberty of digging for helping or renewing pipes for carrying water to the city". As the housing estates of Comiston and Oxgangs developed in the 1940s the danger of contamination to the various Comiston springs led to their no longer being used, the considerable supply of water being allowed, instead, to flow into the Braid Burn. The pipe running under Canaan Lane no longer carries water.

Woodburn House is on the right just beyond the entrance to Canaan Lodge. Adapted in 1966 as the Training Centre for the Scottish Hospital Administrative Staff, it is now occupied by another Scottish Health Service department. This well-preserved elegant and secluded villa stands in pleasant grounds first feued by William Mosman to William Bailie, W.S., in 1806. The house was built in 1812, at a cost of £300. The earliest owner of interest was George Ross, advocate, who resided here between 1818 and 1860. Ross was of course the great benefactor, and for long the sole supporter, of the Old Schoolhouse. It is probable that many meetings of the old school's Management Committee took place in Woodburn House.

In 1861 the house passed to D. R. McGregor of the Merchant Shipping Company of Leith. From 1895 until 1921 a succession of medical men, including Dr Bremner (also at one time of nearby Streatham House) and Dr Mears, resided at Woodburn House. For many years the long wooden pavilion, still extant immediately behind the recently re-built Canaan Lane boundary wall, was a sanatorium. In 1922 the house and the former sanatorium became the Edinburgh Royal Infirmary's Nurses' Home. Many Morningside residents will recall the regular nightly departure of the special bus conveying the red-robed nurses to their night-duty at the Royal Infirmary.

It is possible that the original extremely high boundary wall, recently much reduced in height and moved inwards to widen Canaan Lane at this point, was erected at a time when the building of such walls was undertaken solely to provide employment.

Beyond the southern slope of the pleasant lawn of Woodburn House venerable trees form a glade through which, in a still charmingly rural setting, flows the Jordan Burn. On the high tenement, Woodburn Place, in Canaan Lane is inscribed the builder's date, 1880.

The gateway to the Astley Ainslie Hospital leads us not only into one of the most pleasant and well preserved areas of modern Canaan but also back in time to an era in Morningside's history which stretches over more than four centuries.

By the beginning of the sixteenth century this had already become one of the less forbidding and more pleasantly cultivated parts of the ancient Burgh Muir. Nevertheless, it was still remote from the town. A short distance eastwards across the Burgh Muir stood the primitive keep or tower of the Grange of St Giles. Beyond this and slightly to the north was the small Chapel of St John the Baptist, built in 1512, which in 1517 became the Chapel of the Convent of St Catherine of Sienna. Its site is near the present-day Sciennes House Place, and that of the Convent is the junction of St Catherine's Place and Sciennes Road. A light perpetually burning in the tower of the little chapel guided those bold enough to traverse the Burgh Muir after nightfall.

In the grounds of the Astley Ainslie Hospital today are several early nineteenth-century villas. Once privately owned, they were purchased soon after the establishment of the hospital to accommodate patients. One of them is named St Roque after the earliest building erected in this part of the Burgh Muir, the ancient chapel of St Roque or St Roch, the exact site of which is now impossible to determine. The first Ordnance Survey Map of this area (1852) indicates that it stood a little to the north-west of the present-day villa, perhaps on the site of the hospital school. Another possible location is just outwith the southern boundary wall of Southbank Villa, until quite recently the residence of the hospital's Medical

Woodburn House in Canaan Lane
Photograph by Mr W. R. Smith

Superintendent. In this area there are the remains of an early building and an old draw-well. There is also a traditional belief, for long held by successive hospital gardening staff, that the chapel stood in what became the garden of Canaan Park; here again there are the remains of a very old sunken draw-well. The *Inventory of Monuments in Edinburgh* published by the Historical Monuments (Scotland) Commission in 1951 stated that the chapel stood within the grounds of Canaan House, now the hospital's administrative centre.

Grose, in his *Antiquities of Scotland,* provides an illustration, prepared in 1789, of the chapel, indicating that it consisted of a nave and chancel of equal width. The former was entered from the south and lit by a large, arched window in the west gable. The nave opened into the chancel by an obtusely-pointed chancel-arch of a later period. The chapel was, however, already derelict when Grose drew it. Arnot described it as large and Sir Walter Scott (in *Provincial Antiquities of Scotland*) as "oblong and without any architectural ornament". In the account in the Burgh Records of the Riding of the Marches in 1701, reference is made to the chapel, its surrounding cemetery and an adjacent font. The latter is also noted by Sir Walter Scott. Finally, Lord Cockburn in his *Memorials* recalled playing beside the ruins of the chapel as a boy and he perhaps gives a hint as to its location: "A large portion", he wrote, "including the great window of the Chapel of St Roque, on the northern base of Blackford Hill, then survived. There was a pond close by it where I learned to skate . . ." This presumably was Blackford Pond.

If the chapel's exact location and precise size and appearance are difficult to determine, it is certain that it did exist at the beginning of the sixteenth century within what were to become the grounds of the Astley Ainslie Hospital: this much is borne out by Burgh Records and other sources. It is possible that it was built some time between 1501 and 1504, though the first definite reference to its existence occurs in the Lord High Treasurer's Records for 1507. Here it is noted that, in November of that year, James IV visited the little chapel out on the Burgh Muir. On returning from one of his many pilgrimages to St Ninian's shrine at Whithorn, James rested at West Linton and then continued to Edinburgh via Fairmilehead and the old Braid Road. Before reaching the brow of

Ruins of the Chapel of St Roque

From "Macaulay's Poems", by courtesy of Mr R. Copeland of the Astley Ainslie Hospital

223

Churchhill, he turned eastwards into the ancient lane across the Burgh Muir which is now Newbattle Terrace and Grange Loan, and, on November 13th, 1507, visited the Chapel of St Roque. There he heard Mass and, according to the Royal Treasurer's Accounts, gave fourteen shillings to the celebrant, who placed the offering on the altar.

It may well have been James who had encouraged Edinburgh Town Council to build the chapel and he may himself have contributed towards its cost as he was greatly devoted to the French Saint, venerated throughout Europe as patron of the plague-stricken. His interest in St Roque was also evidenced in 1502, when he dedicated a chapel in his honour at Stirling. In the same year he paid £10 Scots to a French monk "for to bring a bane from Sanct Rok to the King". In 1512 James paid a stipend for Mass to be offered in St Giles Church, at which he was present. It was possibly a Requiem Mass for a close friend who had died from plague.

It is possible, however, that the chapel on the Burgh Muir might have been built in about 1503 by Richard Hopper who endowed an altar to St Roque in St Giles in 1502. Yet another suggestion is that it was built to serve as a chapel-of-ease for those coming south from the town to the more pleasant and habitable parts of the Burgh Muir when feuing first began in 1508.

Despite the many and varied explanations proffered of its origins, there is strong evidence to suggest that the little chapel was at the centre of the group of rough wooden huts built out on the Burgh Muir as a quarantine area for the thousands of plague victims taken there during successive epidemics in the hope of recovery as a result of Masses and prayers offered daily in the little chapel, or to be buried in the cemetery surrounding it.

Six years after the first reference to it in 1507, the chapel became the focal point of a very different assembly, destined to bring to Edinburgh, and indeed to Scotland, sorrow as great as that arising from the frequent ravages of the plague. In the summer of 1513 James IV, in the face of advice to the contrary and mysterious and ghostly premonitions of disaster, decided to march against England in support of France. His declaration of war on England was presented to Henry VIII on August 11th, 1513, while the latter was campaigning in France. Soon afterwards, on September 5th, 1513, James issued the following proclamation:

All sic sensabile persons habill
for weir between the ages of sixteen and
sixty are to assemble on the Burgh Muir in
their best array, bodin for weir under
tynsal of lyfe, land and guid.

In compliance with the royal command there assembled in the vicinity of St Roque's Chapel the largest Scottish army ever to muster — if not the hundred thousand men of some accounts, then at least thirty thousand. It is most unlikely that the entire Scottish army would have assembled on the Burgh Muir: the Borderers, for example, would have joined the army as it moved south, and those from the west would more likely have made their way directly to the border muster at Ellem in Berwickshire. This great Scottish army included men from the highest and from the most humble social ranks: the Archbishop of St Andrews and other bishops, abbots of monasteries, the nobility and professional men, and peasant folk compelled to muster by their feudal lords. The provosts and bailies of every royal burgh were required to provide equipment and provisions. Edinburgh Town Council appointed a temporary provost with four bailies to look after the town while Sir Alexander Lauder, the official provost, and his bailies and council rode out to join the muster on the Burgh Muir. Sir Alexander was one of the countless who did not return from Flodden. With Edinburgh's councillors was a great contingent of burghers and craftsmen, the latter proudly carrying their famous flag, the "Blue Blanket", presented to the Incorporation of Trades by James III in 1482. Unlike so many of its followers, it survived the disastrous battle and is today preserved in the Trades Maiden Hospital in Melville Street.

The Scottish artillery cannons, made in a special factory set up by James at Hawkhill and supervised by Robert Borthwick, the royal "Master Meltar", where trundled out of the Netherbow Port by teams of oxen or men, other men going ahead with spades to level the rough ground *en route* to the border. At the head of the Scottish fleet which sailed from Newhaven was the *Great Michael,* to construct which "all the woods of Scotland were laid bare save for Falkland".

The King himself did not encamp with his great host of followers on the Burgh Muir but he did attend Mass in St Roque's Chapel to pray for Scotland's cause as the army prepared to march south.

The scene when the flower of Scotland's manhood mustered in allegiance to their King in these autumn days of 1513 has been described most graphically (if with some romantic exaggeration) by Sir Walter Scott in Canto IV of *Marmion*. The English knight, on a special mission to the Scottish Court, makes his way towards the Scottish camp:

> Suffice it that the route was laid
> Across the furzy hills of Braid.
> They passed the glen and scanty rill
> And clim'b the opposing bank until
> They gained the top of Blackford Hill.

Sir Walter then compares the view from Blackford Hill which he saw as a schoolboy with that which Marmion beheld:

225

But different far the change has been,
Since Marmion from the crown
Of Blackford saw that martial scene
Upon the bent so brown:
Thousand pavilions white as snow,
Spread all the Borough-Moor below,
Upland and dale and down —
A thousand did I say? I ween,
Thousands on thousands there were seen,
That chequer'd all the heath between
The streamlet and the town:
In crossing ranks extending far,
Forming a camp irregular;
Oft giving way, where still there stood
Some relics of the old oak wood,
That darkly huge did intervene,
And tam'd the glaring white with green:
In these extended lines there lay
A martial Kingdom's vast array.

After relating how the King's lieges assembled from diverse parts of
Scotland and describing in colourful detail the preparations for
departure, he continues:

Highest and midmost, was descried
The royal banner floating wide;
The staff, a pine tree strong and straight
Pitch'd deeply in a massive stone,
Which still in memory is shown ...
Still on the spot Lord Marmion stay'd
For fairer scene he ne'er survey'd ...

Sir David Lindesay, the Lord Lyon, then comments to Marmion on the
scene before them:

The whilst the bells, with distant chime,
Merrily toll'd the hour of prime,
And thus the Lindesay spoke:
"Thus clamour still the war notes when
The King to Mass his way has ta'en,
Or to St Katherine's of Sienne,
Or Chapel of Saint Rocque
To you they speak of martial fame:
But me remind of peaceful game,
When blither was their cheer."

Then the Lindesay's premonition:

226

Nor less, he said "I moan
To think what woe what chance may bring,
And how these merry bells may ring
The death-dirge of our gallant King."

All too soon were the "merry bells" to toll their death dirge not only for the King but also for innumerable followers who fell at Flodden: the Archbishop of St Andrews (James's natural son) bishops, abbots, thirteen earls, clan chiefs and many, many of humbler origin once part of that great assembly on the Burgh Muir, the "martial kingdom's vast array".

So vivid is Sir Walter's picture of the muster on the Burgh Muir that its inaccuracies and anachronisms are unimportant, though for the historical record they merit some reference. While the King might well have made his way to the Chapel of St Roque, he could not have gone to "St Katherine's of Sienne": this convent had not been established when the Scottish army gathered in 1513. It was not founded until four years later, and then largely as a consequence of the disaster of Flodden. Again, the "royal banner floating wide . . . Pitch'd deeply in a massive stone" is, as discussed in an earlier chapter, more colourful than historical.

One feature of Sir Walter's description of the scene does, however, remain. The men, we are told, assembled between "The streamlet and the town", the former being a reference to the Jordan Burn which today still flows through Morningside and the grounds of the Astley Ainslie Hospital as it had since long before the Scottish army camped on its banks.

The bells of St Roque's had not long ceased tolling for the dead who lay where they had fallen on Flodden's fatal field when they were heard to toll again for a more familiar reason: the invasion of Edinburgh by yet another plague epidemic. Many of those following James IV had never reached Flodden, falling victims to the plague *en route,* and, when the sad remnant of the Scottish army returned to Edinburgh, "the pestilence" accompanied them. Once again the huts around St Roque's Chapel, so recently overshadowed by the "Thousand pavilions white as snow", became crowded with victims of the plague.

The first major European epidemic of plague, known as the "Black Death" or "the pest", was recorded as early as 669. Then, while England and Ireland suffered, Scotland, according to Fordun, escaped, "save for Lothiane". St Cuthbert at Lindisfarne fell a victim but recovered. In 1350, as a result of developing trade with the Continent, Scotland shared something of the devastation which swept Europe when nearly a third of its population died. In 1498 Edinburgh suffered an alarming outbreak, quickly spread, as were later epidemics, by the rat and flea-infested living conditions in the congested closes of the Old Town.

Soon after the 1498 epidemic — possibly only five years later — the little Chapel of St Roque was built on the remote Burgh Muir and here plague victims and suspected cases were lodged in rough wooden huts,

227

usually to die. Some might have been buried individually in the little cemetery surrounding the chapel, but during severe outbreaks most were laid in nearby mass graves, some of which may still be seen as large grass or shrub-covered mounds in the Astley Ainslie Hospital grounds.

"The Holy Confessor, Sanct Rok", patron Saint of the plague-stricken, was born at Narbonne in France in 1295 and died at Montpelier in 1327 at the age of thirty-two. He forsook his wealthy family background and set out as a pilgrim to Italy, where he lived as a hermit, tending and bringing comfort to plague victims, and, reputedly, bringing miraculous cures to some. When he himself eventually fell a victim, in his concern not to spread the infection he withdrew into isolation. Food was brought to him by his dog: herein, some say, originated the saying, "Love me, love my dog". On his death-bed, St Roch prayed that whoever invoked his name should be protected from the plague. After his death many cities in Europe attributed their escape from the ravages of the plague to the Saint's intercession. Many churches in Europe were dedicated to St Roch and his relics are preserved in the Church of San Rocco in Venice, which also has a series of paintings by Tintoretto illustrating the Saint's life.

The first chapel in Scotland dedicated to St Roch was that built by James IV at Stirling in 1502. The King also provided money to build a house "for the seik folk" beside the chapel. Other chapels soon followed at Glasgow, Paisley and Dundee. All, like the little chapel on the Burgh Muir, have long since disappeared.

The first "hospital chaplain" at St Roque's on the Burgh Muir, appointed by the Town Council and bailies in 1530, was Sir John Young, whose meagre income was drawn from voluntary offerings and burial fees. He may have been assisted by the monks of St Giles and Holyrood Abbey. The first reference to the Chapel in the town records is a proclamation, issued by the magistrates on December 15th, 1530, whereby Sir John Young was bound "to uphold the said kirk in sclatis, watterticht, glaswyndois and other necessair thingis in efferis", and was granted by the provost and bailies of Edinburgh three acres of land. At the same time James Barbour was appointed "master and governor of the foul folk on the mure".

During successive plague epidemics over nearly three centuries, the Edinburgh Town Council enforced various regulations, often extremely strict. From the earliest times there was an awareness of the need for isolation and quarantine, even though prevention and cure were unknown. Isolation on the Burgh Muir eventually became a well organised "municipal service". All known or suspected plague victims had to be reported to the authorities within twenty-four hours, or, in later times, within twelve hours. Horse or hand-drawn wooden carts conveyed the hapless victims out to the Burgh Muir between the hours of 9 p.m. and 5 a.m. These primitive ambulances were preceded by "Bailies of the Mure", voluntarily recruited men wearing black or grey tunics and St Andrew's

Crosses. They carried long staffs used to touch infected materials and rang hand-bells to warn citizens of their dangerous charges. The carts halted at the Burgh or South Loch, now the Meadows. On its south bank were prepared large cauldrons of boiling water in which other Bailies of the Mure, known as "clengeris", carrying long staffs with metal hooks at the tips, attempted to disinfect the victims' clothes. Early versions of the later, and now obsolete, standard hospital bed-gowns were provided, relatives then being required to collect the victims' disinfected clothes at strictly statutory times.

The patients were taken to the wooden huts around St Roque's, where relatives could not visit them before 11 a.m., under penalty of death. In later centuries only suspected cases or contacts were taken to St Roque's, actual victims being lodged around the chapel of St John the Baptist, in what is now the Sciennes district, where in 1517 was built the Convent dedicated to St Catherine of Sienna. Many victims never reached these early hospitals but died *en route* and were buried by the wayside — hence the human remains unearthed in private gardens in the wide area which was once the Burgh Muir. For long a tombstone to a plague victim stood in the grounds of Bruntsfield House, where it was eventually built into the boundary wall. On certain occasions plague sufferers were also isolated on the shore at Leith, or taken out to Inchkeith and Inchcolme in the Firth of Forth.

While some of the measures enforced by Edinburgh Town Council bordered on the superstitious, others indicated a gradual progress towards some more rational method of containing the plague's worst ravages. Many decrees were issued including the following: the windows of houses in which a case was reported or suspected were not to be opened; after the removal of a victim and the placing in quarantine of all residents in contact, a house was to remain empty for fifteen days. During the severe epidemic of 1645 Mary King's Close, under the site of the present-day City Chambers, was completely evacuated. It has been preserved virtually as it was then, with an old butcher's shop still to be seen.

All furniture from infected houses was to be washed in the running Water of Leith and then left untouched for eight days before being collected by its owners. The washing of furniture in the town's stagnant lochs was forbidden. In later times articles of furniture and other possessions from infected households were laid out in the frost in winter. The fumigation of houses was carried out by the burning of heather.

James IV, whose many interests included medicine (the original body of Edinburgh's Royal College of Surgeons was given its Royal Seal by him in 1506), not only placed his trust, during plague outbreaks, in the intercession of St Roque but also enforced certain measures which, in an era when the scientific treatment and bacterial origin of infectious diseases were undreamed of, now seem remarkably enlightened. For "the staunching of the contagious plaige of pestilence now ringing in diverse places in our realm", he decreed "that Edinburgh be divided into four areas, each, during a plague epidemic, to be supervised by a bailie, and, in each section, cases to be notified to the Barber Surgeons", Edinburgh's earliest general medical practitioners.

Punishments for failure to observe the regulations promulgated were severe and included branding on the cheek, the cutting off of a hand, and banishment. For the most serious disregard of decrees the punishment was hanging from the gibbet erected on that part of the Burgh Muir where Preston Street Primary School now stands. In June 1585 two men were hanged for stealing infected clothing.

"Those whom God relevis of the pestilence and givis their health must converse nocht with other persons for 40 days," it was also decreed. Children under fifteen were not to appear in the streets during an epidemic and dogs were to be kept indoors. Travel between towns and villages was forbidden. Beggars, outlawed from Edinburgh, were housed in rough huts on the Burgh Muir.

To deal with the excessive dirtiness of many old Edinburgh streets five highly-paid street "clengeris" were appointed. Their duties also included the cleaning of infected houses. They carried long staffs tipped with rings of white iron and, before undertaking their dangerous duties, were required to hear Mass in a hospital chapel in St Mary's Wynd. The name of one of these earliest "Cleansing Department" officials was Alexander Pennecuik. In 1527 he appointed a full-time supervisor of the street cleansers, with twelve assistants responsible to him to "dicht and clengeit" the streets every eight days.

Records of the severe epidemic of 1585 reveal several interesting facts. Terror enveloped the town and the Lord Provost James Stewart, Earl of Arran, fled with many of his bailies. On his return, Stewart was deposed. With him had also fled most of the students of "the toun's college". As a consequence of the epidemic, Edinburgh's treasury was so depleted that in the following year the Town Council decided to raise revenue by feuing the Burgh Muir which, since its donation to the town by David I in the twelfth century, had never been profitably developed.

Records of the 1585 plague, as we have seen, also refer to Robert Fairlie, the Laird of Braid's providing ale from his breweries at Littil Egypt for "the seik folkis on the mure". A large storehouse for bread and ale had been erected near St Roque's Chapel. Another citizen whose services were appreciated was Edinburgh's "Medical Officer", Dr James Henrysoun, whom the Town Council appointed "surgeon in charge of all plague procedures". Supervising the sick in their homes, at St Roque's and elsewhere, Dr Henrysoun's services were apparently at the disposal of the town night and day, and "through his guid care and diligence, he sparit nocht the hazard of his own lyfe." He was supplied with all "medicaines" required, paid a stipend of £20 per annum for life and exempted from all burgh taxes during his lifetime. In December 1585 the

230

Old stones depicting symbols from the Passion of Christ, traditionally believed to be from the Chapel of St Roque but probably from Trinity Church on the site of Waverley Station

Photographs by Mr Brian Smith

Edinburgh Town Council thanked Dr Henrysoun for his good services, especially since he himself had contracted the plague and his wife had died during this most severe visitation.

Worthy as were Dr Henrysoun's gallant services, the devoted labours of his colleagues, the Barber Surgeons, and the well-meaning decrees, all had failed to take measure against the real culprits responsible for the frequent reappearance and lightning spread of the disease — infected rats. It was the black rat from Europe, coming ashore from ships at Leith, which brought the plague to Edinburgh. Soon the considerable native rat population became infected and so the disease spread, transmitted by fleas gorged with rat blood infected with bacteria which was passed on to human beings they fed from. While bubonic plague, causing bubos or sores, was not so easily transmitted from person to person, the more lethal pneumonic type readily spread by droplets from the respiratory tract and by the inhalation of infected dust in the congested, dusty closes and houses of old Edinburgh. When the infected person developed septicaemia, the skin turned black, making him easily recognisable as a victim of the dreaded "Black Death".

While Edinburgh Town Council was probably the first in Scotland to make plague a notifiable disease, other town authorities in Scotland had come to suspect rats as the source much sooner than had those of Edinburgh. In 1647 Aberdeen Town Council was the first to lay rat poison, Glasgow taking such measures soon afterwards.

Edinburgh's last outbreak of plague was in 1645, and the last in Scotland occurred in 1648. The final epidemic in Edinburgh is commemorated by the small private burial ground of John Livingston of Greenhill in Chamberlain Road: he was one of the victims in an epidemic so severe as to kill half the population of Leith. Edinburgh was gripped by such terror that many members of the Town Council and other officials fled so as "to leave scarcely sixty men to guard the town". During this outbreak Joannes Paulitius, M.D. was appointed doctor in charge and paid £80 Scots per month.

After the Reformation proscribed the offering of Mass and prayers before "idolatrous shrines", the original function of the Chapel of St Roque would have come to an end, though the isolation of plague victims there continued. Perhaps Protestant services of intercession for the sick were held in the chapel, which certainly continued to exist. For some time it was known as Sir Simon Rollock's Chapel: why is not known, except that it may have been a corruption of "St Roque's". When it was first proposed to demolish the chapel, many citizens objected, and their pleas were upheld. In 1749 the chapel and its surrounding land were purchased by Bailie John Dewar, who began demolition. While this was being done, the scaffolding used collapsed and several workmen were killed. After the accident, widely regarded as a judgment on sacrilegious destruction, no workman would continue, despite the appeals and bribes of Bailie Dewar.

232

By 1789 the chapel was derelict. Two years later it finally was demolished.

Since the chapel's disappearance many stones of ecclesiastical origin have been found in the grounds of the Astley Ainslie Hospital and in private gardens in the neighbourhood. A collection of these, some bearing initials and dates, was built into a specially constructed stone panel by Colonel John Fraser, when Medical Superintendent of the Astley Ainslie Hospital, in the southern boundary wall of his residence, South Bank. Also to be seen in the hospital grounds are a draw-well and a font or trough at the foot of the lawn of Morelands, a very old sunken well in what was the garden of Canaan Park, and, just beyond the southern boundary wall of South Bank, the remains of another old draw-well and those of an early building of some kind. To the west of the lean-to greenhouse in what was formerly the garden of Millbank villa, are, embedded in the ground, a row of four large cylindrical stones. Each bears sculpted emblems of the Passion of Christ: the crown of thorns, the nails and a hammer, and an open hand bearing the print of the nails.

Traditionally, these remains were believed to have been part of the Chapel of St Roque, suggesting that it was a relatively large church. Expert antiquarian opinion now suggests, however, that they originate from the fifteenth-century Trinity College Church which, until 1848, stood on the site of the present-day Waverley Station. When this church was demolished stone by stone, each was carefully numbered and laid out on Calton Hill. Eventually it became fashionable, especially for residents of developing outlying districts such as Canaan, to have some of the more interesting and ornate of these stones transported to their large private gardens. Another possibility is that the stones were brought to the gardens of Canaan during the restoration of St Giles by William Burn in 1829, as were a considerable number to the garden of Swanston Cottage.

Long before the Astley Ainslie Hospital's first small units were opened in Canaan Park House in 1923, the ancient medical traditions of this district of Canaan were fittingly continued by the advent of James Syme, who moved into the villa Millbank in 1842. He became Professor of Surgery in Edinburgh's already world-renowned Medical School and, eventually, one of the leading surgeons in Europe.

Early in his career as a medical student, young James Syme distinguished himself as a chemist by making a discovery which, had he patented it and pursued it commercially, might have brought him great wealth and altered the course of his career. At the age of eighteen he had founded a chemical society with some young friends. In the course of his own researches he produced a pure form of naphtha which was capable of dissolving rubber more effectively than any substance then known. He used his discovery to demonstrate that silk cloth could be waterproofed. Syme relinquished the opportunity of exploiting his process commercially, commenting that "he was then about to commence the study of a profession with which considerations of trade did not seem consistent". In

1823 Charles Macintosh of Glasgow was credited with the discovery which was rightly Syme's and he not only made a fortune by it but, of course, had his name immortalised as an eponym for a raincoat.

Many of Syme's chemistry experiments were carried out in the early University teaching laboratories of John Deuchar at 27 Lothian Street, now the site of the lecture hall of the Royal Scottish Museum. Deuchar was a member of the notable family who for long resided in Morningside House.

Before qualifying, Syme's first appointment was as a trainee-assistant in the Edinburgh Fever Hospital, then in the Queensberry House Barracks in the Canongate and administered from the Infirmary in what is now commemoratively named Infirmary Street.

In 1821 Syme became a Member of the Royal College of Surgeons (London) and, two years later, a Fellow of the Royal College of Surgeons (Edinburgh). After teaching anatomy for some time he fell out with his colleagues who were involved with the body-snatching activities of Burke and Hare. He again found himself at variance with his surgeon colleagues in the extra-mural medical school in Brown Square at the west end of Chambers Street, so boldly established his own private surgical hospital in Minto House in Argyle Square, entered from Horse Wynd near College Wynd leading off from the Cowgate. (The original Minto House was demolished in 1870 and the site is now occupied by the Edinburgh University Staff Club in Chambers Street.) Syme's hospital prospered and his lectures and operations were attended by increasing numbers of students, many of whom were, through his training, to become distinguished surgeons. Despite the demands on his services, Syme dispensed with the assistance both of a secretary and of an appointments diary, yet never failed to be punctual.

Professor James Syme of Millbank in Canaan Lane. Sketch by one of his students, R. Peddie

Many interesting and colourful features of Syme's life, both professional and private, were recorded by his principal assistant, Dr John Brown, author of *Rab and His Friends*. The latter contains a pathetic and moving account by Brown ("the Charles Lamb of Scottish Literature") of James Noble, the Howgate carrier bringing his wife Ailie on a cart, drawn by his old horse Jess and accompanied by his faithful dog Rab, to Syme's hospital, and conveys vividly the atmosphere of the place and the time. The day after Ailie's arrival, the students hurried up the stair of the hospital and read the simple notice on the board: "An operation today." In the crowded operating theatre tears clouded the students' eyes as "the serenely elderly old lady" endured the ordeal without an anaesthetic. She seemed to recover, then, almost inevitably, as in so many cases before the advent of antiseptic surgery, she died from general septicaemia.

In those early days, surgery was not lacking in skilful technique but two essential advancements were still to come, anaesthesia and the use of antiseptics. In addition to Dr John Brown's graphic description of Ailie's bravery during her operation for cancer of the breast, another of Syme's patients recorded his own ordeal during surgery without anaesthesia. Professor George Wilson, a distinguished lecturer in chemistry, founder of the Scottish Industrial Museum (forerunner of the Royal Scottish Museum in Chambers Street) and a pioneer in the study of colour-blindness, who resided for some time at Elm Cottage at the west end of Blackford Road (not far from Syme's house at Millbank), had his foot amputated by the distinguished surgeon. After the operation, Wilson wrote to Professor James Y. Simpson strongly advocating the use of an anaesthetic and describing "the black whirlwind of emotion, the horror of great darkness and the sense of desertion by God and man" during his operation.

Syme was to become involved in an unfortunate controversy and a bitter personal vendetta with his illustrious contemporary Simpson. This aspect of his career and much else of biographical interest is described in *Simpson and Syme of Edinburgh* by John A. Shepherd.

If Syme's relationship with Simpson, pioneer of one of the two revolutionary developments in surgery, anaesthesia, was regrettable, his association with Lord Lister, the pioneer of the other great breakthrough, antiseptic surgery, gave Lister both support and inspiration. Having become Professor of Surgery in the Edinburgh Medical School, Syme invited young Joseph Lister to join his staff for a month. So valuable was their collaboration and so encouraging and beneficial was Syme's influence on his young assistant that Lister remained with his "Chief" for eight years.

While working with Syme at the Infirmary (which had been established in the old Edinburgh High School in what is now Infirmary Street in 1832) Lister was a frequent and welcome visitor to Millbank. There he met and fell in love with Syme's daughter, Agnes. They were married in the drawing-room of the villa on April 24th, 1856. Lister was later converted from his Quaker beliefs to the Episcopalianism of his wife and father-in-law. A plaque in the present-day Millbank Hospital pavilion commemorates the marriage in the villa on the site of which this ward now stands.

Syme had purchased Millbank, with its extensive and pleasant gardens, meadows and greenhouses, in 1842. It was an ideal retreat from the pressures and harrassing duties of hospital life. His chief joy and relaxation was his garden and the greenhouses in which he cultivated rare plants, fruit trees and shrubs, including, as Dr John Brown records, "matchless orchids, heaths and azaleas, bananas and grapes and peaches". Part of the original greenhouse and much of Syme's garden still remain, kept in excellent condition by today's hospital staff.

Millbank was, however, never simply the retreat of a recluse. Here Syme, with the ready help of his second wife, Jemina Burn, entertained many guests. Among the most notable of these was Thomas Carlyle who, during his visit to Edinburgh in 1868 to deliver his University Rectorial address, consulted Syme professionally and underwent a minor operation. After convalescing for two weeks at Millbank, Carlyle was Syme's principal guest at a dinner party which included many distinguished guests, honoured, no doubt, to meet the Sage of Chelsea. After dinner Syme and Carlyle sat on the verandah talking and watching the sunset reflected on Blackford Hill.

Charles Dickens, in Edinburgh in 1869 to give one of his celebrated readings in the Music Hall in George Street, consulted Syme about his lameness.

Millbank, the residence of Professor James Syme, in Canaan Lane
By courtesy of the late Colonel John Cunningham, M.D.

Perhaps the most scintillating social occasion at Millbank took place during the meeting of the British Association in Edinburgh in 1850, when "one hundred noblemen and gentlemen including many distinguished foreign scientists were entertained to a sumptuous dinner at Millbank."

Largely through the encouragement and influence of his father-in-law, Joseph Lister was appointed to the Chair of Surgery at Glasgow University in 1860 and there pioneered and established his techniques in antiseptic surgery. In 1869 he succeeded Syme as Professor of Surgery at the Edinburgh University Medical School. Eventually he returned to London. Syme, latterly one of the great protagonists for a new Royal Infirmary, at last built at Lauriston Place in 1879, spent the evening of his life at his beloved Millbank, where he died on June 26th, 1870. He was interred in St John's churchyard at the west end of Princes Street.

Millbank witnessed not only the marriage of Joseph Lister to Agnes Syme in 1856 but, thirty-six years earlier, it had been the scene of another marriage which was something of a sensation at the time. On September 26th, 1820, Miss Anne Neilson, fourth daughter of James Neilson of Millbank, married Alexander Ivanovitch, Sultan Katte Gherry Krim. Sultan of the Crimea, Ivanovitch had been converted to Christianity by Scottish missionaries at Carass in the Caucasus. At the expense of Alexander, Czar of Russia, he was sent to Edinburgh to receive further Christian education in the hope that he would return to his country as a missionary. After their wedding, he and Anne settled in Morningside, where the Sultan's wife came to be known in the village as the "Sultana". Little is known of her husband's subsequent missionary activities.

The Astley Ainslie Hospital owes its establishment to David Ainslie of Costerton, a village near Crichton Castle in Midlothian. A successful sheep-breeder, whose many trophies are preserved in the hospital board-room, Ainslie, a bachelor, willed his considerable estate to a nephew who, however, pre-deceased his uncle, who then established a trust charged with "the holding, applying and disposing of his estate for the purpose of erecting and maintaining a hospital or institution to be known as the Astley Ainslie Institution for the relief and behoof of convalescents in the Royal Infirmary of Edinburgh".

David Ainslie died on May 24th, 1900, but many years elapsed before the accumulated monies of his estate were used. In 1921 a Board of Governors for the projected new institution was established. It was, they specified, "to deal with patients suffering from curable conditions who have definitely passed the crisis of their illness and who with proper care, sufficiently prolonged, may reasonably be expected to regain normal health and fitness for their usual avocations. The functions of the hospital include the scientific investigation of the process involved in the gradual restoration of health which constitutes 'convalescence' ". Such has continued to be the policy of successive hospital boards. Until 1948 and the establishment of the National Health Service, all patients were from

Lord Joseph Lister, son-in-law of Professor James Syme of Millbank

the Edinburgh Royal Infirmary. Since that date, however, many have been admitted from different hospitals under the aegis of what was the South East Scotland Regional Hospital Board and, since 1974, has been the Lothian Health Board.

The original site acquired by David Ainslie's trustees included a nine-hole ladies' golf course. One of the holes lay just south of the Jordan Burn which still flows through the hospital grounds. It also included the villa and extensive policies of Millbank. In 1922 Canaan Park was purchased. This mansion-house, once the residence of a member of the Forbes family of Pitsligo, had been, from 1909 until its purchase by the hospital, a girls' school known as Canaan Park College. Certain issues of the college magazine are still filed in the Edinburgh Room of the Edinburgh Central Public Library and former pupils of the college, calling themselves the "Canaanites", have held re-unions in recent years.

In October 1923 an experimental unit for women patients was opened in Canaan Park. At about this time, the old villa of Millbank having proved unsuitable for use as a hospital ward, the present-day Millbank Pavilion was built on the site of the demolished mansion-house. In 1930 the east and west butterfly-design pavilions facing Blackford Hill were opened, along with the scientific laboratories. Soon afterwards the Occupational Therapy Department, the Nurses' and Maids' Residences and the Children's School were opened. In 1948 the other two villas, Morelands, near the hospital's east entrance from Whitehouse Terrace, and St Roque were purchased. The two newly-acquired villas accommodated ambulant patients. Canaan House, built in 1805, became the hospital's administrative centre. Southbank, formerly known as Canaan Bank, became the residence of the Medical Superintendent. The Children's Pavilion was opened in 1965 and the Day Centre in 1971.

238

The hospital now has two hundred and fifteen beds. One of its most notable features is its Occupational Therapy Unit. When first established in 1930 it was staffed by Canadians. The subsequently established training school, the first of its kind in Scotland, has attracted trainee therapists from all over the world. Thus, with the most modern scientific techniques, the hospital proudly maintains the ancient traditions of healing first associated with its district over four centuries ago.

Returning from the pleasant Astley Ainslie Hospital grounds to Canaan Lane and proceeding northwards towards its junction with Newbattle Terrace and Grange Loan, we pass a number of interesting villas. On the north garden wall of one called Bloomfield is a sculptured artist's palette bearing the date "1881", possibly the work of Robert McGregor, R.S.A. who resided here at that date. In the garden of Norwood, just within its northern boundary wall at Grange Loan, are the remains of Bloomsberry Cottage, and on the Grange Loan side of this wall may still be seen its long-bricked-up windows. In Bloomsberry Cottage, it will be remembered, lived Gorge Meikle Kemp, architect of the Scott Monument. From the cottage Kemp, in May 1838, wrote to his brother Thomas: "I am quite satisfied with the change I have made from Stockbridge to the land of Canaan. We have more accommodation for the same rent, a very pleasant little garden enclosed with a high wall, well stocked with flowers and fruit trees, and very few taxes." This charming rural atmosphere still surrounds the villas beside which Bloomsberry Cottage once stood. For a period prior to its demolition, the cottage was a laundry. Immediately to the east stood, at one time, Canaan Villa, also long since demolished.

In 1821 the remoteness from Edinburgh of Canaan is referred to in an article in *Blackwood's Magazine,* the writer remarking that "the calls of the fishwives have even reached the lands of Canaan". Canaan itself he describes as, "the grounds to the south of the city where a number of snug boxes attest to the taste of the inhabitants for country retirement and the pleasures of rustication". "Box" was a term used for "a small country house or shooting-box". Of the "snug boxes", none would then have merited the description more than Woodville, the entrance drive of which is opposite the gates of Norwood. The feu contract for the building of Woodville is dated 1803 and the villa was built soon afterwards.

Of the owners of Woodville, most interesting was James Wilson, F.R.S.E., who came to reside here shortly after his marriage in 1824. A distinguished naturalist and "a less rollicking blade" than his brother "Christopher North", the famous literary figure, Wilson wrote at Woodville the whole section on Natural History in the 7th Edition of the *Encyclopaedia Britannica.* It may have been his awareness of failing health which led him to decline the Chair in Natural History at Edinburgh University in 1854. He died two years later.

Something of the atmosphere of Canaan in the early nineteenth

239

Woodville, Canaan Lane, the residence of James Wilson
By courtesy of the Rt Hon. Lord Strachan

century is conveyed by Wilson's biographer, the Rev. James Hamilton, who wrote: "It would be difficult to find a more charming retreat than, in Mr Wilson's possession, Woodville became. In his domain of two acres, snugly ensconced amidst the groves of Morningside, he caught the whole sunshine of the winter noon, forgetful of biting blasts and easterly fogs." It has been suggested that this reference to "the whole sunshine of the winter noon" is a clue to the origin and meaning of the name Morningside. Another, already mentioned, is that the original entrance to East Morningside House faced east — to the "morning side" of the sun.

Apart from his prolific writings on natural history, which included *Illustrations of Zoology* (1826) and the "Notes of a Naturalist" in Porter's *Illustrations of Scripture,* depicting animals referred to in the Bible, Wilson's other literary works included *A Voyage Round the Coasts of Scotland and the Isles,* illustrated by his versatile neighbour and fellow-voyager, Sir Thomas Dick Lauder of Grange House.

On a window-pane of what was the villa's dining-room, now the study and library, are scratched the initials of James Wilson and his wife, "J.W. — I.W. 1826". Mrs Wilson's name before marriage was Isabella Keith. After Wilson's death, soon followed by that of his wife, his niece Henrietta Wilson came to reside at Woodville. The house and its attractive garden are described in her book *Chronicles of a Garden : Its Pets and Pleasures.*

A later owner of Woodville was Sir James Alexander Russell, M.D., Lord Provost of Edinburgh 1891-4. Dr Russell, during his period in office, did much to advance public health, clearing many of Edinburgh's worst slums. In the early 1940s, Thomas Usher, a well-known Edinburgh brewer, added the east wing to the house. The present owner, a distinguished Scottish judge, now retired, has further enhanced the charm of both house and garden.

Leaving Canaan Lane and turning westwards along Newbattle Terrace, we notice, on the right-hand side, a wooden door which was once a rear entrance to the grounds of a villa named Woodcroft, on the site of which an important telephone exchange now stands. Here begins a fine avenue of beech trees, originally the entrance drive to East Morningside House in Clinton Road. On the left, immediately beyond Woodville, stands another typical red sandstone Canaan villa, of the early nineteenth century, Canaan Grove, now the pavilion for the pleasantly situated municipal tennis courts and bowling greens. In the garden of this house are a number of carved ecclesiastical stones similar to those in the Astley Ainslie Hospital grounds.

Immediately beyond Canaan Grove we come to yet another of Morningside's Biblical names — Eden. Eden Lane leads into one of the quaintest little communities in the district. While the location of Eden appears on the Ordnance Survey Map of 1852, it is not shown in Kirkwood's map of 1817 as the first house was not built here until about 1822. This was Harmony House, named as such by 1852 and still standing today.

In 1816 a small area of land in what came to be called the district of Eden had been disponed to Robert Haxton, whose surname also appears as Halkerston. Whether the house he built in Eden was named Harmony House by him or by a subsequent owner is not known. There are two possible explanations of the name. An owner following Haxton might have been a devotee of Charles Dickens and might have found the name in one of his novels. Alternatively, there is some traditional support for a second theory. Robert Haxton was the Chief Armourer at Edinburgh Castle and it is possible therefore that local people came to call Haxton's house "the armourer's house". eventually corrupted to Harmony House. The traditional occupations of armourer or gunsmith continued in Haxton's family though they did not long reside in Harmony House. A little to the north of Harmony House, the 1852 Ordnance Survey Map shows Ellen Cottage and Jane Cottage, built by Robert Haxton for his daughters. Both remain but have been renamed.

Also indicated in the informative 1852 Ordnance Survey Map is Eden Hermitage, a small cell-like building which may still be seen opposite the side entrance to Harmony House. Some part of the little building may have very early origins as the retreat of a hermit, though the cast-iron Celtic cross formerly surmounting it and the apparently antique hinges once on the doorway of the "cell" were found by an expert to have been relatively modern. The cross, considered to be in danger of collapse, was removed some years ago by the owner of Eden Lodge, in whose property

Eden Lane, Canaan
By courtesy of Mr Brian Smith

Eden Hermitage now stands. In the 1830s a curio dealer lived in Harmony House and it is probable that he was responsible for the Celtic cross and the hinges which perpetuated the belief that a hermit had once lived there. On the lintel above the side entrance to Harmony House are carved the initials "A.S.L.", which cannot be identified with any previous owner. On the old wall on the left-hand side of Eden Lane are several bricked-up doorways and windows believed to be the remains of cottages once part of the adjacent Canaan Farm.

Beyond Eden Lane, in Newbattle Terrace, are a number of pleasant nineteenth-century villas which also formed part of the old Eden community. Falcon Gardens to the left commemorates one of the largest estates within the lands of Canaan, the Falcon estate, which eventually extended to eighteen acres, from Newbattle Terrace to Canaan Lane in the south, where most of the old boundary wall still remains, and from Morningside Road eastwards to, approximately, the line of the present-day Falcon Gardens. Within its pleasant, tree-shaded confines there came to be built in 1815, by Alexander Falconar, the majestic and ornate mansion, Falcon Hall, from which the streets of today take their names. The site of the house was the junction of Falcon Court and Falcon Road West. The main entrance drive from Morningside Road was half-way between Steel's Place and Falcon Road West, where two short rows of

Falcon Hall, Canaan Estate

tenements, notably different in design and date, meet above the shops at 193 and 195 Morningside Road. Several writers have stated that the main gateway of the drive leading off Morningside Road to Falcon Hall was at what is now the entrance to Falcon Road West, opposite Morningside Public Library. That this was not so has, however, been revealed by a valuable old photograph kindly provided by a Morningside resident. In fact, the tall stone pillars of the gate, each surmounted by a stone falcon, stood immediately north of what is now 195 Morningside Road. At the time of the photograph, about 1900, only the tenements on the east side of Morningside Road, extending from Steel's Place to No. 195, had been built. Those from No. 193 to Falcon Road West were built after the Falcon Hall gates had been demolished, probably around 1909. The architectural difference between the two blocks of tenements is obvious, especially when studied from the rear. A porter's lodge used to stand just within the gates. Another driveway led from what is now Falcon Avenue, near Falcon Road.

There is some confusion over the origins of Falcon Hall. Mair claims that it was built by Lord Provost William Coulter in 1780, the facade and other embellishments being added by Alexander Falconar in 1815. Grant

Falcon Hall
Photograph by the late Mr John Bartholomew

244

wrote, in 1880: "Falcon Hall, eastward of the old village, is an elegant modern villa erected early in the present century by a wealthy Indian civilian named Falconar, but save old Morningside House or Lodge, before that time no other mansion of importance stood there." Grant, the *Scots Magazine* and the *Edinburgh Eveing Courant* also state that Coulter died at Morningside Lodge on April 14th, 1810, but the feu which Coulter held in Morningside was not in the Morningside (originally Wester Morningside) estate on the west side of Morningside, but in Canaan. Furthermore, the sasine records for Edinburgh for the period 1781-1815 reveal that Coulter seised, in 1803, three acres and, in 1806, a further three acres of the lands of Canaan. On February 2nd, 1814, four years after William Coulter's death, Margaret Thomson, Coulter's widow, purchased a further three and a quarter acres. Fifteen days later, on February 17th, 1814, Mrs Coulter disponed to Alexander Falconar her part of the Canaan Estate, approximately nine acres. It may therefore be concluded that the house which Coulter built in his original three acres of Canaan in 1780 was Morningside Lodge and that it was this house which Alexander Falconar purchased with almost nine acres of land in February 1814 and then proceeded to redesign and embellish, naming it, as a play on his surname, Falcon Hall.

William Coulter, head of a large hosiery business in the High Street, became, after many years' service as a Town Councillor, Lord Provost in 1808, but died after only two years in office. He pressed for the foundation of a fever hospital in the City, which was not opened until 1903. He also laid the foundation stone of Edinburgh's "first proper asylum for the insane", the original East House, completed, on a site between Maxwell Street and Millar Crescent, in 1813. He was a captain in the Edinburgh Volunteers and as such earned a biographical note and sketch in Kay's *Portraits*. Great pride in his "military" rank led him in an after-dinner speech, when well fortified with port, to remark: "It is true I have the body of a stocking weaver but I have the soul of a *skyppyo afreekanus*." His audience were puzzled over his claim until one of the more learned guests suggested that Coulter was comparing himself with the renowned Roman general, Scipio Africanus. In another unhappy speech he expanded upon the progress of history by proclaiming: "Gentlemen, we live in a great area." He was honoured by a public funeral from Morningside Lodge, conducted, according to one critic, "with a parade and show that was gratefully overdone". The Edinburgh Volunteers preceded the *cortège;* the city bells were tolled and black streamers draped Nelson's Column on Calton Hill. The Coulter monument in Greyfriars churchyard is an altar-tomb supported by six ornamental pillars.

The Falconar family has been the subject of recent research. Alexander Falconar who built Falcon Hall was the eldest son of William Falconar, one-time adjutant of Fort St George in Madras, and was born in

Whisky label incorporating a view of Falcon Hall

By courtesy of John Bartholomew & Sons Ltd

Nairn. He too had a successful career in Madras, becoming, in 1809, Chief Secretary to the Governor. In 1811, having become very wealthy, he retired at the age of forty-four, and soon afterwards returned to Scotland, settling in Morningside. In 1792, in India, Falconar had married his cousin, Elizabeth Davidson, whose father, a solicitor in the East India Company, had come from Cromarty. They had fourteen children, twelve daughters and two sons, five dying in early childhood. There is a portrait of Falconar's wife at the age of fifteen in the Dulwich Art Gallery.

The luxurious mansion-house which became the Falconars' Morningside home was known to the villagers as "the big house". Certainly it had many impressive features. Stone falcons of varying size predominated, the first of which were to be seen perched atop the stone pillars of the Morningside Road entrance. It is interesting that the house named Falcon Hall as a play on Falconar's name should have been situated close to a hunting falconry once used by James IV. Twelve pillars, great monoliths of Craigleith stone, formed the impressive main entrance of the house, flanked by statues of Nelson and Wellington, while more falcons adorned the frontage. A great bronze-railed staircase led to the upper floor, the striking feature of which was an oval drawing-room suggesting the sweep of the Bay of Naples. Its pale blue domed ceiling was embossed with gold stars, while the walls were decorated with panoramic water-colours of Athens, Venice and Rome, painted, it is believed, by Hugh "Grecian" Williams, an important early nineteenth-century Scottish artist.

The owners of "the big house" had the image of lords of the manor but theirs was a benevolent feudalism. Alexander Falconar was a generous

246

benefactor of Morningside Parish Church and five of his daughters had headed the list of subscribers towards its establishment in 1838. The village schoolhouse also benefited greatly from his financial support and interest, and two of his daughters made regular donations and presided over the annual prizegiving ceremony. The little school's winter soirees and summer outings also received their generous support. A colourful spectacle in old Morningside village high street was the yellow horse-drawn carriage with two footmen which conveyed five Falconar daughters into town.

Alexander Falconar kept a strict vigil over the affections of his daughters, but one man was to break through the barrier: Henry Craigie, who married Jessie Pigou Falconar.

After Falconar's death in 1847 Henry Craigie succeeded to Falcon Hall and continued to reside there with his family and four of the Falconar daughters till his own death in 1867. Craigie was also a generous benefactor of the schoolhouse and Parish Church. A memorial stained-glass window in three parts was installed in the latter by his widow. The poor of Morningside also benefited from his kindness. The surviving Falconar daughters continued to live in Falcon Hall, the last dying in 1887, at the age of ninety. It was she who met the cost, some £3,400, of building the chancel and spire of Christ's Episcopal Church at Holy Corner, in memory of her father. She also provided several small stained-glass lights for the five lower windows in the processional aisle behind the altar. The Falconar family tomb, in which are buried also three of Henry Craigie's children, is in the western section of Greyfriars churchyard, not many yards from the grave of William Coulter, first owner of what became Falcon Hall. The Craigie family tomb is in Newington Cemetery, where it was originally marked by a very large stone.

In 1889 Falcon Hall became a high-class boarding school for boys, the original objective of which was to prepare Edinburgh boys for entry into the Indian Civil Service, Sandhurst and Woolwich—training hitherto available only in England and Ireland. The school had first been established as Morningside College in 1883, in the impressive five-storey hydropathic near the junction of Morningside Drive and Morningside Grove. When this building was taken over temporarily by the Royal Hospital for Sick Children, the college moved to Rockville, the renowned baroque villa built by James Gowans in Napier Road in 1858. This eventually became too small and the college moved in 1889 to Falcon Hall, becoming Falcon Hall College. The director was Dr Fearon Ranking and the masters were all ex-Oxford or Cambridge dons. The setting and facilities of the college were unique and especially suitable for outdoor activities and physical training, an important part of the educational programme.

The last owner of Falcon Hall was John George Bartholomew, of the world-renowned Edinburgh cartographic firm. When the mansion-house

The pillars of the facade of Falcon Hall rebuilt as the frontage of Bartholomews' the cartographers' premises in Duncan Street, off Causewayside.

Photograph by Mr W. R. Smith

was demolished in 1909, the regret of many Morningside residents at its disappearance was lessened when the pillared façade was re-built to form the main entrance to Bartholomew's premises in Duncan Street. Neither were the many stone falcons which had dominated the mansion-house and its grounds to be lost: several of these were built on to the frontage of the house at Corstorphine which belonged to Cameron McMillan of Andrew Melrose & Company, the tea merchants. This house, eventually purchased by the Royal Scottish Zoological Society, still displays its now appropriate falcons.

The Falcon Estate was sold by auction to the Edinburgh Merchant Company in 1889 for £33,000 — £8,000 above the upset price. Among those bidding at Dowell's for the extensive properties was one gentleman who had plans to lay out the estate as a race-course. Had he been suc-

248

cessful the future development of Morningside would have taken a different direction.

St Peter's Roman Catholic Church, built on the Falcon estate in 1907, is notable not only for its architecture. Its first parish priest, Canon John Gray, himself prominent in the world of letters, in association with his close friend André Raffalovitch, who largely financed the building of the church, brought to Morningside many of the country's most distinguished literary figures.

John Gray, the eldest of nine children, was born at Woolwich in 1866, where his father was a carpenter in the dockyard. A scholarship from the local Wesleyan day school took him to Roan Grammar School in Greenwich, which he left at the age of thirteen to become a metal worker in order to supplement the family's meagre income. At evening classes, however, he became proficient in French and Latin, and later entered the Civil Service. After matriculating at London University he became a librarian in the Foreign Office.

For some time young John Gray had cut a dashing figure as a man of fashion, a regular attender at London theatrical first nights, becoming well known in literary and theatrical circles, where he met Oscar Wilde.

Then residing in Park Lane, Gray's articles and poetry began to attract attention. He had come a long way from his humble origins in Woolwich, but the direction of his life was soon to change. In 1888 he had first met young Marc André Raffalovitch in a house in the Temple. Raffalovitch's family, Russian Jews, had fled to Paris in the wake of an anti-Jewish edict in 1863. André's father became a successful international banker and his mother, a lady of great beauty and high intelligence, one of Paris's leading hostesses, entertaining distinguished writers, artists, financiers, diplomats and politicians, whose interest she skilfully enlisted in aid of the poor of Paris. When André Raffalovitch came to London, soon enjoying a literary reputation, he and Gray were drawn to each other immediately, and became close and life-long friends.

By 1895 Gray's writing, especially his poetry, became increasingly religious in theme and spirit and, in the autumn of 1898, he resigned from his post in the Foreign Office and entered the Scots College in Rome to study for the Catholic priesthood, having earlier become a convert. On December 21st, 1901, he was ordained in Rome, to work in the Archdiocese of St Andrews and Edinburgh. He was appointed curate at St Patrick's Church in the Cowgate, a vicinity then noted for its lodging-houses and slum tenements. In an area in which policemen patrolled in pairs and outbreaks of violence were frequent, young Father Gray, the former social and intellectual dandy, soon impressed people by his willingness to tackle any situation, to do anything for anyone in the face of the greatest difficulties.

Andre Raffalovitch regularly came to Edinburgh to meet Father Gray and, finding the climate agreeable to his indifferent health, in 1905

St Peter's Church, Falcon Avenue

he purchased the large villa at 9 Whitehouse Terrace where he and his housekeeper Miss Florence Gribbel took up residence. The same year an important conversation took place in the Scots College vineyard in Marino near Rome between Archbishop James Smith of Edinburgh, Father John Gray, and others, as a result of which Gray's proposal for the building of St Peter's in Falcon Avenue received support. In May 1905 Sir Robert Lorimer, the leading Scottish architect of the time, especially noted for his creation of the Shrine of the National War Memorial at Edinburgh Castle, was commissioned. In consultation with Father John Gray, the design for the new church was conceived. A site was purchased from the Edinburgh Merchant Company and the foundation stone was blessed by Archbishop James Smith on April 17th, 1906; the church was opened a year later, Andre Raffalovitch, then living at nearby Whitehouse Terrace, bore the major cost of the building. Father Gray was appointed the first parish priest.

Now that his friend was established in nearby St Peter's, Raffalovitch initiated the regular Sunday luncheons and Tuesday dinner parties which were to make his house in Whitehouse Loan a mecca for men of art, music and literature. With Florence Gribbell's genius for hospitality, Raffalovitch and Father (later Canon) Gray stimulated remarkable dinner conversations. Their guests, it is said, included Henry James, Max

250

Beerbohm, Robert Hugh Benson, Professor Sayce, Lady Margaret Sackville, Eric Gill, Father Bede Jarrett, O.P., Gordon Bottomley and, in later days, Compton Mackenzie, Herbert Grierson and Moray McLaren. The celebrated talker Oscar Wilde was, alas, no longer alive.

On February 14th, 1934 the long friendship between Raffalovitch and Gray ended: the generous benefactor of St Peter's was found dead when his daily taxi called to take him to Holy Communion. Four months later Canon Gray died. In his latter years he had devoted some time to writing religious articles, poetry for meditation and hymns, while remaining an active mountaineer and enthusiastic member of the Royal Scottish Zoological Society. Thus ended a great partnership, uniting diverse origins and adding a fascinating chapter to the chronicles of Morningside.

When in recent times, the interior of St Peter's, a church of unique architectural interest, was radically transformed, reputedly to conform with the spirit of Vatican Council II, there was much adverse criticism. Many of the features which were the subject of the late Paul Shillabeer's masterly illustrated brochure, produced for St Peter's Golden Jubilee, have now disappeared or fallen into disuse.